Twayne's English Authors Series

EDITOR OF THIS VOLUME

Arthur F. Kinney

University of Massachusetts, Amherst

Ben Jonson

TEAS 268

Ben Jonson

BEN JONSON

By CLAUDE J. SUMMERS and TED–LARRY PEBWORTH

The University of Michigan–Dearborn

TWAYNE PUBLISHERS
A DIVISION OF G. K. HALL & CO., BOSTON

Published in 1979 by Twayne Publishers,
A Division of G. K. Hall & Co.
All Rights Reserved

Printed on permanent/durable acid-free paper and bound
in the United States of America

First Printing

Library of Congress Cataloging in Publication Data

Summers, Claude J
Ben Jonson.

(Twayne's English authors series ; TEAS 268)
Bibliography: p. 221-25
Includes index.
1. Jonson, Ben, 1573?-1637—Criticism and inter-
pretation. I. Pebworth, Ted-Larry, joint author.
PR2638.S69   822'.3   79-12102
ISBN 0-8057-6764-9

For
John Edward and Willene Schaefer Hardy

May windes as soft as breath of kissing friends,
  Attend thee hence; and there, may all thy ends,
As the beginnings here, prove purely sweet,
  And perfect in a circle alwayes meet.

Contents

About the Authors

Preface

A Note on the Texts

Chronology

1. The Man and His Age   17

2. The Comedies   42

3. The Tragedies   110

4. The Masques   121

5. The Poetry   133

6. Jonson's Reputation   202

Notes and References   207

Selected Bibliography   221

Index   226

About the Authors

Claude J. Summers and Ted-Larry Pebworth are Professors of English at the University of Michigan–Dearborn. They have collaborated on a number of notes and articles and are coeditors of *The Poems of Owen Felltham*. They are the principal organizers of the University of Michigan–Dearborn Biennial Renaissance Conferences.

Claude Summers earned his Ph.D. at the University of Chicago. He is author of *Christopher Marlowe and the Politics of Power* and has published articles on Marlowe, Shakespeare, Herrick, Vaughan, Marvell, Auden, Isherwood, and others. Associate Editor of *Seventeenth-Century News*, he serves on the executive committee of the Milton Society of America and on the Modern Language Association Delegate Assembly.

Ted-Larry Pebworth received his doctorate from Louisiana State University. Author of *Owen Felltham* (TEAS 189), he is an assistant editor of *Seventeenth-Century News*. His essays on seventeenth-century critical and textual problems have appeared in *Bulletin of the New York Public Library*, *English Literary Renaissance*, *Journal of English and Germanic Philology*, *Modern Philology*, *Papers of the Bibliographical Society of America*, *Studies in the Literary Imagination*, and elsewhere.

Preface

This book attempts to satisfy the need for a one-volume critical survey of Ben Jonson's achievement. A prolific writer who attempted most of the major seventeenth-century poetic and dramatic genres, Jonson resists easy categorization. Best known for *Volpone, The Alchemist,* and a handful of nearly perfect lyrics, he is also the author of other superb comedies, two tragedies, a host of masques, and a large canon of excellent poetry. This book seeks both to reveal the diversity of his art and to emphasize the social vision which unifies such disparate modes as the masque and the comical satire. We have tried to respect the integrity of individual works while relating them all to Jonson's poetics of human possibilities.

The two largest chapters in the book focus on Jonson's comedies and on his nondramatic poetry. Jonson contributed five comedies to the permanent repertory of English drama. These five, *Every Man in His Humour, Volpone, Epicoene, The Alchemist,* and *Bartholomew Fair,* receive careful attention and close study. In addition, the comical satires and the late plays are also discussed. Jonson's seriousness of purpose, masterful craftsmanship, and boisterous comic spirit render his comedies significant works of literature. The study of the nondramatic poetry examines Jonson's three collections, *Epigrams, The Forest,* and *The Underwood,* and, to a much lesser extent, his uncollected verse. Although his poems have been undervalued in comparison with his greatest comedies, they are remarkably rich and varied. The chapter offers close readings of many individual poems and stresses Jonson's mastery as a social poet whose poetic commonwealth includes space for private as well as public emotions. The gracefulness of his lyrics, the dignity of his odes and epistles, the variety of his epigrams, and the surprising accomplishment of his love poetry merit Jonson recognition as a great nondramatic poet.

Brief chapters consider Jonson's tragedies and masques. The two tragedies, *Sejanus* and *Catiline,* both failed on the Jacobean stage, and they are not likely ever to win popular favor. Nevertheless, they have enduring value as imaginative reenactments of ancient history and as gripping reminders of the consequences of social decay. The chapter on the tragedies emphasizes their historical settings and didactic purpose. The masque did not survive the Stuart court which produced it, but Jonson invested the glittering spectacle with dignity, learning, and ethical force, and his masques repay careful study. The chapter on the masques defines the ritualized mode and its courtly function, sketches Jonson's career as the greatest masque writer of his age, and analyzes *The Masque of Queens* as a representative Jonsonian masque.

The first chapter sketches Jonson's life and era, emphasizing the shape of his career and the artistic stance which he assumed. The final chapter briefly outlines his reputation, from his acclaim in the seventeenth century, through his precipitous decline in the eighteenth and nineteenth centuries, to his current recognition as one of the great writers in English literature. The book concludes with a selective bibliography. Space limitations have necessitated restricting that annotated list to the most important, book-length studies of recent years. Readers are urged to consult the notes and references to each chapter for important articles on individual works. In addition, readers should be aware of the numerous modern editions of Jonson's plays which are excluded from the bibliography. Limitations of space have also precluded discussion of Jonson's achievement as a prose stylist and critical theorist in *Discoveries*. But the frequent quotations from that fascinating book, especially in Chapters 1 and 5, should give some idea of its forthright expression and acute insight.

We gratefully acknowledge grants from the University of Michigan's Horace H. Rackham School of Graduate Studies and the University of Michigan–Dearborn Campus Grants Committee, which provided financial assistance in our research. The Huntington Library, San Marino, California, offered a pleasant and congenial atmosphere in which to work; and our typist, Sue Falconer, proved unfailingly cheerful. We are also indebted to a number of stimulating essays and books which have appeared in recent years, a debt only imperfectly acknowledged in the notes and bibliography.

A Note on the Texts

Quotations from Jonson are from *Ben Jonson*, edited by C. H. Herford, Percy and Evelyn Simpson, 11 volumes (Oxford, 1925–52). Titles of the plays, masques, and collections of poetry have been modernized; the use of "i," "j," "u," and "v" has been regularized; troublesome contractions have been expanded; and lengthy quotations in italics have been silently reversed. Quotations from classical authors, unless otherwise noted, are from the Loeb Classical Library. The following abbreviations are used in citations:

Alch.	*The Alchemist*
Conv.	*Conversations with William Drummond of Hawthornden*
Disc.	*Timber, or Discoveries*
E.	*Epigrams*
E. M. I.	*Every Man in His Humour*
E. M. O.	*Every Man out of His Humour*
F.	*The Forest*
H. & S.	C. H. Herford, Percy and Evelyn Simpson, eds., *Ben Jonson*, 11 vols. (Oxford, 1925–52)
Hym.	*Hymenaei*
Ind.	Induction
L. T.	*Love's Triumph through Callipolis*
M. Bl.	*Masque of Blackness*
M. L.	*The Magnetic Lady*
M. Q.	*Masque of Queens*
Poet.	*Poetaster*
Pro.	Prologue
Sej.	*Sejanus*
U.	*The Underwood*
U. V.	Uncollected Verse
Vol.	*Volpone*

Chronology

1573 (?)	Ben Jonson born, probably in or near London, 11 June (?), one month after the death of his father, a minister.
1574–1583	Jonson's mother marries a master bricklayer living in Westminster. Jonson attends a private school in St. Martin's Church.
1583–1588	Attends Westminster School, studying under William Camden.
1588–1596	Apprenticed as a bricklayer to his stepfather. Serves briefly as a volunteer soldier in Flanders.
1594	Marries Anne Lewis of the parish of St. Magnus the Martyr, London, 14 November.
1597	Acts in a strolling company of players. Employed by the Admiral's Men as a playwright. Collaborates on *The Isle of Dogs* (now lost). Imprisoned for sedition.
1598	*The Case Is Altered* performed by the Children of the Chapel Royal. *Every Man in His Humour* performed by the Lord Chamberlain's Men in mid-September. Kills a fellow actor in a duel, 22 September; imprisoned in Newgate, where he converts to Roman Catholicism. Tried in October and freed on a plea of right of clergy, but branded on the thumb and his goods confiscated. Obtains the freedom of the Company of Tilers and Bricklayers.
1599	Resumes collaborative writing for the Admiral's Men. John Marston's portrait of Jonson in *Histriomastix* sparks the War of the Theaters. *Every Man out of His Humour* performed late in the year by the Lord Chamberlain's Men.
1600	*Cynthia's Revels* performed late in the year by the Children of Queen Elizabeth's Chapel.
1601	*Poetaster* produced early in the year by the Children of Queen Elizabeth's Chapel. Thomas Dekker's *Satiromastix* concludes the War of the Theaters.
1601–1602	Paid by Henslowe to revise *The Spanish Tragedy*.

1602–1607	Leaves his wife; lives with Esmé Stuart, Lord Aubigny.
1603	Queen Elizabeth dies, James I succeeds her. Begins era of Jonson's "entertainments" and court masques. His son Benjamin dies. *Sejanus* acted by the King's Men and hissed off the stage. Forms "The Mermaid Club."
1605	Voluntarily joins Marston and George Chapman, his collaborators on *Eastward Ho!*, in jail for mockery of the Scots.
1606	*Volpone* performed by the King's Men. Jonson and his wife charged for failure to take Anglican communion.
1608	Returns to the Church of England.
1609	*Epicoene* produced by the Children of Her Majesty's Revels.
1610	*The Alchemist* acted by the King's Men.
1611	*Catiline* produced by the King's Men.
1612–1613	Travels in France as tutor to the son of Sir Walter Ralegh.
1614	*Bartholomew Fair* performed by the Lady Elizabeth's Men.
1616	Publishes a folio edition of *Works*, including nine plays, *Epigrams*, *The Forest*, and several masques and entertainments. *The Devil Is an Ass* acted by the King's Men. Granted a royal pension.
1616–1625	Presides over meetings of the "Tribe of Ben" at London taverns.
1618–1619	Makes a walking tour of Scotland; visits Drummond of Hawthornden.
1619	Awarded an honorary M.A. by Oxford University.
1623	Jonson's house and library destroyed by fire. Contributes a commemorative tribute to the first folio collection of Shakespeare's plays.
1625	King James dies, Charles I succeeds him. Jonson's prestige at court declines.
1626	*The Staple of News* performed by the King's Men.
1628	Partially paralyzed by a stroke. Appointed Chronologer of the City of London.
1629	*The New Inn,* "most negligently play'd" by the King's Men, hissed by the audience.
1632	*The Magnetic Lady* produced by the King's Men.
1633	*A Tale of a Tub*, revised from an early draft, presented by Queen Henrietta's Men.

1637	Dies August 6. Buried three days later in Westminster Abbey. The epitaph "O rare Ben Jonson" carved into his blue marble grave stone.
1638	Publication of *Jonsonus Virbius*, a collection of commemorative verse in Jonson's honor.
1640–1641	Sir Kenelm Digby publishes the *Works* in two folio volumes.

CHAPTER 1

The Man and His Age

AMONG the most important figures in English literature, Ben Jonson resists neat classification. Capable of delicate lyricism as well as savage mockery, he is remembered as both the genial host of the Apollo Club and the stern moralist of the comical satires. A learned neoclassicist, he is also the master of coarse jests and earthy humor. The author of some of the most popular plays on the Renaissance stage, he was as well the greatest masque writer of his age, endowing with intellectual substance the extravagant court spectacles of King James I. A convicted felon who became the earlier seventeenth century's foremost man of letters, he articulated a code of civilized values for an era he believed in imminent danger of social and political decay. In his work, he alternately portrayed the men and women of his age as gross and vulgar beasts and as reincarnations of ancient grace. But what animated all of Jonson's work, from the satiric epigrams to the royalist encomia and the love lyrics, was an abiding vision of human possibilities. This idealism informed even the scorn he heaped upon the vices and follies he found rampant in his society, and it explains how he was able to reconcile in his work the contradictory impulses of satire and celebration, rage and commendation which his age aroused in him.

I *The Age*

Ben Jonson was born fifteen years into the long reign of Queen Elizabeth I, who ruled England from 1558 to 1603. The Elizabethan Age was an exciting time, a period of national self-awareness, of global exploration, and of intellectual ferment.[1] The queen, her nobility, and even wealthy commoners founded scores of new schools and colleges and refounded with handsome new endowments many older ones. The writing, publication, and dissemination of books flourished. While they read widely in the works of continental authors, both modern and ancient, Englishmen became increasingly aware of the importance of their own native literature. Sophisticated men like Sir Philip Sidney even began to theorize about contemporaneous literature and to write critically about it, and discussions of poetry were no longer confined to the universities but spread into the taverns of London.

Unlike his peripatetic medieval predecessors, Elizabeth's grandfather, Henry VII, firmly settled the bureaucracy of England in one place, the royal city of Westminster. Although he and subsequent monarchs occasionally held parliaments in such places as Oxford and frequently took themselves and their courts into the countryside, spending time in the numerous royal palaces scattered throughout the kingdom or accepting the hospitality of their nobles at great country houses, the political and commercial business of the realm remained centered in Westminster and its giant neighbor, London. By far the largest city in England, London was a crowded metropolis of narrow, crooked streets; of magnificent residential, public, and commercial buildings; and of squalid tenements. It was a city of buying and selling, of opulence and poverty, of hard work and boisterous leisure. Already sprawling beyond its medieval walls, it stretched toward Westminster to the southwest, into the open fields of the north and northeast, and south to the villages across London Bridge. By the end of Elizabeth's reign, the city and its suburbs had a total population of over 200,000 inhabitants.

When Jonson was three years old, an important building went up in a northern suburb of London. At Shoreditch, James Burbage constructed a public playhouse, called simply The Theatre. It was the first permanent home for a professional company of actors in England, and with its construction and occupancy, English commercial drama began in earnest.[2] Over the next several years, large and small playhouses proliferated, tenanted both by troupes of adult performers and by companies of child actors. Drawing an eager audience from almost all segments of society, drama flourished for nearly seventy years. On many occasions during the period, the lord mayors and aldermen of London tried to suppress the public performance of plays. Considering actors to be little better than vagabonds and thieves and plays to be lewd and seductive incitements to immorality and civic irresponsibility, they especially deplored the fact that playgoing took the citizens away from their proper task, hard work. But theatrical entrepreneurs wisely constructed most of their playhouses outside the city precincts—initially in the northern suburbs and later south of the Thames on the Bankside—where the London administrators had no authority. In addition, the acting companies sought and obtained the patronage and consequent protection of powerful people such as Lord Chamberlain Hunsdon, Lord High Admiral Howard, and the Earl of Essex. Fortunately, too, for the actors and managers, Queen Elizabeth and her successors, James I and Charles I, enjoyed plays. Although these monarchs exercised censorship through their various Masters of the Revels, they allowed the theaters to flourish, even to the point of supporting the establishment of private playhouses within London itself. Commercial acting companies gave frequent command performances at court, and some of them came to enjoy official royal patronage. The only agent that regularly halted the production of plays prior to 1642 was bubonic plague—something that could resist even the power of royal patrons. From 1592 until the year Jonson died, 1637, virulent outbreaks of the Black Death frequently closed the theaters during the summer months.

The plague was only one of many problems that England faced during Jonson's lifetime. Between the 1570s and the 1630s, serious religious, political, economic, and social issues progressively divided the nation's people until, five years after the poet's death, civil war erupted. Queen Elizabeth inherited most of her problems and managed to deal with them remarkably well. Her Scottish cousin James, who ruled England from 1603 to 1625, was somewhat less adept; and his son Charles was so inept a politician that his reign and his life were ended on an executioner's scaffold in 1649.

Elizabeth's father severed the Church of England from the Church of Rome in 1533. The regents who controlled the minority reign of her younger brother Edward VI (1547–53) made the English church unequivocally Protestant. Her elder sister Mary, who ruled from 1553 to 1558, returned the country to the Roman fold, by force when persuasion failed. Reared a Protestant, Elizabeth was by nature a pragmatist. As soon as she ascended the throne, she and her advisors set about to establish a state church which would be acceptable to all but the most determined Roman Catholics. This doctrinal compromise, figured forth in the thirty-nine Articles of Religion (1563), was frankly anti-Roman; but on questions that divided continental Protestants—election, predestination, the nature and extent of grace—it was purposely vague. Throughout her long reign, Elizabeth refused to be drawn into public controversy concerning her church. As long as her subjects practiced its outward forms, she and her government did not peer closely into their private beliefs. She would probably have ignored the discreet practice of Roman Catholicism had not two popes threatened her throne and her very life. In 1570, Pius V excommunicated her and released English Roman Catholics from all obligations to obey her; and in 1580 Gregory XII went further, endorsing her assassination as a meritorious act: "there is no doubt that whosoever sends her out of the world with the pious intention of doing God service, not only does not sin but gains merit."[3] Reacting to such extreme measures, Elizabeth's government severely repressed Roman Catholicism. In 1605, King James and an entire parliament narrowly escaped annihilation at the hands of Roman Catholic zealots in the infamous Gunpowder Plot, and the repression continued for a while. But in the early 1620s, James made overtures of friendship toward Spain, the most militantly Roman Catholic power in Europe; and in 1625, the year he ascended the throne, Charles married a French princess and thereafter allowed her and members of the court to practice the Roman rite unchecked.

Although few may have realized its full potential at the time, extreme Protestantism proved a far greater threat to the English crown and to national peace than Roman Catholicism. During the persecutions under Queen Mary, many Protestants fled to safety in the reformed areas of the continent. When they returned to England after the accession of Elizabeth, many of them came back as Puritans. English Puritans were never a unified, cohesive group. The various lines of development within their number reflected differing forms of continental Protestantism; and their sects had numerous, often overlapping designations: Precisionists, Anabaptists, Brownists, Presbyterians, and Separatists, to name only a few. All had as a goal the "purifying" of the Christian religion, stripping away the accretions of Rome to discover and recover the true primitive church beneath. Their religious convictions should be distinguished from their political activities. Some remained members of the Church of England and worked for change from within; indeed, for a time Calvinist doctrine dominated establishment theology. Their more extreme brethren separated themselves from the state church; and some eventually separated themselves from England itself, emigrating first to Holland and later to North America. Elizabeth tolerated Puritanism so long as it was not destructive of the commonweal. James, reared in Scotland by dour Presbyterian regents, despised politically active Puritans, whose resolve to have "no Bishops" he feared would lead inevitably to the corollary "no King"; and he harried Separatists out of the realm.

Charles, acquiescing to the impolitic goals of his standardizing and ritualizing Archbishop of Canterbury, William Laud, inflamed many Puritans—even formerly moderate ones—to frenzied political action; and both Laud and the king died at their hands.

During Jonson's lifetime, Puritans played an increasingly large role in English religious and political life. As a political force, they became especially strong in London and among the commercial and professional classes generally. Most English Puritans lived sober, upright lives and were loyal, valuable, hardworking citizens. They educated themselves, studied the Scriptures, and earnestly sought to imitate Christ's example in their own lives. Others, however, were ignorant, narrow-minded bigots who sought to impose their own rigid beliefs on others, who miserably and hypocritically failed to live up to their professed ideals of rectitude, and who determined to destroy the order and beauty which they themselves could not appreciate. Thoughtful, concerned Englishmen, including Ben Jonson, feared and attacked this second kind of Puritan.

The three monarchs under whom Jonson lived were increasingly troubled by growing parliamentary self-assertiveness. Parliaments became less and less tame servants of the crown as well-educated, legalistic, and eloquent men began to stand for public office. By tradition, parliament held the right of taxation; and as the revenue from crown lands declined, the House of Commons began to demand royal concessions in return for the levying of taxes. Elizabeth managed to hold most of her parliaments in check, often by the mere force of her personality. In addition, despite her love of luxury and show, she lived rather frugally, thus making appeals for extra funds an infrequent necessity. And when she engaged in a war, she made certain that it was a popular one, against Spain, so that public sentiment would incline parliament to vote taxes with few strings attached. James succeeded in staying out of costly wars, even declining to fight what would undoubtedly have been a popular one in support of his Protestant son-in-law, the Elector Palatine, who was driven from his lands by Roman Catholic powers. But James lived lavishly, and he was in constant need of money. As his reign wore on, he had increasingly difficult relations with his parliaments. His claim that he was entitled by divine right to unquestioned obedience served only to exacerbate his problems, and he bequeathed to his son a governmental crisis. Early in his reign, Charles called parliaments only to dissolve them quickly when they made virtually unnegotiable demands. For eleven years (1629–40), he ruled without a parliament, plunging ever more deeply into debt. The parliament he was finally forced to call late in 1640, with disgruntled Puritans in the majority, eventually declared war on the crown.

Jonson's age witnessed a drastic and dislocative shift from a medieval economy to capitalism. While ownership of land still carried social status and newly rich merchants and speculators rushed to acquire country estates, wealth and the power consequent to it came to rest in ready money. Furthermore, the influx into the European economy of precious metals from the Americas—particularly silver—cheapened money itself; and prices of goods and services steadily rose, at especially alarming rates during the frequent years of crop failure. The whole basis of land tenancy changed, fostering a litigious spirit the breadth, depth, and passion of which are unique in English history. Landowners enclosed once commonly held lands, and many of them turned from the growing of food crops to the grazing of sheep, displacing large numbers of people who had once made at least a subsistence living from the land. The dissolution of religious houses in the reign of Henry VIII and the decay of manorial cohesiveness and responsibility throughout the next several reigns destroyed the old ways in which the poor were relieved and threatened the web of traditional relationships between landowners and tenants. Many of the old families who stayed on the land—such as the Sidneys, whom Jonson praises in "To Penshurst" (F. 2)—had increasingly less money available to take care of the tenants and neighbors to whom they felt obligated by long tradition. Many of the squires who managed to remain wealthy, by charging exorbitant rents or by involvement in trade, began to live most of the year in London and to spend their money there, leaving the people in and around their estates to fend for themselves. And the newly rich who bought land and built great country houses felt no obligation at all toward their rural neighbors. Elizabeth's government recognized a social responsibility and tried to meet it, sponsoring a succession of comparatively enlightened Poor Laws. But the problems of inflation and unemployment persisted, and most of the progress made against these two evils was quickly offset by a rapid rise in the country's population. This economic upheaval explains, if it does not totally excuse, the often fantastic schemes of exploration, trade, and exploitation of land and people that mark the Elizabethan, Jacobean, and Caroline periods.

One of the most abusive and frequently decried forms of exploitation was the monopoly system. Under it, the crown granted an individual or a group of people the exclusive right to provide a product or a service to the nation. In some ways monopolies were beneficial. They often provided employment for displaced agricultural workers; they channeled large amounts of money into useful, even necessary enterprises which could never have been accomplished without vast outlays of capital, such as the development of coal mining and transport to offset the swift disappearance of timber fuel; and they provided Englishmen with desirable items that they could not have acquired so easily otherwise—wines, spices, and furs, for example. But monopolists were allowed to set the prices on the goods and services they provided, and the greed of many added significantly to the country's inflationary spiral.

Even with their many economic problems, however, Englishmen on most levels of society generally lived better than most of their continental neighbors; and those who could acquire the money to do so usually lived exceedingly well. They were not misers. What they got, they immediately spent; and not a few borrowed heavily against nebulous expectations to buy present luxuries. They lived in fine houses and apartments, collected expensive possessions, pursued with enthusiasm the latest fads, ate and drank magnificently and immoderately, and wore fortunes on their backs. In 1574, according to Jonson's schoolmaster William Camden, a "very great excesse of Apparell spred it selfe all over *England*, and the habite of our Countrey through a peculiar Vice incident to our apish Nation, grew into such contempt, that men by new-fashioned Garments, and apparell too gawdy, discovered a certaine deformitie and insolencie of minde, whilest they jetted up and downe in theyr Silkes, glittering with gold and silver eyther imbroydered or laced. . . . And withall crept in ryot in banquetting, and braverie in building. For now began more Noblemens and private mens houses, to bee raised here and there in *England*, built with neatnesse, largenesse, and beautifull shew, then ever in any other age, and surely to the great ornament of the Kingdome, but decay of the glory of Hospitalitie."[4] In the next several decades, this extravagance did not abate, but intensified.

At the head of this glittering society, and sharing both its virtues and its vices, stood the court: the royal presence and the advisors to and chief administrators of the monarchy. Comprising over the years both aristocrats of ancient lineage and new men who were accorded place through personal wealth or merit, the courts of Elizabeth and James governed surprisingly well considering the problems they faced. But there were frequent abuses, some of them leading to scandal. Offices were bought and sold, and their incumbents frequently took advantage of their hard-won positions to demand bribes and to embezzle the funds that they administered. Anyone doing business with the crown, and often with the judiciary, needed money or powerful friends or both if his suit was to fare well. Having direct and frequent access to the monarch, royal favorites were particularly cultivated and were both flattered and resented. Elizabeth and James each had a series of handsome young favorites whose chief recommendations seem to have been beauty and charm. Elizabeth was usually astute enough to enjoy her favorites without allowing them undue influence in the government of the realm. James permitted his favorites to grow rich and allowed them some power in domestic matters but gave them little voice in international affairs. Charles inherited, along with the crown, his father's last and most charming favorite, the handsome George Villiers, Duke of Buckingham. The young king allowed his headstrong friend to lead the nation into a disastrous foreign policy; and in the duke's defense, Charles antagonized an already obstreperous parliament. After Buckingham's assassination in 1628, the king did not replace him with a similar kind of favorite, but the advisors that he did look to were inept politicians. Though sincere and often selfless, they were not sensitive to the delicacy of their monarch's increasingly tenuous hold on the government, and they led him into foolish and ultimately fatal mistakes.

The sometimes sordid reality of the royal court was often at odds with the celebration accorded that body by poets. Elizabeth, though a huntress and perhaps a perpetual virgin, was no goddess of the moon; James, though learned, was no Solomon; Charles, though a patron of the arts, was no Apollo. These monarchs and their courts did not in actuality signal a return of the Golden Age, and astute Englishmen never really believed that they did. But the royal person and court represented the nation's potential for greatness and goodness, its very soul; and poets like Ben Jonson, loyal but clear-sighted, told the rulers and courtiers of England what they should be, chided them when they fell short, and gloried with them in their successes.

II   *The Man*

The exact date and place of Jonson's birth are unknown.[5] The year 1572 has been the traditional conjecture, but he was probably born on June 11, 1573. Of Scottish ancestry, he was the son of a Church of

England minister who died one month before the poet's birth. His widowed mother soon married a bricklayer, and the family settled in what was then the village of Charing, midway between London and Westminster. Jonson was fortunate in his early education. He began his studies in a school attached to St. Martin-in-the-Fields, but soon entered the venerable and prestigious Westminster School, located within the precincts of the abbey.

At Westminster, he came under the influence of William Camden (1551–1623), who was to become one of the age's greatest classicists, antiquarians, and teachers. Best known for his *Britannia* (1586), an historical compendium which achieved wide popularity both in its original Latin and in the English translation by Philemon Holland (1610), Camden was also a conscientious schoolmaster. He earned the adulation of serious students such as the young Ben Jonson, who in a famous poem later credited him with "All that I am in arts, all that I know" (*E*. 14, l. 2). The young master taught the boys in his charge to keep commonplace books, he encouraged his students to compose poetry by first drafting a prose version, and he instilled in them a profound love of the classics. Jonson's posthumously published commonplace book, *Timber, or Discoveries,* his characteristic method of poetic composition, and his vaunted classicism probably all stemmed from Camden's influence. Certainly Jonson's love of scholarship, a central aspect of his art as well as his life, sprang from his early immersion in learning at Westminster.

Jonson was forced by financial straits to end his formal education early, perhaps even before completing the Westminster curriculum. He never ceased to pursue knowledge, however. Study remained a lifelong passion, as the learned authorial notes to his masques and tragedies and the markings in the surviving books of his personal library attest. Indeed, he became one of the best educated men of his age, proudly asserting in 1619 that "he was better Versed & knew more in Greek and Latin, than all the Poets in England" (*Conv.*, ll. 622–23). Still, it must have been a disappointment to Jonson that he was unable to attend either Oxford or Cambridge. In 1607, he expressed gratitude that *Volpone* was favorably regarded at "The Two Famous Universities," and he dedicated the published play to them. With understandable satisfaction, he later boasted to William Drummond of Hawthornden that he had been awarded honorary degrees by both institutions (*Conv.*, l. 252).

Instead of attending a university during his late adolescence and young adulthood, Jonson served as an apprentice to his bricklayer stepfather, as a soldier, and as an actor and playwright. In 1598, he obtained the freedom of the Company of Tilers and Bricklayers, thus becoming a journeyman of the craft. Since an apprenticeship normally required seven years, he must have begun working for his stepfather no later than 1591, and probably earlier inasmuch as it is unlikely that he spent seven continuous years as an apprentice. Bricklaying was an ancient and honorable craft, but its practice denoted less than gentle birth and culture; and despite the fact that Jonson came to number nobility and even royalty among his friends and patrons, his antagonists never let him forget that he had been trained as a craftsman. In the second part of *The Returne from Parnassus,* a university play written perhaps as early as 1601, one character described him as "The wittiest fellow of a Bricklayer in England" and another as "so slow an Inventor, that he were better betake himselfe to his old trade of Bricklaying, a bould whorson, as confident now in making of a booke, as he was in times past in laying of a brick."[6] As late as 1632, after Jonson had for sixteen years been virtually poet laureate of England, Alexander Gill the younger remarked of him, in reference to *The Magnetic Lady:*

> A Brickehill's fitter for thee then A stage;
> Thou better knowes a groundsell how to Laye
> Then lay the plott or groundeworke of A playe,
> And better canst derecte to Capp a Chimney
> Then to Converse with Clio, or Polihimny.[7]

Jonson's rise from humble origins may explain the central fact of his personality and of his integrity, that he was impressed by virtue and achievement rather than by title or birth.

In 1594, Jonson married Anne Lewis, who lived in the London parish of St. Magnus the Martyr. The marriage seems not to have been a very happy one. Almost nothing is known of Anne Jonson aside from the poet's 1619 description of her as "a shrew yet honest" (*Conv.,* 1.254). The couple had at least two children, a son named Benjamin and a daughter named Mary, both of whom died young and were mourned by their father in tender epitaphs.[8] Significantly, Jonson never addressed his wife in any literary production. The couple was separated at least from 1602 through 1607, when Jonson accepted the hospitality first of Sir Robert Townshend and then of the king's cousin Esmé Stuart, Lord Aubigny. The poet's marital difficulties may have been exacerbated by his rise in social status after the accession of King James in 1603, when he came more and more often

into intimate contact with members of the nobility who were to
become patrons and friends.

At some point during his late teens or early twenties, Jonson served
as a volunteer foot soldier in the Low Countries where, as he told
Drummond, "he had in the face of both the Campes Killed ane
Enimie & taken opima spolia from him" (*Conv.*, 11.244–46). And by
1597, before officially completing his apprenticeship as a bricklayer,
Jonson began yet another apprenticeship, this one to the theater.
Early in that year, he acted in a touring company of players; and later
in the year, he completed a play begun by Thomas Nashe, *The Isle of
Dogs*. It was a singularly inauspicious beginning for a career of
playwriting. Queen Elizabeth's Privy Council found the play objec-
tionable, stopped its production, destroyed the script, and imprisoned Jonson and at least two of the actors for sedition. Since the play
does not survive, we do not know specifically what dangerous matter
it contained; but Jonson must have been able to convince the
authorities that he had no seditious intention in his portion of the
writing, for within two weeks he and the actors obtained release from
Marshalsea Prison. Undaunted by the close call, Jonson assiduously
pursued his new career as playwright. During the next two years, he
collaborated on at least three plays for the Admiral's Men, all of which
are now lost: *Hot Anger Soon Cold*, with Henry Chettle and Henry
Porter (1598); *The Page of Plymouth*, with Thomas Dekker (1599);
and *Robert the Second, King of Scots* (also called *The Scot's Tragedy*),
with Chettle, Dekker, and others (1599).[9] Of more importance, he
wrote at least three plays wholly his own: *The Case Is Altered* (1598)
for the Children of the Chapel Royal; and both *Every Man in His
Humour* (1598) and *Every Man out of His Humour* (1599) for the Lord
Chamberlain's Men, the most prestigious acting ensemble in London. By the end of 1599, Jonson was an established and successful
playwright.

He was also a convicted felon and a Roman Catholic convert. On
September 22, 1598, Jonson was provoked to fight a duel with the
young actor Gabriel Spencer and "Killed his adversarie, which had
hurt him in the arme & whose sword was 10 Inches Longer than his"
(*Conv.*, 11. 247–48). Indicted for manslaughter, he was held in
Newgate Prison and escaped execution only by pleading the ancient
right of clergy. He was entitled to such a plea by virtue of the fact that
he could read. But his goods were confiscated, and he was branded on
the thumb.

While in Newgate, he was visited and converted by a Roman

Catholic priest, probably a member of a Jesuit missionary squad who was himself imprisoned there. It was a dangerous time in which to convert to Roman Catholicism, and Jonson's action provides another instance of his innate bravery or, as some would allege, his perversity or foolishness. Jonson always equated valor with Christian fortitude, an unflinching determination to do what is right even in the face of certain danger. He also had a strong sense of history and a love of antiquity to which Roman Catholicism could justifiably appeal. These, rather than theological niceties, were probably at the heart of his conversion. He and his wife remained faithful to the Roman Church for at least ten years. They refused communion in their parish church and in 1606 were cited for recusancy in a document which accuses Jonson of being "by fame a seducer of youthe to ye popishe Religion."[10] He denied the charge of seduction but was ordered to consult an approved priest of the Church of England to resolve his questions of conscience. When he finally reconverted to the established church, he did so without pressure and wholeheartedly. Of his return to the Church of England, he reported to Drummond that "at his first communion in token of true Reconciliation, he drank out all the full cup of wyne" (Conv., 11. 315–16). Although religion is not the most important subject of Jonson's work, a deeply felt religious vision does inform much of his poetry, offering consolation in times of grief and faith in times of trouble. Christian stoicism particularly fortified the poet's repeated depictions of isolated virtue in a gilt age.

The plays that Jonson wrote for the Lord Chamberlain's Men in 1598 and 1599 mark the beginning of his mature production, work that he himself deemed worthy of preservation. But even though he had begun to make a significant mark for himself with plays of his own devising, in the early years of the seventeenth century Jonson could not afford to forego play doctoring and collaboration when they were offered to him. Particularly irksome must have been the revisions he undertook for a new production of Thomas Kyd's *The Spanish Tragedy*, a popular and bloody melodrama he more than once criticized as a prime example of a bad play. He may have taken more delight in his 1605 collaboration with John Marston and Thomas Dekker on a rollicking comedy incorporating the ancient motif of the prodigal son, *Eastward Ho!* Unfortunately, King James was not amused by the play's mockery of the Scots. Marston and Dekker were jailed for their presumption, and in a characteristically magnanimous gesture, Jonson voluntarily committed himself to prison as a display of solidarity with his collaborators. The exact way in which the trio secured their release is unknown, but it was probably through the intervention of influential friends and patrons, including the powerful Robert Cecil, Lord Salisbury, to whom Jonson appealed for help.

Eastward Ho! must have become a cause célèbre, for it was published immediately and went through three editions in one year. Although Jonson's name was given on the title page, along with Marston's and Dekker's, he likely took no part in the publication; and he omitted the play from his collected *Works*. Indeed, he did not himself preserve any of his collaborations. The stage version of *Sejanus* which was produced in 1603 was a collaborative effort, probably with George Chapman, a leading tragedian; but when Jonson published the play two years later, he noted in a preface that he had rewritten the portions originally composed by "a second Pen" and that the published play was wholly his own work. Using documentary evidence from the period, G. E. Bentley has shown that dramatic collaboration usually followed much the same pattern. After one author had written a scenario approved by the acting company, the playwrights involved were assigned to compose specific acts and scenes individually.[11] This is probably the way in which *Eastward Ho!* was written. Either Marston or Jonson plotted the comedy. Marston apparently wrote the first act; individual scenes in the middle acts were assigned to each of the three collaborators; and Jonson, who had a reputation as a master of the denouement, probably composed most of the final act.

Jonson's negative attitude toward his collaborative works may reflect both his ambiguous attitude toward the stage itself and his self-conscious artistry. As Bentley has noted, Jonson was only now and then a professional playwright.[12] Unlike Shakespeare and, at various times, Dekker, Thomas Heywood, John Fletcher, Philip Massinger, James Shirley, William Rowley, and Richard Brome, he was not attached to an acting company as resident writer; and after his theatrical apprenticeship, he did not earn his entire living from the theater. After 1603, most of Jonson's income derived from his authorship of entertainments and masques written at the behest of noble and royal employers and from the patronage of the king and members of the aristocracy. Indeed, for the ten years from 1616 to 1626, he avoided writing for the popular stage altogether. Jonson's particular relationship to the theater had both advantages and disadvantages. He never became rich from it, as did Shakespeare, nor did he derive even a steady income from it, as did the resident playwrights who were not shareholders in their companies. On the other hand, he was free to sell his scripts to the company which offered the most money or the most sympathetic production, and he was able to exercise an unusual degree of artistic independence from both the acting companies and the audiences. Moreover, he was less restricted in the publication of his plays than were the attached playwrights.

For Jonson, publication was extraordinarily important. It countered the ephemerality of theatrical production and allowed the careful shaping of an artistic canon. His first published book was the quarto of *Every Man out of His Humour* issued in 1600. With it, he began a practice which was unusual for playwrights of his time, the careful publication of plays under authorial supervision. A quarto of *Every Man in His Humour* was issued the following year; and all but one of the plays which he wrote over the next ten years, among them his most popular stage successes, such as *Volpone* and *The Alchemist*, were published, under his supervision, shortly after theatrical presentation. Jonas A. Barish explains Jonson's passionate concern with the publication of his plays as a measure of his distrust of the stage: "Jonson belongs in a Christian-Platonic-Stoic tradition that finds value embodied in what is immutable and unchanging, and tends to dismiss as unreal whatever is past and passing and still to come. What endures, for him, has substance, what changes reveals itself thereby as illusory."[13] Publication stills in a permanent artifact works which less self-conscious artists might have considered fully alive only in the flux of the stage.

Jonson considered himself foremost a poet and his plays and masques species of poetry. He wrote nondramatic poetry thoughout his life, and during the reign of King James he was frequently commissioned to write masques and entertainments. James I and his consort, Anne of Denmark, were fond of lavish spectacle; and Jonson invested the masque with new dignity and ethical force. His career as masque writer provided him with money and recognition, and it may have helped mold his conception of himself as a public poet. Certainly access to court provided him the opportunity to study at close hand the ruling class whom he undertook to counsel in his poetry. Generally, Jonson's work advises how best to achieve a good society, inspiring through praise and shaming through ridicule. In his nondramatic poetry, he addressed familiarly some of the most powerful men and women of his age, usually tactfully but sometimes boldly offering counsel. His conviction of the true utility of poetry helped him maintain an essential integrity and protected him from any temptations toward sycophancy. He became friends with such aristocrats as Lucy, Countess of Bedford; Sir Robert Sidney; Lady Mary Wroth; and William Herbert, Earl of Pembroke, the latter a particularly generous patron. He cultivated friendships with such members of the intellectual aristocracy as John Selden, Sir Robert Cotton, Sir Francis Bacon, and Sir Walter Ralegh, whose highspirited son Jonson accompanied as tutor on a journey to France in 1612. Jonson's position as social poet was solidified by the publication in 1616 of his folio *Works,* a book which deliberately and provocatively integrated the two aspects of his career as poet and playwright.

The 1616 folio is one of the most important books published in seventeenth-century England. A massive, beautifully produced, physically imposing volume, it established Jonson as an important poet whose literary domain encompassed modes as diverse as the masque and the comical satire. Perhaps even more significantly, it gave new dignity to the playwright's craft. The deliberate inclusion of plays originally composed for the popular theater in a folio entitled *The Works of Benjamin Jonson* boldly asserted the right of plays to be considered serious literature as well as popular culture. Previously, plays had been printed almost invariably in cheap, often inaccurate quartos. Some measure of the low esteem in which published plays were held can be gauged from the fact that when the insatiable book collector Sir Thomas Bodley made plans for establishing his magnificent library at Oxford, he specifically excluded the acquisition of plays.[14] Jonson's own quarto publications were produced in texts distinctly superior to those of his fellow dramatists. But the act of collecting his plays, including them with his poems and masques, constituted a daring claim for their permanent value. Jonson was roundly ridiculed for his presumption. One epigrammatist asked, "Pray tell me *Ben*, where doth the mystery lurke, / What others call a play you call a worke."[15] Despite the chiding of his contemporaries, however, Jonson's confidence was vindicated. The 1616 *Works* set a precedent which undoubtedly inspired the greatest folio publication of them all, the 1623 collection of Shakespeare's plays, for which Jonson composed his famous tribute, "To the memory of my beloved, The Author *Mr. William Shakespeare:* And what he hath left us" (U. V. 26).

Jonson scrupulously controlled the contents of the *Works*. He included nine plays *(Every Man in His Humour, Every Man out of His Humour, Cynthia's Revels, Poetaster, Sejanus, Volpone, Epicoene, The Alchemist,* and *Catiline)* along with two collections of

poetry *(Epigrams* and *The Forest)* and several masques and entertainments. The prefatory matter features commendatory verse by
John Selden, George Chapman, John Donne, Francis Beaumont,
and others. As W. David Kay remarks, the publication of the folio
and the careful choice of its contents represent Jonson's attempt "to
interpret himself to his age as a writer whose individual works formed
a unified corpus animated by his conception of the poet's function."[16]
Although it does not account for the curious absence of *Bartholomew
Fair* (1614), this self-conscious making of a canon explains Jonson's
decision not to include early works or collaborations in the folio.
The care which Jonson lavished on the volume is apparent from his
revision and expansion of *Cynthia's Revels* and the minute polishing
of *Volpone* and other plays which had already been published in
quarto. The inclusion of the masques, often accompanied by descriptions of their productions, especially reveals his desire to "borrow
a life of posteritie" for his work *(M. Bl.,* 1.5).

The publication of the 1616 folio established Jonson as the leading
man of letters in London. King James awarded him a pension, and he
became unofficially poet laureate of England. He gathered about him
a host of younger poets and wits, including such individual talents as
James Howell, Robert Herrick, and Thomas Carew, who styled
themselves "Sons of Ben." Jonson was a notably gregarious man. As
early as 1603, he formed "The Mermaid Club" at the tavern of that
name, noted for its excellent wine. Like the coffeehouse clubs of the
eighteenth century, the Mermaid Club was a group of convivial
writers and lovers of literature who met regularly to talk of their
common trust in good verses. In 1616, and for many years afterward,
the "Tribe of Ben" met at various London establishments, especially
at the Apollo Room of the Devil Tavern, to discuss life and literature
in feasts of wine and wit. Jonson composed an amusing set of rules or
"laws for the beaux esprits," the "Leges Convivales," which were
engraved in marble over the fireplace in the Apollo Room; and in a
comic poem which was painted on a panel in the tavern, he declared
"Truth itself doth flow in wine."

The position Jonson assumed as father figure and teacher was one
peculiarly appropriate to him. This status and the new honors he
received recognized his attempts to dignify the art of playwriting and
to reassert the social function of poetry. Jonson regarded himself as a
lawgiver to the stage, and he attempted to make comedy a more
serious mode of literature than it had been. As satirist, he was intent
on exposing hypocrisy and puncturing pretension. As social poet, he

attempted to enunciate a vision of a harmonious society based on enduring ideals. The public recognition he enjoyed after 1616 not only rewarded his past efforts but also placed him in a position to continue as a self-nominated arbiter of civilized values.

Not surprisingly in light of his employment at court and his dependence on noble patrons, Jonson was politically conservative and an ardent royalist. But the poet's conservatism was not merely an opportunistic stance. Most profoundly, his political convictions stemmed from his classically rooted conception of his function as a public poet, of his responsibility to lead forth the "many good, and great names" of his time so that they might serve as exemplars of good conduct for his own and future ages. He was always conscious of his role as advisor to the ruling class and of his special obligation to remind those in power of their opportunities and responsibilities. He honored those nobles who were "so addicted to the service of the *Prince*, and Common-wealth, as they looke not for spoyle" (*Disc.*, 11. 1127–29); but he was fiercely independent. He almost never fawned, and he frequently satirized courtiers and indicted the shallowness and misplaced values of the nobility, particularly deriding those who were lazy or who "remove themselves upon craft, and designe . . . with a premeditated thought to their owne, rather then their *Princes* profit" (*Disc.*, 11. 1134–36). In an age of political strife and religious dissension, he saw the monarch as a unifying force. "*After God*," he remarked, "nothing is to be lov'd of man like the Prince" (*Disc.*, 1. 986). For Jonson, the rise of capitalism and of Puritanism signaled a real danger to the ideal of a united commonwealth. He associated capitalism and Puritanism with financial exploitation, vulgar ostentation, hypocrisy, and intolerance. Puritans were the most persistent targets of Jonson's satire throughout his career. Significantly, he never attacked their religious beliefs. Instead, he focused on their political disruptiveness and hypocrisy, characterizing them as divisive and ignorant charlatans who would ruthlessly impose their beliefs on others.

In 1618, Jonson set off on a walking tour to Scotland. The journey attracted much attention among the literary circles of both London and Scotland. To Jonson's delight, Sir Francis Bacon wittily remarked that he "loved not to sie poesy goe on other feet than poetical dactils & spondaes" (*Conv.*, 11. 333–34). Less delightfully from Jonson's point of view, John Taylor the Water Poet promptly embarked on an imitative journey. Throughout his trip, Jonson was warmly greeted. The Edinburgh town council staged a dinner in his honor, and various dignitaries entertained him lavishly. Among the literary figures whom Jonson visited in Scotland was William Drummond of Hawthornden (1585–1649), a wealthy squire who kept notes on the famous poet's visit.

Actually, the so-called *Conversations with Drummond* is not so much a record of conversations as a listing of comments made by Jonson, frequently without contexts, and a portrait of him by Drummond. Much of what Drummond reports is literary gossip which Jonson probably did not realize would be recorded for posterity. According to Drummond, Jonson remarked "that Done for not keeping of accent deserved hanging" (*Conv.*, 11. 48–49); "That Shaksperr wanted Arte" (1. 50); that Sir Philip Sidney "was no pleasant man in countenance, his face being spoilled with Pimples & of high blood & Long" (11. 230–31); and that Jonson himself once "beate Marston and took his pistoll from him" (1. 160). Jonson also related to Drummond such revealing personal details as that "he heth consumed a whole night in lying looking to his great toe, about which he hath seen tartars & turks Romans and Carthaginions feight in his imagination" (11. 322–24); that "of all stiles he loved most to be named honest, and hath of that ane hundreth letters so naming him" (11. 631–32); and that "In his merry humor, he was wont to name himself the Poet" (1. 636).

Conversations with Drummond is an important document, a source of valuable and curious information; but it ought not to be regarded as an authoritative source for Jonson's considered opinion on any particular subject. Jonson's true estimate of Shakespeare, for instance, was actually far more complex, and far more favorable, than Drummond's account indicates. In *Discoveries*, Jonson condemned "the *running Judgements* upon *Poetry,* and *Poets*" as a preposterous exercise (1. 588), one which he almost certainly would not have engaged in had he known his comments to his Scottish host were being recorded. Drummond was apparently a naive and sober, isolated and sheltered young man; and Jonson probably delighted in shocking him with quick judgments and candid observations. As guest, he may have felt an obligation to perform for his host, to regale him with outrageous anecdotes and bits of gossip. The impression he left with Drummond, however, was that of a blustery and opinionated martinet, too proud and too passionate to please the sensitive Scotsman. "He is a great lover and praiser of himself, a contemner and Scorner of others, given rather to losse a friend, than a Jest, jealous of every word and action of those about him (especiallie after drink) which is one of the Elements in which he liveth," Drummond concluded of his guest (11. 680–84).

Drummond's assessment of Jonson's personality may be a fair-minded account of the young man's impression of his famous visitor.[17] Nevertheless, it is only a partial account. Jonson's was a proud and self-assertive nature, and there was indeed a coarseness in his manner. Throughout his life, he made enemies and engaged in many quarrels, including particularly those with his sometime collaborators John Marston and Inigo Jones, the latter of whom described him as "the best of Poetts, but the worst of men."[18] Yet Jonson always had more friends than enemies, and he inspired the personal devotion of many of his poetic "sons." The most gifted of them, Robert Herrick, canonized him as "Saint Ben."[19] Jonson passionately pursued friendships, and in this pursuit he revealed much generosity and a great deal of self-awareness, sometimes disarmingly acknowledging his own character flaws. Physically imposing but not attractive, in middle age he was a mountain-bellied, rocky-faced, gray-haired man. He prided himself on his achievements, yet he could playfully mock his appearance. He valued his honesty and independence, yet he articulated a genuinely felt code of courtesy. He was capable of tenderness as well as bluntness. Jonson's personality was not a simple one, and he imposed its many facets on his poetry, where he is alternately enraged satirist and amused observer, bitter enemy and loving friend, proud poet and courteous host, grieving father and vulnerable lover.

In his later life, Jonson functioned as a kind of literary eminence, the most famous man of letters in England. The honorary degree he received from Oxford in 1619 recognized his scholarship as well as his artistry. He may also have been awarded a deputy professorship of rhetoric by Gresham College; and his name headed the list of candidates to be nominated for a proposed academy of letters. King James offered to confer a knighthood on him, which he refused. He was nominated to the office of Master of Revels, a position he never actually achieved since it was to come to him by reversion, on the deaths of two other appointees. Jonson used his literary prominence well, writing commendatory poems for other authors and apparently urging his friends John Heminges and Henry Condell to collect Shakespeare's plays in the folio of 1623 to which he contributed his own triumphant celebration of his fellow playwright and friend.

But Jonson's years of glory did not extend to the end of his life. A number of misfortunes marred the final years of a career which had been far more successful than the young Jonson could have dreamed it would be. In 1623, a fire destroyed his library, consuming his books and several unpublished manuscripts. At court, as his antagonist Inigo Jones gained ascendancy, Jonson was viewed with less favor. With the accession of King Charles in 1625, he was called upon less frequently to write masques and entertainments. His return to the stage with *The Staple of News* in 1626, after a ten-year absence, was relatively unsuccessful; and that play's unenthusiastic reception was followed in 1629 by the most thorough disaster of Jonson's theatrical career, *The New Inn*. In 1628, the fat, aging poet was paralyzed by a stroke and confined to bed for a long period. In his last years, he was often impoverished. Although King Charles honored his request for an increase in the pension which King James had originally awarded him in 1616, the payments were frequently late.

Thus Jonson's last years were marred by poverty, illness, and a decline of prestige at court. Nevertheless, he maintained an honored position even under these difficult conditions. Jonson was visited both by the young wits of the town and by such wise old friends as the Earl of Pembroke; John Selden; Brian Duppa, later Bishop of Chichester; and George Morley, later Bishop of Winchester. Although his final plays were neither popular nor critical successes, they represent continued experimentation with theatrical form. When he died, he left an unfinished manuscript of a pastoral drama, *The Sad Shepherd*, perhaps his most lyrical dramatic composition. He continued writing nondramatic poetry in his last years, too, and his final poems show no great diminution of poetic power. Perhaps most remarkably, they avoid despair and sentimentality, embracing instead quiet dignity and gentle humor. Jonson died on August 6, 1637. Three days later he was buried in Westminster Abbey. His funeral cortege included "all or the greatest part of the nobilitie and gentrie then in the town."[20] His death was mourned with an outpouring of elegies and tributes, but perhaps the most memorable epitaph is the simple phrase which was carved into the blue marble stone marking his grave, "O rare Ben Jonson."

III   *The Artistic Stance*

Few writers have had a more noble conception of literature than Ben Jonson. He considered poetry among the highest and most useful of human expressions, and for him poetry included comic and tragic drama as well as masques and lyrics. Paraphrasing Cicero, he described poetry as an art which "nourisheth, and instructeth our Youth; delights our Age; adornes our prosperity; comforts our Adversity; entertaines us at home; keepes us company abroad, travailes with us; watches; divides the times of our earnest, and sports; shares in our Country recesses, and recreations; insomuch as the wisest and best learned have thought her the absolute Mistresse of manners, and neerest of kin to Vertue" (*Disc.*, 11. 2389–96). The principal end of poetry, he declared, is "to informe men, in the best reason of living" (*Vol.*, Dedication, 11. 108–109). Precisely because he thought literature so important, he took it seriously. By instinct a reformer, Jonson endeavored throughout his career to impose form and order on the rich but unruly literary traditions to which he was heir.

The literary milieus in which Jonson matured were various and disparate. The late sixteenth century was an age of humanism, of the rediscovery of classical texts and literary theory. It was also a moment ripe for satire, for both the "Toothless Satyres" based on Horace and the "Byting Satyres" imitative of Juvenal.[21] Coming of age artistically in the 1590s, Jonson was profoundly influenced by the humanistic desire to incorporate classical values into his own life and era and by a satirical impulse to cleanse a society widely perceived as corrupt. These two predilections shaped his attitudes toward the literary traditions, both dramatic and nondramatic, which he inherited. On the one hand, the Elizabethan popular theater, while vital and exuberant, seemed too discursive and too reliant on noisy bombast and improbable action to satisfy Jonson. On the other hand, the lyric poetry of the day appeared too decorative, too artificial, and too monotonous to please him. What Jonson attempted in his plays was to fuse classical precepts of structure and decorum with native English vigor and contemporary subject matter. In his nondramatic poetry, he sought to develop an individualized speaking voice and to revitalize classical forms such as the epigram and the epistle.

Unlike many of his contemporaries, Jonson often commented on the nature and aims of his art. In the dedicatory epistles, prologues, and epilogues to his plays and especially in his commonplace book, *Timber, or Discoveries*, he announced his artistic principles.[22] For him, literature was fundamentally didactic. Echoing the ancients, he proclaimed "the impossibility of any mans being the good Poet, without first being a good man" (*Vol.*, Dedication, 11. 22–23). He declared that his aim "In all his *poemes*, stil, hath been this measure, / To mixe profit, with your pleasure" (*Vol.*, Pro., 11. 7–8) and that "this

pen / Did never aime to grieve, but better men" (*Alch.*, Pro., 11.
11–12). Even masques, he contended, "ought alwayes to carry a
mixture of profit, with them, no lesse then delight" (*L. T.*, 11. 6–7). In
Discoveries, he observed that poetry "offers to mankinde a certaine
rule, and Patterne of living well, and happily" (11. 2386–87). It is, he
continued, "a dulcet, and gentle *Philosophy*, which leades on, and
guides us by the hand to Action" (11. 2398–99). Of the poet, he said,
"Wee doe not require in him meere *Elocution;* or an excellent faculty
in verse; but the exact knowledge of all vertues, and their Contraries;
with ability to render the one lov'd, the other hated, by his proper
embattaling them" (11. 1038–41). The satiric intent of the comedies
also clearly mirrors Jonson's essential didacticism. In these plays he
imitated human follies, and occasionally crimes, in order to cure
them by exposure to the wholesome remedies of laughter. He hoped
that foolish people would recognize themselves in the comedies,
realize the absurdity of their follies and vices, and determine to rid
themselves of them. Significantly, however, while Jonson was always
didactic in his work, he was very seldom self-righteously or oppressively moralistic.

Central to Jonson's artistic stance was a respect for discipline and
scholarship. In *Discoveries*, he announced "three Necessaries" for a
person to write well: "reade the best Authors, observe the best
Speakers: and much exercise of his owne style" (11. 1697–99). He also
enumerated five requirements for the poet: natural wit, exercise,
imitation, study, and art. By natural wit, Jonson meant genius or
poetical rapture, an ability "by nature, and instinct, to powre out the
Treasure of his minde" (11. 2412–13). True poets, Jonson believed,
were inspired by "a divine Instinct" (1. 2420), and without this
natural genius, study and learning are profitless. He quoted Petronius to the effect that only a king or a poet is not born every year (11.
2433–34). But as he remarked in his famous celebration of Shakespeare, "a good *Poet's* made, as well as borne" (U. V. 26, 1. 64), and
the other four requirements he listed are means of imposing discipline on natural genius. By exercise, he meant the capacity for
arduous revision. By imitation, he did not mean the Aristotelian idea
of mimetic representation, but more simply the ability "to convert
the substance, or Riches of an other *Poet*, to his owne use" (*Disc.*, 11.
2468–69). In addition, the poet must also possess a critical faculty, "an
exactnesse of Studie, and multiplicity of reading" (11. 2483–84). And,
finally, the poet must achieve art, the sum of the discipline necessary
to regulate spontaneous genius: "it is Art only can lead [the poet] to

perfection" (1. 2495). The qualities Jonson most valued in the poet
may seem pedestrian to the romantic imagination: discipline, study,
control. Yet they crystallize his rebellion against the excesses of
Elizabethan literature and serve as an index to his own scrupulous
artistry.

In the dedication of *Volpone* to the two universities, Jonson
audaciously promised to "raise the despis'd head of *poetrie* againe,
and stripping her out of those rotten and base rags, wherwith the
Times have adulterated her form, restore her to her primitive habit,
feature, and majesty, and render her worthy to be imbraced, and kist,
of all the great and master-*spirits* of our world" (11. 129–34). Jonson
proposed to reform "th'ill customes of the age" (*E. M. I.*, Pro., 1. 4).
He determined to refine comedy by observing "The lawes of time,
place, persons . . . / From no needfull rule he swerveth" (*Vol.*, Pro.,
11. 31–32). He particularly objected to his fellow playwrights'
violations of the unities of time, place, and action, and of their
frequent mixtures of comic and tragic characters and action. He
complained that even Sir Philip Sidney, presumably in his epic
romance *The Arcadia*, "did not keep a Decorum in making every one
speak as well as himself" (*Conv.*, 11. 18–19). In contrast, Jonson
confined himself in his comedies to "deedes, and language, such as
men doe use: / And persons, such as *Comoedie* would chuse" (*E. M.
I.*, Pro., 11. 21–22). In his nondramatic poetry, he embraced a plain,
though resonant style, reflecting his preference for "Pure and neat
Language . . . yet plaine and customary" (*Disc.*, 11. 1870–71). He
would, he wrote, "rather have a plaine downe-right wisdome, then a
foolish and affected eloquence" (*Disc.*, ll. 343–45).

Jonson must be regarded as one of the most thoroughgoing
neoclassical writers in English literature. His neoclassicism can be
seen most clearly in the observance of the classical unities, the
verisimilitude and decorum of the comedies, the dignity of the
tragedies, and the plain style of the nondramatic poetry. The superb
plotting of the mature comedies and the sophisticated tone of the
poetry also reflect classical literary influence. More profoundly,
Jonson's classical bent made him emphasize the integrity of the whole
in producing a work of art, and made him conscious of the relationship
of the parts to the whole. His discussion of unity of action in
Discoveries, echoing Daniel Heinsius's 1611 redaction of Aristotle,
pointedly stressed the necessity for a prior conception of the whole:
"The Fable is call'd the *Imitation* of one intire, and perfect Action;
whose parts are so joyned, and knitt together, as nothing in the

structure can be chang'd, or taken away, without impairing, or troubling the whole; of which there is a proportionable magnitude in the members" (11. 2681–86). Most significantly of all, Jonson's acute consciousness of the social role of poetry and the didactic nature of literature was itself a function of his classicism.

Yet Jonson was as independent in his classicism as in every other aspect of his life. In *Discoveries*, he wrote that "*Nothing* can conduce more to letters, then to examine the writings of the *Ancients*," but he also advised "not to rest in their sole Authority, or take all upon trust from them" (11. 129–31). In addition, he declared that "I am not of that opinion to conclude a *Poets* liberty within the narrowe limits of lawes, which either the *Grammarians*, or *Philosophers* prescribe" (11. 2555–57). He remarked that "Nothing is more ridiculous, then to make an Author a *Dictator*, as the schooles have done *Aristotle*" (ll. 2095–97); and he regarded the ancients as "Guides, not Commanders" (11. 138–39). In his classical tragedy, *Sejanus*, he violated the unity of time and omitted "a proper *Chorus*," explaining that it was unnecessary and impossible "in these our Times, and to such Auditors, as commonly Things are presented, to observe the ould state, and splendour of *Drammatick Poemes*, with preservation of any popular delight" (To the Readers, 11. 8, 12–15). Indeed, for all Jonson's appreciation of classical literature and critical theory, he was also very much steeped in native English drama and poetry. English poets and playwrights such as Sir Philip Sidney, Christopher Marlowe, George Chapman, William Shakespeare, and John Donne influenced him as much as his hallowed classical writers, Homer, Horace, Vergil, Martial, Catullus, Cicero, and Plautus. His works reflect a fusion of classical and English traditions. More accurately, they mirror an English sensibility broadened and refined by thorough immersion in classical scholarship.

Jonson's conscious and scrupulous artistry yielded works which are shapely and controlled, weighty and didactic. But his works are also playful and witty, earthy and raucous. They provide ample evidence of that divine instinct which marked a true poet according to his own definition. His work incorporates those classical virtues of "clarity, unity, symmetry, and proportion," as Douglas Bush enumerates them;[23] but it also embodies the spontaneity, vigor, and excitement of the age he sought to portray. As well as a neoclassical theorist, Jonson was a master of realism. "The true Artificer," he declared, "will not run away from nature, as hee were afraid of her; or depart from life, and the likenesse of Truth" (*Disc.*, 11. 772–74). As likenesses of truth, Jonson's various works transcend the rigid barriers suggested by such terms as classical or contemporary. They express the lives of men and women in "fit measure, numbers, and harmony" (*Disc.*, 11. 2349–50).

CHAPTER 2

The Comedies

BEN Jonson is one of the greatest writers of comedy in the English language. Energetic and vital, realistic and satiric, Jonson's comedies are the product of a self-conscious artist who took seriously the Horatian maxim that poetry should entertain and instruct. Best known today as the author of *Every Man in His Humour, Volpone, Epicoene, The Alchemist,* and *Bartholomew Fair,* Jonson actually wrote many comedies during the course of a career which spanned forty years. The fourteen complete comedies which survive are extraordinarily varied, for throughout the four decades Jonson restlessly experimented with approach, point of view, characterization, language, and plotting. But each of them bears the identifying stamps of his artistry: moral seriousness, robust humor, careful structure, and comic realism.

The master of urban comedy of manners, Jonson is primarily a social poet. He believed that the purpose of art was the betterment of society. More specifically, he believed that the aim of comedy was the exposure of those vices and follies which weaken society and disrupt the web of human relationships necessary to a commonwealth. Consequently, his comedies generally have a strong satirical bent, and all are infused with didacticism. Most often, they attack "the ragged follies of the time" (*E. M. O.,* Ind., 1. 17) in an attempt to shame through ridicule. False values, foolishness, greed, pretentiousness, hypocrisy, and especially self-deception are Jonson's chief targets, both because they are individual failings and because they typify the failures of the age itself. Writing at a time when inflation inspired greed, when social climbing was rampant, when religious unrest threatened domestic tranquility, and when the old manifestations of *noblesse oblige* seemed dormant,[1] Jonson heaped scorn on his society by exposing the sordid reality which gave urgency to the ideal commonwealth he sought to construct in his nondramatic poetry.

But Jonson is not the rigid moralist he is sometimes thought to be. He never forgets that comedy has a primary responsibility to amuse, and other than in prologues, epilogues, and other extradramatic framing devices, he seldom preaches. In the Prologue to *Volpone*, he declares that his purpose, "In all his *poemes*, still, hath been this measure, / To mix profit, with your pleasure" (ll. 7–8), a formulation which emphasizes delight as well as instruction. His conviction that a major function of comedy must be moral edification is supported by both classical example and Renaissance theory. But these two sources also warn that the most effective way to teach through art is to clothe the lesson in a fable so delightful that the audience relaxes its all too human defenses against instruction, and Jonson embodies his moral themes in robust entertainment. Moreover, Jonson's didacticism is tempered by his awareness of the complexity of moral choice and by a characteristic ambiguity. He frequently points out the dangers in passing easy judgment on others, and he creates ambiguous situations in which folly and even evil are seductively enjoyable. For instance, the evil of Volpone's enticement of Celia, the false values which underlie Sir Epicure Mammon's dreams, and the baseness of Subtle's trickery are never in doubt, yet the reader is manipulated into admiring—emotionally if not intellectually—all three men and even, at least momentarily, wishing them well. This ambiguity is implicit in the enjoyment with which the plays sport with their galleries of fools. Although Jonson's comedies use the stage as an intellectual forum to impart a didactic vision, they do so through genial, often broad, and even low humor; and their lessons recognize the reality of flawed human perception and admit the necessity of adaptability and compromise. Sophisticated and worldly, the comedies collectively mirror a moral vision which is serious without being grim.

Jonson's moral seriousness is matched by his artistic seriousness. When he began writing for the stage in the mid-1590s, few were willing to admit that popular drama could be considered literature. Plays were published almost invariably in cheap, hastily produced, often inaccurate quartos which were read once or twice and then either thrown away or sold to wastepaper dealers. In 1616, when Jonson included seven of his comedies and two of his tragedies in a folio publication of his *Works,* conferring on them the status then reserved for a writer's serious production, he was chided by his friends and ridiculed by his enemies for his presumption.[2] But Jonson had a noble conception of drama. To him, plays, whether written in verse or prose, were or should be poems; and he considered poetry one of the highest and most useful of human expressions. Preeminently a humanist, Jonson attempted to make popular comedy a more serious mode by adapting classical ideals of comedy to his contemporary material.

The neoclassicism of Jonson's comedies consists largely in their observance of the classical unities of time, place, and action and in their sense of decorum: their reliance on "deedes, and language, such as men do use: / And persons, such as *Comoedie* would chuse" (*E. M. I.*, Pro., 11. 21–22). From classical comedy, Jonson appropriated disciplined structure, concentrated action, and serious purpose; and he imposed them on the rich vitality of the middle- and lower-class London material he knew so well. The result is a comedy which is carefully shaped but earthy, artfully designed but unlabored, enriched by ancient tradition yet contemporary and topical. Although the comedies are informed with the self-conscious artistry of a determined neoclassicist, they have very little of the scholarly affectation sometimes attributed to this lawgiver of the stage. Jonson insisted that the ancient writers he admired were "Guides, not Commanders" (*Disc.*, 11. 138–39), and he was never a slave to theory. As he remarked, "rules are ever of lesse force, and valew, then experiments" (*Disc.*, 11. 1757–58).

The conscious artistry of Jonson's comedy can best be appreciated by comparing it to the carelessly conceived and artlessly executed comedy of many of his contemporaries. Almost exclusively concerned with the problems encountered and eventually overcome in romantic pairings, most of these comedies were far removed from the everyday lives of their audiences. Characters and situations were frequently brought up only to be dropped without resolution or explanation. Comic materials were mixed with pathetic and even tragic elements. Plots were improbable, relying heavily on coincidence and accident. Settings were exotic in place and time. Locales often changed drastically from scene to scene, and two-hour plays often galloped through ten or twenty years of action. Dukes and cobblers mingled freely and even joined in unlikely fraternity, and the dialogue of both was sentimental and artificially poetic.

By contrast, Jonson's comedies possess internal unity and coherence. All characters and situations are carefully integrated into the fabric of the whole play. Pathetic and tragic materials are excluded. While the plots are far from simple, they are composed of believable action which gives the impression of spontaneity. Characters are restricted to the middle and lower classes; and whether in verse or prose, they speak in the words and rhythms appropriate to them. The passage of time is held within the bounds of credibility; usually no more than twelve hours elapse during a play. And locales are restricted to places within easy walking distance of each other. Moreover, Jonson moved comedy to his own milieu and that of his audience, the city; and he made its setting contemporaneous. The formal limitations he imposed on his comedies actually led to a broadening of scope and theme. Rather than focusing on amorous adventures or any other single aspect of life, Jonson sought to paint an "Image of the times" (*E. M. I.*, Pro., 1. 23), realistically detailing the men and manners of his age. Peopled with representatives of nearly all segments of the broad middle class, the plays are fully grounded in the contemporary reality of London.

Jonsonian comedy does not begin with a plot which is then fleshed out with characters, but rather with characters whose natures are the source of the action. Each of his plays brings together people who have individual eccentricities, or "humours"—follies, and occasionally vices, which cause them to act in ways counterproductive to themselves and to society. These people may be ruled by single passions, such as greed or anger or self-righteousness; or they may have pretensions to abilities or positions which they do not actually possess, such as wit, learning, fashion, or social prestige. Their passions and their distorted views of themselves lead them into ridiculous action and interaction and make them easy prey for manipulators of all kinds. The gulling of them or the sporting with them to make them display their follies to the world constitutes the action of Jonson's plays. Many of his comedies also contain individuals of genuine cleverness and integrity who, as representatives of the best aspects of society, serve both as normative figures and as moral pointers. All of Jonson's comedies from *Every Man in His Humour* onward are humor comedies; some, notable among them *Epicoene*, are also comedies of manners, balancing criticism of an imperfect society against the implied faith that the wit and sophistication of its intelligent members are sufficient to discover and root out shortcomings. Except for the sophisticated gallants, Jonson's characters tend not to be unambiguously sympathetic, and the result is unsentimental, tough-minded comedy.

Although most of Jonson's characters begin as types, almost all are given individualizing traits or aspects which contribute to their credibility as actual, albeit exaggerated human beings. Most of them have prototypes or sources in classical comedy, in native English drama, and in nondramatic literature of all periods; but all of them are given fresh life by the playwright's own acute observations of the world about him. He consistently gives clues to his characters' natures by the names he assigns them.[3] Some, such as Clement, Bonario, Morose, Truewit, and Purecraft, are transparent names; others are recondite, but no less revealing. Fabian Fitzdottrel in *The Devil Is an Ass*, for example, translates as "licentious son of silliness"; Dauphine Eugenie in *Epicoene*, as "well-born heir." Many of Jonson's major characters have extraordinary, memorable presence: Volpone, Subtle, Sir Epicure Mammon, and Zeal-of-the-Land Busy, to name only a few. A real mark of his ability as a comic writer, however, is his capacity for making even minor characters unexpectedly affecting: Bobadill, Sir Politic and Lady Wouldbe, the Ladies Collegiate, Dapper, and Ursula the pig woman are unexpectedly complex characters. Moreover, Jonson is always careful to distinguish between characters and to individualize them even when they appear superficially similar, as Volpone and Mosca, for instance, and even when they function collectively, as do Truewit, Clerimont, and Dauphine. Jonson's characters frequently have a one-dimensional singlemindedness; yet they are fully and realistically, recognizably human even in their comic exaggerations.

Perhaps the most obvious excellence in Jonsonian comedy is the superb execution of the plots. The kinds of plots Jonson uses vary widely, from the apparent structural sprawl of *Every Man in His Humour* and *Bartholomew Fair* to the tightly wound construction of *The Alchemist*. But all his plots are animated by characters with believable motives, and all events are realistically accounted for, even in plays which employ a *deus ex machina*. He generally uses the five-act form in which the first two acts introduce the characters and set up the conflicts, the third act provides a complication, and the fourth act ends in a false conclusion, only to have a new twist introduced in the final act, which effects the real conclusion. Often the action is accelerated, event piled on event, episode interlocked with episode, until finally a perceptive character steps forward to sort out the confusion and to dispense the comic justice. The enormous number of incidents and the unpredictable yet realistic action of Jonson's plays contribute immensely to their exuberant vitality.

Another source of the excitement of Jonsonian comedy is the brilliant manipulation of language.[4] Although he eschewed the artificial wordplay of romantic comedy, he nevertheless fills his comedies with the cant and jargon of contemporary London, from the alchemical technicalities of Subtle to the biblical cadences of Zeal-of-the-Land Busy. He perfectly matches speech to character, and the large number of characters in the comedies provides him the opportunity for a broad range of style. There is Marlovian richness and seductive power in the exalted celebrations of luxury which pour from the mouths of Volpone and Sir Epicure Mammon. There is the crystal purity of lyric song in Clerimont's "Still to be neat." There is the polite but witty banter of Truewit and Clerimont. There is the testy railing of Humphrey Wasp and the beleaguered dignity of Celia. But most of all, there is the energetic billingsgate of rogues and cheaters, whose vigorous vituperation becomes intoxicating. The plays are filled with catalogues of exotic unguents, cosmetics, chemical elements and processes, news items, and misquoted canon law, all designed to tempt the unwary and the foolish. And when the low characters strip down to reveal their true selves, they sling epithets of stable, street, and privy with exuberant abandon. Jonson is a master of colloquial dialect and speech rhythm, and the characteristic speech of each figure is a kind of signature which reveals him as concretely as his actions. The sheer vitality of Jonson's language energizes his comedies, and the range of his style contributes to the comprehensiveness of that "Image of the times" he sought to portray.

I *The Early Comedies (1596–1601)*

The first phase of Jonson's career may be conveniently terminated in 1601, when he took temporary leave of "the *Comick* MUSE" to "trie / If *Tragoedie* have a more kind aspect" (*Poet.*, To the Reader, ll. 222, 223–24), a sabbatical from comedy which was to last three years. The plays of this early period include *Every Man in His Humour* (1598), *Every Man out of His Humour* (1599), *Cynthia's Revels* (1600), and *Poetaster* (1601), which Jonson collected in his *Works* (1616); as well as an unknown number of apprentice efforts of which only two survive, *A Tale of a Tub* and *The Case Is Altered*. The variety of these comedies is instructive, for Jonson's early career can be described as a struggle to find his most comfortable and effective voice. The early plays include experiments in uncharacteristic modes—rustic and romantic comedy—as well as types which were to become particularly identified with Jonson—the "humour" play and the "comicall satyre." Near the beginning of his career, Jonson moves toward the compression of time, place, and action; toward the development of realistic dialogue; and toward the themes and the artistic stance which were to be uniquely his. This movement culminates in an early masterpiece, *Every Man in His Humour*, only to be followed by an excursion into satire. Significantly, by the expiration of his three-year hiatus from writing comedy, Jonson came to realize where his true genius lay. He masterfully revised *Every Man in His Humour* and produced even greater successors in the comedic triumphs of his middle years.

Jonson chose not to preserve his earliest plays, and *A Tale of a Tub* and *The Case Is Altered* are extant only in late texts. Although they are in different ways problematic, they may reflect Jonson's earliest surviving dramatic work. Thus they provide useful gauges by which to measure the playwright's maturity. *A Tale of a Tub* survives only in the revised version of 1633 and now elicits primarily biographical interest directed toward the late additions to the text, scenes which attack Jonson's one-time collaborator in the production of masques, the architect and theatrical designer Inigo Jones. These interpolations are easily detached from the play as a whole, however, and the original version may very well have been written as early as 1596.[5] A comedy of rustics, its central action is the marriage of the daughter of the High Constable of Kentish Town. Its pastoral setting distinguishes *A Tale of a Tub* from Jonson's mature comedies, which are set in cities and nearly always feature country people only as bumpkins come to town. Moreover, the characters of *A Tale of a Tub* are superficially drawn and betray nothing of Jonson's subsequent interest in humor types. In addition, the play is set in a bygone age, a practice Jonson was to follow only once again in comedy. But *A Tale of a Tub* is thoroughly Jonsonian in some ways. Its concern with pretentiousness and the comic zest of its dialogue look forward to the mature comedies. The characters of *A Tale of a Tub* speak in a dialect appropriate to them, indicating that very early Jonson was already striving toward realistic speech on the stage. And, finally, the play adheres to the unities of time and action and makes the typical Jonsonian compromise in the unity of place, its scenes set in several places but all within a relatively small area.

The other surviving example of Jonson's apprentice work, *The Case Is Altered,* is probably the last of his compositions before *Every Man in His Humour*. It exists only in a revised state as well, but the revisions were probably made only a few years after the original version. Coincidentally, the revisions, like the added scenes in *A Tale of a Tub*, consist largely of an interpolated attack on a contemporary figure, the pageant poet Anthony Munday. *The Case Is Altered* is a romantic comedy, a genre Jonson was later to attack for its absurdities of plotting, characterization, and diction. Its two plot lines, drawn from different Plautine comedies, double the instances of long-lost children ultimately restored to their families and multiply the love interests and eventual pairing of couples. The play follows the pattern of romantic comedy in freely mixing noble and base characters, even to the point of having noblemen and clownish servants vie for the hand of the same young lady. But despite its genre, there are actually relatively few love scenes, and Jonson imposes on the play some of the formal strictures characteristic of his later work. He compresses the passage of time as much as possible, allowing only a few weeks to transpire between the first and last acts; he restricts place to a few locales in close proximity; and he carefully ties the two plots together and integrates the concerns of the low characters with those of the nobility. Moreover, *The Case Is Altered* contains incidental speeches and episodes, most notably the exaggerated mourning of Count Ferneze for his wife (I.vi and ix), which anticipate the humor characterization and comedy of manners of *Every Man in His Humour*.[6]

Jonson's first undisputed success, *Every Man in His Humour*, premiered in 1598 at The Curtain, the second oldest of the Elizabethan playhouses. Produced by the Lord Chamberlain's Men, its original cast included Will Kempe, the most famous comic actor of his generation; Richard Burbage, a player of both comic and tragic genius; William Shakespeare, the company's leading playwright-actor; and John Heminges and Henry Condell, the pair who in 1623 (perhaps with the aid and encouragement of Jonson) collected and published Shakespeare's plays. In its original version, issued in quarto in 1601, *Every Man in His Humour* is set in Italy and most of its characters have Italian names, although both setting and characters are recognizably English. Some years after its original production, perhaps for presentation at court in early February of 1605, perhaps as late as 1612, Jonson rewrote the play, abandoning the Italian locale and names in favor of a London setting and descriptive English names. He also tightened the play, most notably by abbreviating the speeches in praise of poetry which slow the original fifth act.[7] In its revised form, Jonson placed *Every Man in His Humour* first among the plays in the 1616 *Works*, indicating thereby his own judgment of the play's importance as the earliest of his comedies worthy of preservation. A brilliant comedy of manners molded from both classical and native English traditions, the play bears the impress of Jonson's genius.

Although original in its details, Jonson's first major play owes much of its shape to Latin comedy, particularly to Plautus. In a frenetic series of episodes, two witty gallants and a wily, frequently disguised servant manipulate their foolish relatives and companions to supreme heights of folly, all for the sport of it. When the numerous threads of the action are thoroughly complicated, a fun-loving old magistrate sets everything right; and the play ends with an invitation to a banquet celebrating the marriage of one of the gallants to a wholly appropriate young woman. A deliberate synthesis of diverse elements, both dramatic and nondramatic, the play self-consciously adheres to classical ideals of structure and decorum; but its characters, situations, and language are informed and enriched by native English dramatic traditions, by the rogue literature and the humor psychology of the Elizabethan period, and by Jonson's own robust enjoyment of city life in all its manifestations.

In the Prologue to the revised version of the play, Jonson expounds on his adherence to classical structure and decorum by contrasting the virtues of his comedy with "th'ill customes" of other playwrights (1. 4). Unlike his contemporaries, including Shakespeare, he will not allow, in a two-hour play, "a child, now swadled, to proceede / Man, and then shoote up, in one beard, and weede, / Past threescore yeeres" (11. 7–9). After the scene is set, he will allow no chorus suddenly to waft his audience "ore the seas" (1. 15). And he will not mix comedic and tragic personages, actions, or language, but will confine himself to

> deedes, and language, such as men doe use:
> And persons, such as *Comoedie* would chuse,
> When she would shew an Image of the times. (11. 21–23)

Jonson in effect describes *Every Man in His Humour* as a decorous comedy which illuminates contemporary life and manners while observing the unities of time, place, and action.

In *Every Man in His Humour*, the classical strictures which Jonson voluntarily adopts never intrude as artificially enforced rules. In Jonson's hands, they serve to strengthen design and to reenforce theme. The settings of *Every Man in His Humour* are the streets, warehouses, and residences of a single city and a house in the countryside a short walking distance away; and when characters move from one locale to another, they do so at a natural pace. Furthermore, when Jonson uses letters and messengers, those old standbys of Greek and Roman drama, he does so in functional ways that do not violate probability. They are not used to relate events which, because of the confinement to a single locale, cannot take place within the audience's view. They serve instead to bring characters together and to complicate the plot. Similarly, though few plays call attention to the exact hours of the day as insistently as *Every Man in His Humour*, the unity of time is as unforced as the unity of place. All of the action transpires between the early morning and the early evening of a single day. Those twelve or so hours are crowded with events, but the crowding does not strain credibility. Indeed, the frequent references to the passage of time and the tumbling-together of events have thematic points, reflecting the crowded and hurried nature of urban life. The many decisions which have to be made must be made quickly, without the luxury of prolonged consideration. To survive in the city, and certainly to flourish, one needs a wit both quick and penetrating.

While *Every Man in His Humour* is crowded with events, it is unified in action. The one action is the making of "sport with humane follies" (Pro., 1. 24), and all the events in the play contribute to that end. Each event is designed to show either the folly of the fools, the perception of the wits who manipulate them, or both simultaneously. And just as the action of the play is of one piece, though crowded with details, so is the theme single but multifaceted. Fools lack self-knowledge and, as a consequence, do not perceive the true nature of the world and fail to participate positively in human society. Wits, on the other hand, know themselves and thereby the world about them. Such knowledge makes them able both to perceive and to uphold desirable social values. The conclusion of the Prologue states this theme, though it avoids overt moralizing. If loved and perpetuated, rather than despised and banished, human follies can become crimes. Jonson's term for these failings, "popular errors" (1. 26), not only indicates that they are widely accepted and practiced, but also suggests that they are faults harmful to society as a whole. This implication is strengthened in the final line of the Prologue. There Jonson expresses the hope that his comedy will cause the audience to purge itself of its affection for "monsters" and to appreciate "men," well-balanced human beings in a harmonious society. The playwright is, however, somewhat disingenuous here, for the obvious delight which the play takes in the antics of fools

actually reveals a more ambiguous attitude than the Prologue allows. Nevertheless, the moral intention of the play is manifest, if expressed in robust entertainment.

Although the action of *Every Man in His Humour* is of one piece, it is woven of many strands. Preeminent is the sport made with the pretentiousness of the three fools, Bobadill, Matthew, and Stephen. Another strand has older men (Knowell and Downright) foolishly attempting to protect their young relatives (Edward and Wellbred) from corruption by loose society. Closely related to this concern is the jealousy plot, centered on Kitely and his wife. Also included, though minimized in importance, is the courtship motif, with Bridget as the prize and Matthew and Edward as the juxtaposed foolish and sensible suitors. Finally, though it is more prominent in the earlier version than in the revision, there is a concern with distinguishing true and false poetry, again pitting Edward against Matthew as well as against his father. All of these plot lines may be combined into two large considerations, one focusing on gentility and the other centering on human relationships, both familial and sexual. The true gentility of Wellbred and Edward contrasts with the futile aspirations of Bobadill, Matthew, and Stephen, who think that to be gentlemen they have only to fight, swear, and parrot verse. The concern with relationships subsumes blood ties, notably represented by Downright's anxiety over his brother Wellbred and old Knowell's fear about his son Edward, and conjugal relationships, including the jealousy of Kitely and the courtship of Bridget. These two parts of the main plot are masterfully parodied in a subplot centered on the low characters Cob and Tib. Cob mirrors the pretentiousness of the would-be gentlemen of the main plot in his admiration of outrageous oaths and in his concern with his own distinguished lineage, tracing his family back to King Herring, while at the same time he professes disgust with the gentlemanly affectation of tobacco. The waterbearer also reenforces the jealousy of Kitely in his own suspicions of Tib, while Tib duplicates Dame Kitely's essential blamelessness in her own innocent but raucous behavior.

A comedy deliberately composed within the strictures of the unities runs the risk of appearing mechanical and contrived in its plotting. In *Every Man in His Humour*, Jonson avoids that pitfall. Once the various parts of the plot are set in motion, specific incidents give the impression of flowing naturally from unpremeditated occasions. For instance, Edward decides to "furnish our feast with one gull more" only because the foolish Stephen happens to be at the

Knowell house when Wellbred's letter arrives (I.iii.70–71). Similarly, Wellbred apparently has no thought of matchmaking when he
invites Edward to London for a day of sport. Only after he perceives
that Edward has fallen in love with Bridget does he determine to aid
their union (IV.v). Stephen's altercation with Downright comes
about entirely through a happy convergence of circumstances. The
character who most often improvises is the witty servant Brainworm.
Without premeditation, he takes advantage of the situation at hand to
gull Stephen into buying a cheap sword at a dear price (II.iv). He uses
Formal's offer of a drink to disguise himself as "the Justices man"
(IV.viii.50). And he grabs occasion by the forelock in the quarrel
between Bobadill and Downright, selling the blustering soldier and
Matthew a warrant against the angry squire (IV.ix). Throughout, the
plot of *Every Man in His Humour*, while unified and tightly controlled, gives the impression of spontaneity, as actions seem to arise
naturally from unexpected situations.

As is clear from the Prologue, Jonson is concerned with decorum in
the selection of characters, voluntarily restricting himself to "persons, such as *Comoedie* would chuse" (1. 22). His model of decorum is
Greek New Comedy, as transmitted to the Renaissance through the
comedies of republican Rome. Inspired by Athenian democratic
ideals, this comedy is peopled with characters from the middle and
lower classes only. To the squires and burghers of these classical
prototypes, Jonson adds a third group of middle-class citizens
prominent in Elizabethan England, the merchants; and for the slaves
of Roman comedy, he substitutes free servants and menial laborers.
Although restricted by considerations of decorum, the range and
number of characters in the play are nevertheless large enough to
"shew an Image of the times" (Pro., 1. 23), particularly since Jonson
places them in realistic settings which accentuate social relationships.
Most of the characters may also be described as "humourous," or
eccentric in one way or another. Cash's definition of humor as "a
gentleman-like monster, bred, in the speciall gallantrie of our time,
by affectation; and fed by folly" (III.iv.20–22) explains Jonson's title
for a comedy of manners intent on exposing pretension and folly.

The sources for the specific characters are many and varied, and
Jonson often mixes traits from two or more sources in a single
character or subtly modifies a stock figure to give it fresh life.
Bobadill, for instance, is ultimately the *miles gloriosus*, the braggart
soldier of Roman comedy, but with a significant difference. Unlike his
classical ancestors, he is poor. He has no mistress or parasite in his

retinue. His only companion is the equally poor and pretentious Matthew. The result of this modification is that while Bobadill is a ridiculous liar and coward, he is also curiously affecting. His desire that Matthew "possesse no gentlemen of our acquaintance, with notice of my lodging" (I.v.33–34) reveals his affected gentility; he wants no one to know that he is reduced to renting a room from a waterbearer. But it also indicates how poorly society treats its soldiers when there are no wars in which they are needed. Moreover, while Bobadill is a coward, he faces his poverty with a kind of bravery, as well as bravado, making do with radishes, salt, wine, and tobacco "to close the orifice of the stomach" (I.v.167).

In another instance, Jonson adds to a characterization a self-awareness not usually found in its prototype. The old husband of a young and pretty wife, Kitely is dominated by jealousy and is basically a humor character. But Jonson makes him aware of the irrationality of his behavior. In a long speech (II.iii.57–74), Kitely warns himself that jealousy works "upon the phantasie," that it "soone corrupts the judgement," and that it "Sends like contagion to the memorie." He tries to "shake the feaver off," and as a consequence he becomes a much more complex figure than the stock jealous husband of Roman and Elizabethan comedy. Finally, for comic effect and thematic point, Jonson sometimes places characters in positions where they seem, at least for a time, to be types which they actually are not. Old Knowell, for instance, is not the *senex amans*, the lecherous old lover of Latin comedy, although his appearance at Cob's door makes Kitely think that he is, and the old man suffers much verbal abuse as a result (IV.x). Similarly, Wellbred and Edward appear to be the dissolute gallants of earlier comedy, prodigal young men who need to be rescued from bad company, but in fact they are not dissolute. They revel in the antics of what could be corrupting companions, but both are in reality wise enough not to be tainted by their associates.

The low characters of *Every Man in His Humour* are carefully drawn, and even the least important of them are used to brilliant effect. Cash, with whom Kitely would "trust my life" (II.i.23), is quite easily persuaded to desert his master's cause for his mistress's (IV.viii). The stuffy Formal is a perfect foil to his fun-loving master, Clement, and his formality is comically compromised by his affection for drink and shattered entirely when he is reduced to appearing before his employer in Brainworm's rusty armor. Cob and Tib, the quarrelsome but fundamentally devoted peasant couple of medieval drama, provide a farcical element in the play and underscore some of its more serious concerns. And, finally, Brainworm, whose complex ancestry includes the wily slave of Roman comedy, the vice character of medieval and early Renaissance drama, and the coney-catcher of Elizabethan pamphlet literature, is a kind of comic overreacher, anticipating such later creations as Mosca in *Volpone* and Face in *The Alchemist*. Successful beyond expectation in his early manipulations, he becomes so enamored of his wit that he takes a dangerous risk which leads to his comic fall.

The duped characters in the play may be divided into two groups: those who are permanently foolish and those who are foolish for a time only. The three gulls, Bobadill, Matthew, and Stephen, are all pretenders to what they are not; and they are all so insensitive to their own realities that they are incapable of becoming rational creatures. Bobadill is a pretender to gentility and to martial prowess. Although he may actually have fought in a battle or two, he is ridiculous in the role of officer and tactician. He is a fencer out of books and a coward. Matthew, a fishmonger's son, is a pretender to gentility and to poetry. But the verse he claims as his own is invariably stolen and mutilated in the process. He pretends to melancholy because it "breeds your perfect fine wit" (III.i.90), but he has none of the useful introspection that accompanies that humor and in no way is his wit improved by it. Stephen, a dense young man of "rusticall cut" (III.i.18), is the country bumpkin come to town to learn the latest fashions of gentlemanly deportment. He is so out of touch with polite society that he is just now taking up the sport of hawking, already passé. Like Matthew, he affects the melancholy humor; and from Bobadill, he is anxious to learn to swear and to take tobacco. All three are such fools that they are easily manipulated. As Justice Clement perceives, they are unable to abandon their folly and must be exiled from convivial society, Bobadill and Matthew to fast in the courtyard, Stephen to eat with the menials in the kitchen.

Old Knowell, Kitely, and Dame Kitely are fools for a time only and then only partially so. Dame Kitely is fundamentally sensible. She recognizes and is untouched by the folly of the gulls. Wellbred is able to persuade her that Kitely is a lecher (IV.viii), however, and for a time she is outraged without true cause. Old Knowell, though somewhat too self-satisfied and pompous, is a loving father of good motives. He knows that Edward is a dutiful young man, but he is concerned that his son, having studied only poetry, knows so little of the real world that he may be led astray. The father's failure to appreciate the true utility of poetry and his lack of faith in his son are failures of perception. And like Knowell, Kitely acts foolishly against his own better judgment. At the end of the play, Justice Clement asks the three "to put of[f] all discontent. . . . you, master KNO'WELL, your cares; master KITELY, and his wife, their jealousie" (V.v.70–72). There is every reason to believe that the exposure of their foolishness has cured them of it.

Downright is a special case among the manipulated characters. A no-nonsense country squire, he is a humor character; but his humor, anger, is potentially more dangerous to society than the affectations of simpletons, the misplaced anxiety of a parent, or the jealousy of a husband. Wellbred and Edward recognize the difference. They comment on Downright's anger, and they bait it; but they cannot find the same kind of amusement in it that they find in the irrational behavior of the other dupes. Although a misanthrope may despise the follies and vices of mankind, his all-engrossing anger is not an answer to them, and his rantings disturb the comic spirit. Downright cannot distinguish between relatively harmless folly and more harmful vice; and in treating the two alike, he makes a serious error in judgment. Justice Clement tells him to leave off his anger, but his destructive humor is so fundamentally a part of his personality that it is unlikely he can alter it.

The positive aspect of the play's moral thrust is embodied in Wellbred, Edward Knowell, Justice Clement, and, to a lesser extent, Bridget. All four recognize folly when they see it; and although they make sport of it, their own actions and essential natures remain untouched. Bridget obviously enjoys the outrageous wooing of the false poet, Matthew, but she comes to love and to marry the true poet, Edward. Ironically, he does not court her with verse. The play's focal characters, Wellbred and Edward Knowell, are, of course, more thoroughly developed than Bridget. Wellbred is a spirited but sane young man. As his name indicates, he is a true gentleman. He is the prime mover of the action, which begins as a lark to expose the follies of two gulls, progresses through some unexpected fun with Kitely's jealousy, and ends with the romantic and sensible match of Edward and Bridget. Edward is a studious young man, but one who can enjoy a jest. He respects his father, but thinks him too sober and too protective. He has the exuberance of youth and the good sense to fall in love with a wholly suitable young woman.[8]

Justice Clement is the play's *deus ex machina,* but "a god with a sense of humour."[9] As his name indicates, he tempers justice with mercy, though, as in the cases of both Cob (III.vii) and Brainworm (V.iii), he finds amusement in making a culprit squirm. As the embodiment of justice, Clement resolves all the plot complications and metes out appropriate rewards and punishments. In the comic spirit of the play, his role of judge is primarily one of seeing through foolish pretension and irrational conduct. He banishes Bobadill, Matthew, and Stephen from the festivities; he cautions Old Knowell, the Kitelys, and Downright; and he creates the appropriate conditions for the happy reconciliation of master and servant, husband and wife, and father and son. Tellingly, he pardons Brainworm "for the wit o' the offence" (V.iii.113–14).

Every Man in His Humour is a considerable achievement. In it Jonson synthesizes both classical and native traditions of drama, concretely illustrating the adaptability of ancient practice to his contemporary stage; he reveals insight into the complexities of human character, adding unexpected dimensions to stock figures; and he captures the excitement of Elizabethan city life in fast-paced scenes of comic realism. Perhaps most important of all, however, the play's exuberant comic spirit and its serious social intent perfectly complement each other. The attitude the work expresses toward human follies is serious but urbane and sophisticated. It recognizes the dangers of social pretension and of failures of perception, but it delights in the city's sport. This balance of moral seriousness and comic joyousness distinguishes *Every Man in His Humour* from the harsh works which immediately followed it.

One difference between *Every Man in His Humour* and the three subsequent plays is revealed by Jonson's designation of *Every Man out of His Humour, Cynthia's Revels,* and *Poetaster* as comical satires rather than comedies. Unlike the earlier comedy, these plays are not goodnatured correctives which delight as well as instruct. Rather, they instruct by means of overt and biting attacks on faults and individuals seriously harmful to society. While they are frequently amusing, these plays present a less appealing vision than that "Image of the times" incorporated in *Every Man in His Humour*. Moreover, they lack the mastery of organic form and complex characterization which enriches that comedy. Indeed, the comical satires may represent an attempt to dramatize the verse satires of the period; plot and characterization are thus subordinated to the presentation of didactic episodes and abstractions which contribute to a generalized thesis. Although the comical satires are interesting, even revolutionary, experiments and reveal Jonson's conception of the poet's role as censor or moral arbiter of the age, they do not much engage the emotions or capture the imagination.[10]

Every Man out of His Humour premiered late in 1599. Like its immediate predecessor, it was first acted by the Lord Chamberlain's Men, but in the newly completed Globe Theater. During the Christmas season, it was also presented at court. Although its title might imply that it is either a sequel or a companion piece to *Every Man in His Humour*, it is neither, though both plays expose and reform humors. In contrast to the earlier comedy's intent to "shew an Image of the times," *Every Man out of His Humour* is designed to show "the times deformitie / Anatomiz'd in every nerve, and sinnew" (Ind., ll. 120–21). In it, Jonson sets forth a gallery of grotesques: a self-commending, vainglorious knight; an affected courtier; an empty-headed lady of the court; a greedy farmer who would let the masses starve while his barns are full; and two aspiring courtiers, one a country fool, the other a law student in love with fine clothes. Even the two characters who expose the deformities of the others are themselves representatives of undesirable passions. One is an envious malcontent, the other a profane jester. The only sensible character is Cordatus, but his role is to comment on the play as an ideal spectator rather than to participate in it. The framing device of which he is a part heightens the sense that the diverse characters and episodes are intended as object lessons, not illusions of real human beings engaged in actual human behavior. The result is that the play fails to evoke empathy. Whereas Jonson's best comedies appeal simultaneously to the mind and to the emotions, *Every Man out of His Humour* speaks only to the intellect.

The second and third of Jonson's trio of satirical comedies, *Cynthia's Revels* and *Poetaster*, were written for the Children of Queen Elizabeth's Chapel. Both premiered at Blackfriars Theater, the former late in 1600, the latter early in the next year. *Cynthia's Revels* is an attack on false courtiers, *Poetaster* on false poets. Even more so than *Every Man out of His Humour*, these plays sacrifice structure to portraiture, and both are collections of good and bad exempla only occasionally animated by drama.

In *Cynthia's Revels, or the Fountain of Self-Love*, Jonson deserts the milieu he knew best and could best represent on stage, the world of the middle and lower orders of London society, to present a confusing mixture of mythological, allegorical, and humor characters centered in the court of the virgin huntress-queen of Gargaphie, a "fustian countrie" (Ind., l. 43). In a progression of loosely connected scenes, characters whose names translate into such abstractions as voluptuousness, impudence, prodigality, money, and self-love, exhibit their respective follies and, rather superfluously, drink from the Narcissan fountain. With the encouragement and support of a lovely woman whose name means sobriety, Crites, a discerning critic-poet ("A creature of a most perfect and divine temper. One, in whom the humours and elements are peaceably met" [II.iii.123–25]), exposes their follies and, in a pair of masques presented before Queen Cynthia, delineates the characteristics desirable in courtiers: natural affection, pleasant conversation, wit, simplicity, elegance, courage, and good nature.

Cynthia's Revels may best be understood as an attempt by Jonson to fulfill his perceived role of advisor to the ruling classes, a role he would assume in fact only after the death of Queen Elizabeth. With its static plot, overt moralizing, predictable didacticism, and tedious allegorizing, the play is not exciting theater. Yet it is among Jonson's most interesting early works, a profoundly serious experiment to create an idealistic, intellectual form of comedy capable of excoriating pretentiousness and moral failure in the highest levels of society.[11] The play was frankly designed as a revolutionary departure from the "beaten path" of popular drama and directed toward "learned eares" (Pro., ll. 10, 11). It contains some of Jonson's loveliest lyrics, such as Echo's Song (I.ii.65–75) and the Hymn to Cynthia (V.vi.1–18); and the masques within the play adumbrate Jonson's later role as court poet. If the play is an unsuccessful amalgam of scarcely compatible modes—comedy, satire, allegory, lyric poetry, masque—it usefully anticipates Jonson's later achievements as the greatest masque writer of his age and a supremely accomplished lyric poet.

While *Every Man out of His Humour* and *Cynthia's Revels* may both contain incidental skirmishes in the so-called War of the Theaters, *Poetaster, or His Arraignment* is unquestionably a major attack in the conflict. Several theories have been offered as to the exact nature of the altercation: that it was a personal quarrel between Jonson and his antagonists John Marston and Thomas Dekker; that it expressed the rivalry between the public adult acting companies and the private children's companies; that it centered in the conflicting artistic principles of Shakespeare and Jonson; and that it was merely a ploy to increase box-office revenue for all parties concerned. In any case, the war apparently began in the summer of 1599, when Marston, in revising the old play *Histriomastix,* modeled the character of the pedant Chrisoganus on Jonson. Later in that same year,

Marston may have sensed a counterattack in the inflated diction of the
fop Clove in *Every Man out of His Humour* (III.iv); and the next year
Marston and fellow playwright Thomas Dekker recognized themselves in the characters of Hedon and Anaides in *Cynthia's Revels*. To
revenge these unflattering portraits, they began a collaborative play
entitled *Satiro-mastix, or the Untrussing of the Humourous Poet*. But
before that work could be staged, Jonson recaptured the offensive by
a devastating satire of his opponents in *Poetaster*.

Poetaster is, however, more than an attack on Marston and
Dekker, who are actually represented in the rather small roles of
Crispinus and Demetrius. Written in the unusually short time of
fifteen weeks, the play is set in imperial Rome, where Augustus
Caesar as a matter of course looks to poets for advice. The subject of
the play is poetry itself, and more particularly the relationship of
poetry and society.[12] In the initial plot revolving around Ovid and
Julia, Jonson raises questions about the effect of the poet's private life
on his public role. In the major plot, activated by the satirist Horace,
Jonson examines the public obligations of the poet. Horace explains
that his satirical bent is motivated by his love of virtue and hatred of
vice. He will "spare mens persons, and but taxe their crimes"
(III.v.134). The ideal poet is Vergil, and his poetry is of indisputable
utility, as Tibullus explains:

> That, which he hath writ,
> Is with such judgement, labour'd, and distill'd
> Through all the needfull uses of our lives,
> That could a man remember but his lines,
> He should not touch at any serious point,
> But he might breathe his spirit out of him. (V.i.118–23)

With Vergil as judge and Caesar as supporting authority, Horace
arraigns greater and lesser enemies of poetry. Among the lesser
malefactors is the "play-dresser" Demetrius, easily recognizable as
Dekker; among the more serious culprits is Crispinus, representing
Marston, who in the play's climactic scene is given an emetic and
forced to vomit up bombastic words and phrases.

Poetaster is the most successful of Jonson's comical satires. It does
seem to have been written too hurriedly; its plots are not well
integrated; and the incidental action is not always focused clearly. But
the play is genuinely amusing. It contains some of Jonson's most
interesting characters, particularly the complex Ovid and the wonderfully boorish Captain Tucca. As in the best of Jonson's comedies,

the satiric force of the play does not preclude delight in sporting with folly. And although it may have originated in a personal quarrel, *Poetaster* transcends the topical to express a lasting vision of the poet's active function in a receptive society.

The first period of Jonson's career is marked by experimentation and innovation. In *Every Man in His Humour* he successfully imposes classical ideals of form and decorum on contemporary material. The result is realistic comedy which breathes an air of city life. The excursion into comical satires did not yield great plays. But Jonson's restless experimentation indicates an attempt to make the popular stage a forum for intellectual issues. And if the War of the Theaters no longer interests us—however bitter Jonson's quarrel with Marston, the two were sufficiently reconciled by 1604 to join George Chapman in collaboration on *Eastward Ho!*—it provided an opportunity for Jonson to assert in *Poetaster* the profound seriousness of poetry and its usefulness to society, a lifelong theme. After *Poetaster,* Jonson abandoned the comic muse for a time to attempt tragedy. When he returned to comedy with a play of his own devising, he produced *Volpone,* a work which combines the organic form and control of *Every Man in His Humour* with the seriousness of the comical satires.

II   Volpone *(1606)*

Jonson's second major comedy, *Volpone, or The Fox,* was first presented by the King's Men (formerly the Lord Chamberlain's Men) at the Globe Theater, probably early in 1606. Within a year, the play was produced at both Oxford and Cambridge; and when it was published, Jonson dedicated it "To the Most Noble and Most Equall Sisters the Two Famous Universities." Jonson wrote *Volpone* in only five weeks (Pro., l. 16), for him an extraordinarily rapid rate of composition, but he was justifiably pleased with the result. When he prepared the play for inclusion in his *Works,* he altered the text only slightly. Although in some respects unlike anything else he was to write, *Volpone* is masterful both in conception and in realization. Its characters and its actions are sources of unflagging interest, and the language of the play is rich and evocative.

The situation from which the action springs in *Volpone* was no doubt suggested to Jonson by a medieval beast fable in which a fox feigns imminent death in order to catch and eat carrion birds.[13] Using details from the legacy-hunting literature of classical Rome and from an important Renaissance satire, Erasmus's *The Praise of Folly,*

Jonson transforms the fable's appetite for food into an appetite for riches and adds a host of complications. With the assistance of his parasite, a Venetian magnifico named Volpone pretends to be terminally ill in order to extract expensive gifts from three wealthy old men, named appropriately Voltore, Corvino, and Corbaccio, leading each to believe that he will be made sole heir if his gifts find favor with the dying man. The "fox" is a luxurious, quick-witted man who becomes enamored of his own ability to scheme. His voluptuous nature manifests itself in his lust for Celia, the virtuous young wife of one of his gulls; and his determination to bed her, culminating in attempted rape, causes the play's first catastrophe. Volpone averts public exposure, but deludes himself into believing that he was saved entirely by his own quick wit. His already high opinion of his cleverness soars, and he elaborates on his scheme so much that he unwittingly provides an opportunity for the parasite Mosca to seize his fortune. The rivalry of master and servant leads to a second and complete catastrophe.

The subjects of *Volpone* are vices, not follies: greed so great that it disrupts both the familial and the broader social order, luxuriousness so excessive and unchecked by conscience that it countenances rape, perversions so fundamental that human beings descend to the level of beasts.[14] Carried to the extent that they are, these human failings cannot be considered merely humors and the major plot of *Volpone* cannot be considered a comedy of manners. It does not contain a single normative figure.[15] On one side are the vicious characters, Volpone, Mosca, and the three gulls; on the other side are Bonario and Celia, their innocent victims, who are so naive that they lack even that moderate amount of calculating wit necessary for self-preservation in a far from perfect world. In the middle stand the Avocatori, who should be the wise guardians of society but who are actually foolish old men easily led astray. If the play had only this one plot, it might be bleak indeed. But Jonson masterfully weaves into its fabric a subplot which is a comedy of manners in miniature, using it both to ameliorate the tension of the major plot and to show the ultimate danger of what appears to be relatively harmless folly.

Scattered throughout *Volpone* are scenes which feature an expatriate English couple, Sir Politic and Lady Wouldbe, and a young gentleman traveler named Peregrine. Both Sir Pol and his wife are pretenders to that which they do not have, the husband to worldly wisdom and an intimate knowledge of state secrets, his wife to beauty, intelligence, and fashion. The manipulation of Lady

Wouldbe by Volpone and Mosca clearly demonstrates the ease with which folly can be used by vice. She is readily made partner to the unjust persecution of Celia and added to the company of greedy legacy hunters. Sir Pol's function is more subtly connected to the play's chief action. His most egregious folly is alleging the existence of political plots where none really exists. This proclivity pointedly complements the inability of the Avocatori to detect the actual conspiracies of Volpone and Mosca. Peregrine, in the manner of the gentlemen wits of other Jonsonian comedies, at first finds amusement in Sir Politic's pretensions. But when he himself becomes a victim of the English couple's foolishness (IV.ii and iii), he exposes the old knight's absurdities in an appropriately humiliating way.[16]

The range of characters in *Volpone* is great, from simply developed figures of minor interest to completely realized individuals of memorable presence and power. The four Avocatori are defined only by their collective judicial blindness, self-satisfaction, and obsequiousness to wealth and social position. The three gulls are somewhat more fully drawn. All are characterized by a greed so great that they are willing to sacrifice for material gain those things they should most love. Voltore, a lawyer, should of all men respect truth. But his tongue is "mercenary" and "His soule moves in his fee" (IV.v.95,96). Corbaccio should cherish his dutiful son, but he is willing to disinherit the young man for the promise of great wealth. Corvino, insanely jealous and defensive of his reputation, should appreciate the virtue of his wife. But after locking her away from the world to avoid even the appearance of impropriety, he then willingly prostitutes her in the hope of increasing his wealth. The manipulation of the gulls abounds in irony. None of them believe that they actually endanger the values they profess, but their subordination of everything to the hope of gold reveals their true natures. In contrast to the gulls, Celia and Bonario are defined by an innocence so complete that they are unequipped to deal with the real world.[17] As their names indicate, Celia is "heavenly" and Bonario is a "good man." When faced with rape, Celia naively believes that she can win over her attacker by appealing to his conscience, honor, and pity. And even after learning of his father's plan to disinherit him, Bonario remains dutifully obedient. Their only defense to counter the perjuries sworn against them in their trial are the touching, but naive and ineffectual witnesses of "Our consciences. / And heaven, that never failes the innocent" (IV.vi.16–17).

Peregrine is characterized in much the same fashion as the witty

gallants of Jonson's other comedies.[18] Basically blameless, he is
clever enough to recognize folly. While he enjoys the city's sport, he
can, when necessary, manipulate a foolish character into an embar-
rassing exposure of his inadequacy. The two humor characters he
confronts are quite thoroughly drawn, and both became enduring
types in comedies of manners. Sir Politic Wouldbe is full of assumed
dignity, self-importance, and even bluster when he is away from his
wife, but a slave to her shrewish tongue when she is present. Some of
his speeches, such as the "advice to travelers" passage that begins Act
Four, are among the most sophisticated bits of comic writing in the
play. But Lady Wouldbe is the masterpiece of humor characterization in *Volpone*. Full of recipes for medicines and cosmetic
unguents, furnished with the names of authors and titles—but not the
contents—of books, completely oblivious to her own ridiculousness
and to the havoc she wreaks on her mother tongue, she chatters her
way through the play, to the frustration of its characters and to the
delight of its audience. She may be used negatively to point up a
moral lesson, but she is a brilliant creation; and her numerous
daughters and granddaughters enliven the comedy of manners
throughout the Restoration and beyond.

Most of Jonson's comedies are focused widely. They present the
actions of people in groups and the audience follows the fates of
several characters simultaneously. In *Volpone*, however, attention is
almost unrelentingly directed toward the title character and his
parasite. Both are superb improvisors of comic action and both
ultimately overreach themselves, but Jonson carefully distinguishes
between them. The keys to Mosca's character are his contempt for
others and his conviction that his wit entitles him to status higher than
that of servant. He recognizes the monstrosity of his deeds. As he tells
Bonario, even here using the truth for his own deceitful purposes,

> I have done
> Base offices, in rending friends asunder,
> Dividing families, betraying counsells,
> Whispering false lyes, or mining men with praises,
> Train'd their credulitie with perjuries,
> Corrupted chastitie. . . . (III.ii.25–30)

But he scorns the social fabric he endangers. Acutely aware of being,
in the words of the judge who sentences him, "a fellow of no birth, or
bloud" (V.xii.112), he is alienated from a body politic which restricts
his ambition and fails to recognize him as "a most precious thing,

dropt from above, / Not bred 'mong'st clods, and clot-poules, here on earth" (III.i.8–9). He takes pleasure in undermining the society from which he feels excluded. The gulls of the play merit his disdain, but his contempt for fools gradually broadens to include Volpone himself. Mosca comes to believe that he is more clever than his master and that his own wit rather than the magnifico's is responsible for cozening the dupes. In this context of social resentment, Volpone's praise begins to smell of condescension. Mosca chafes at the subservient role, and when the opportunity arises, he seizes the wealth and social position he believes due him. Appropriately, Volpone's pride in his own status precludes allowing himself to be tricked by a parasite. If the magnifico must accept defeat, his ruin will be at the hands of his social peers. "My substance shall not glew you, / Nor screw you, into a family" (V.xii.87–88), he declares to Mosca, even though his exposure of the parasite necessarily causes his own severe punishment.[19] By making Mosca resentful of his social position and using this alienation to help motivate his actions, Jonson deepens his portrait and, without mitigating his confessed evil, makes him more complex and affecting than he might otherwise be.

Unlike Mosca, Volpone does not acknowledge the evil he does or causes others to do. Indeed, he congratulates himself that he earns his money by wit rather than by such "destructive" occupations as trading, farming, mining, manufacturing, shipping, or banking:

> I use no trade, no venter;
> I wound no earth with plow-shares; fat no beasts
> To feede the shambles; have no mills for yron,
> Oyle, corne, or men, to grinde 'hem into poulder;
> I blow no subtill glasse; expose no ships
> To threatnings of the furrow-faced sea;
> I turne no moneys, in the publike banke;
> Nor usure private. (I.i.33–40)

He complacently accepts Mosca's praise of his generosity and "sweet nature" (I.i.48), and he apparently misses the irony in his servant's commendation of him for abhorring the ruthlessness of capitalists, though in fact his schemes lead exactly to the abuses catalogued by Mosca (I.i.40–51). Completely egocentric, he is a jaded voluptuary who delights in feasting the senses. He keeps as household entertainers the dwarf Nano, the eunuch Castrone, and the hermaphrodite Androgyno, their physical abnormalities mirroring his spiritual unnaturalness. Even the satisfaction he derives from his clever scheming is sensual. "The pleasure of all woman-kind's not like it" (V.ii.11), he exclaims.

Volpone's lack of conscience makes him a monster, but he is nevertheless enormously appealing, at least for a time. Despite the perversion of values implicit in his worship of gold, he certainly evokes far more admiration than Corbaccio, Corvino, and Voltore; for they share his debased values, but not his appealing wit. When he preys on individuals as monstrous as he, his attractiveness insulates him from moral censure. His vision is larger than theirs and his cleverness far greater. Even when the excess of his luxuriousness grows to outweigh its apparent attractiveness, when he attempts to destroy—in the persons of Celia and Bonario—both heavenly and earthly goodness, his agile wit continues to command respect and interest. His false values represent the dark side of man, but in him that side shines with a brilliant, tempting luster. And despite his profoundly serious moral failings, Volpone remains a comic character, complex and compelling and always entertaining.

A measure of Jonson's genius in *Volpone* is that the play's dark vision of spiritual malaise is presented delightfully. But the play's fun does not obscure its serious social and religious insights. At its center is an animating materialism so complete that it becomes religious; the play studies that worship of riches which translates men into beasts. The inversion of Volpone's values is clear from his opening hymn to gold, "the worlds soule, and mine" (I.i.3):

> O, thou sonne of SOL,
> (But brighter then thy father) let me kisse,
> With adoration, thee, and every relique
> Of sacred treasure, in this blessed roome. (I.i.10–13)

All the characters of the main plot, except the symbolic innocents, join to greater or lesser degrees in the worship of the false god gold. This worship of riches impoverishes them spiritually. Their materialism yields subhuman behavior and the ironic physicality of the sensualist who knows, even as he tries to suppress the knowledge and even as he catalogues the exotic pleasures wealth can buy, that gold cannot purchase health, youth, or eternal life.

The limits of materialism are stretched in Volpone's gorgeous speeches designed to seduce Celia. Although the magnifico dismisses Corvino as one who "would have sold his part of paradise / For ready money" (III.vii.143–44), his own soaring imagination does little more than attempt to buy her. Even the *carpe diem* appeal of the famous song, "Come, my Celia, let us prove," is itself a recognition of limitations: "Time will not be ours, for ever" (III.vii.168). His appeals escalate from predictable offers of "a rope of pearle" and "A diamant" (III.vii.191, 195) to temptations of exotic food ("The heads of parrats, tongues of nightingales, / The braines of peacocks, and of estriches" [III.vii.202–203]) to visions of luxuries which delight the entire body:

> Thy bathes shall be the juyce of july-flowres,
> Spirit of roses, and of violets,
> The milke of unicornes, and panthers breath
> Gather'd in bagges, and mixt with *cretan* wines. (III.vii.213–16)

When these prove no temptation, he lures her with the almost total involvement of sensation implied in the erotic novelty of fantastic role-playing:

>   my dwarfe shall dance,
> My eunuch sing, my foole make up the antique.
> Whil'st, we, in changed shapes, act OVIDS tales,
> Thou, like EUROPA now, and I like JOVE,
> Then I like MARS, and thou like ERYCINE,
> So, of the rest, till we have quite run through
> And weary'd all the fables of the gods. (III.vii.219–25)

Volpone continues, offering more "moderne formes" than those of the ancients, but his imagination is exhausted, and the thematic and metaphorical point has been made. Volpone's materialistic universe, for all its Faustian appeal, is severely bounded by its earth-centeredness, a diminishment emphasized by the earlier reference to paradise and by Celia's symbolic name and function. Moreover, the allusion to Ovid's *Metamorphosis*, in which human beings are not ennobled but transformed into plants or animals, inadvertently acknowledges the bestial proclivities of materialism. Tellingly, when the lady resists his persuasion, Volpone resorts to the brute physicality of rape.

The frequent allusions to physical illness in the play reflect the spiritual sickness of Venice and they also indicate in another way the limitations of materialism.[20] The complexity of Volpone's attitude toward illness and old age, a mixture of contempt and dread, is especially revealing. Shamming disease for profit, Volpone pretends to be ill throughout much of the play. But being a true voluptuary, he scorns the reality he imitates, especially the infirmities which affect the enjoyment of physical pleasures. He unfeelingly catalogues the "feares attending on old age," describing the elderly in contemptuous terms (I.iv.145–50). In the mountebank scene (II.ii), he callously hawks a "precious oyle" which offers false hopes of remedy and eternal youth. Beneath the voluptuary's easy derision of the aged and the ill, however, is a barely submerged dread. Fittingly, while feigning disease to trick the Avocatori, he is struck by the initial symptoms of a real malady. As he recounts to Mosca, with momentary foreboding:

> 'Fore god, my left legge 'gan to have the crampe;
> And I apprehended, straight, some power had strooke me
> With a dead palsey. (V.i.5–7)

He tries to deny this intimation of mortality ("well, I must be merry, / And shake it off"), but his merriment does not last long. When his doom is sealed, the sentence passed on Volpone is grimly ironic:

> thy substance all be straight confiscate
> To the hospitall, of the *Incurabili:*
> And, since the most was gotten by imposture,
> By faining lame, gout, palsey, and such diseases,
> Thou art to lie in prison, crampt with irons,
> Till thou bee'st sicke, and lame indeed. (V.xii.119–24)

The fate which Volpone had most mocked and feared becomes his own. Not only is he stripped of the wealth and freedom which made voluptuousness possible, but the conditions of his imprisonment will also rob him of sensation itself. The punishment is the greater because his materialism has never allowed him to transcend the physical.

The materialism of the gold worshipers limits their human potential and causes them to express the bestiality within, to become less than fully human. Appropriately for a play based on a beast fable, the names of most of the characters suggest their animal natures—fox, fleshfly, vulture, raven, crow, and the diminutive "Pol" for parrot. But these names are only the comedy's most overt identification of human beings with animals. Bestiality abounds in the play, from the epithets applied to nearly all the characters to the actions which reek of carrion. Only Mosca and Volpone admiringly identify themselves with animals, however—Mosca with the "subtill snake" (III.i.6) and Volpone with the fox (e.g., I.ii.94–96). Their frankness makes them more attractive than the other, equally animalistic characters who never admit their resemblance to beasts. Yet the honesty does not alter their bestiality, particularly since the snake and the fox are traditionally potent emblems of evil and cunning. The materialistic limitations and spiritual poverty of animalism are strikingly revealed in Volpone's reaction to the judgment pronounced against him, the single sentence, "This is call'd mortifying of a FOXE" (V.xii.125). The simple phrase—the last words he speaks in the play proper—neatly concentrates a number of important insights and focuses the play's irony. In the early seventeenth century, "mortifying" did not mean "causing extreme embarrassment," its common modern meaning, but "causing to die." Moreover, two specialized meanings are implied as well. As a religious term, it refers to a denial of the physical appetites; and as a kitchen term, it denotes the hanging up of dead animals to allow the first stages of putrefaction to tenderize their flesh before being cooked and eaten. Thus in the one word Volpone acknowledges his fate in three areas. His fears regarding old age and death will be horribly realized; his voluptuousness will be thoroughly checked; and his identification with an animal will be made unpleasantly total.

Significantly, the conclusions of both plots are effected in terms of the pervasive animal metaphor. The subplot ends with a farcical scene in which Peregrine, whose name means "falcon" as well as "traveler," brings down Sir Politic Wouldbe, the parrot of fictional intrigues. He illustrates the foolish knight's descent from the human sphere to the animal by frightening him into a giant tortoise shell (V.iv). Sir Politic's hilarious punishment is the exposure of his foolishness, a fate less harsh than that apportioned to the vicious characters. The main plot ends with an ironically self-congratulatory moral delivered by one of the foolish Avocatori and stated in terms of the slaughterhouse:

> Let all, that see these vices thus rewarded,
> Take heart, and love to study 'hem. Mischiefes feed
> Like beasts, till they be fat, and then they bleed. (V.xii.149–51)

But the play's vision of man's animalistic instincts and its depiction of justice and goodness as impotent have been too complete to allow the Avocatori's smug sententiousness to be reassuring.

Indeed, *Volpone* is not a very reassuring comedy. The discovery of truth is not effected through societal safeguards, or even by a witty,

basically good individual as in other Jonsonian comedies, but solely
through the confession of the play's chief criminal, who decides he
prefers vengeance to safety. The play may illustrate the self-defeating
futility of vice and the ability of true innocence to resist the
temptations of materialism, yet Celia and Bonario are so symbolic as
to be scarcely imitable. But the negative vision of *Volpone* needs no
apology. The brilliant depiction of materialistic corruption is its own
justification, documenting the betrayal of human nature itself by men
in the service of the false god gold. Jonson defended the harsh ending
by remarking, in the letter dedicating *Volpone* to Oxford and
Cambridge, that "the office of a *comick-Poet*" is, among other things,
"to imitate justice, and instruct to life" (ll. 121–22). As instruction and
imitation, *Volpone* achieves the combination of moral seriousness
and delight its author always sought.

  Volpone is a major achievement, a totally successful experiment in
mixing profit with laughter. The aims Jonson confessed in his
Prologue are daringly realized. A play providing serious moral
insight, it is nevertheless a "quick *comoedie*"; with its lessons
conveyed in "salt" rather than in "gall," it is a work of great "pleasure"
(ll. 8, 29, 33, 34). Although "refined, / As best Criticks have designed"
in its adherence to "The lawes of time, place, persons" (ll. 29–30, 31),
it nonetheless seems both spontaneous and plausible. Moreover, its
two plots, though different in kind, are perfect complements to each
other. The comedy of manners in the subplot periodically relieves the
tension built by the main plot as vice temporarily yields the stage to
foolishness. The language of the play, while always highly evocative,
is satisfyingly varied, ranging from coarse bestial invective to soaring
voluptuous fantasy, but always suited to character and situation. And,
finally, the major characters of *Volpone* are so well conceived and so
thoroughly developed that they transcend the limits of time, place,
and custom. By all the tests applied to imaginative literature,
Volpone is a masterpiece.

III Epicoene *(1609)*

  The subplot of *Volpone* touches briefly on the subject of sex roles.
Lady Wouldbe dominates her husband, and in one scene she
mistakes Peregrine for a loose woman in disguise, describing him as
"A female devill, in a male out-side" (IV.ii.56). In his next comedy, a
work very different from *Volpone*, Jonson explores the issue more
fully. *Epicoene, or The Silent Woman* was first presented in late

1609 or early 1610 by the Children of Her Majesty's Revels at Whitefriars Theater. Its plot combines situations from Plautus's *Casina*, the sixth declamation of Libanius, and other sources, but with much elaboration and transformation. The action is so carefully and naturally developed according to classical precepts that John Dryden described it as "the greatest and most noble of any pure unmixed comedy in any language."[21]

In *Epicoene* Jonson returns to the exuberant manners comedy of *Every Man in His Humour*, a mode he abandoned for the comical satires and used only in the underplot of *Volpone*. The action takes place in a single day in a London neighborhood and centers on the efforts of young Dauphine Eugenie to secure his rightful share of his eccentric uncle's estate. Morose, the uncle, is addicted to silence and wrongly believes that his nephew has harrassed him with unnecessary noise. The old man determines to find a mute woman, marry her, beget an heir, and deprive Dauphine of his inheritance. Working in secret, Dauphine creates a "silent woman," Epicoene, and arranges for Morose to discover her. Although the scheme is almost upset by the well-intentioned but misplaced efforts of Dauphine's friend Truewit, the old man proposes to her. As soon as Morose marries Epicoene, however, she turns into an incessantly chattering shrew. When the miserable husband offers his fortune to his nephew if he will rid him of such a hateful wife, the young man reveals the bride to be a boy in disguise.

Although its plot hinges on the disposition of money, *Epicoene* is primarily concerned with sex roles and sexual stereotyping. It has been described as "a grimly serious play which exposes moral disease,"[22] but it is actually a high spirited, even affectionate comedy. Unlike *Every Man in His Humour*, which it resembles in many respects, *Epicoene* does not present an "Image of the times." Although designed for a wide audience, as both its Prologue and its mixture of low comedy and learned wit indicate, it focuses narrowly on a group of Londoners on the periphery of the court. This element of upper middle class society is in flux, especially in the area of sexual expression; and the very absence of unchallenged conventions provides the source of much of the play's laughter. As guides through the competition of aims and ideals expressed by the diverse characters, Jonson places at the comedy's center a trio of young gallants, Dauphine, Clerimont, and Truewit. These handsome youths expose the follies of the other characters and establish the play's criteria of sophistication and wit by which everyone else is measured. The

comedy has a satiric edge. It ridicules violations of decorum by its
bizarre cast. But the play delights in most of the frivolities it criticizes,
and its comic vision is goodnaturedly tolerant.

Dauphine, Clerimont, and Truewit are among the most attractive
characters in Jonsonian comedy.[23] Intelligent, well-educated, and
sensible, they delight in living well and in observing the world about
them. All three are exuberant young men who enjoy the city's sport,
but they are capable of seriousness as well. They are sophisticated in
their casual acceptance of the varieties of sexual expression and in the
high value they place on wit. As Dryden remarked, Jonson "has here
described the conversation of gentlemen in the person of True-wit,
and his friends, with more gaiety, air and freedom, than in the rest of
his comedies."[24] The confident tone of comic banter with which the
young men rally each other is clear in Truewit's early description of
Clerimont as a "man that can melt away his time, and never [feele] it!
what, betweene his mistris abroad, and his engle at home, high fare,
soft lodging, fine clothes, and his fiddle" (I.i.23–26). This passage
probably should not be construed literally as evidence of Clerimont's
bisexuality and indolence, but it does indicate the gallants' easy
familiarity and urbane values.

The three wits function collectively in the play, but they are highly
individualized. Clerimont, for instance, is retiring and writes beautiful poetry. Truewit, on the other hand, is gregarious, even impulsive.
He visits the court, attends sporting events, and enjoys amorous
adventures. Dauphine seems younger and less experienced than the
other two, and he suffers from lack of money. But he has the wit
necessary to improve his finances and an eagerness to learn from his
friends. Indeed, the willingness and ability of all three to learn from
the world and from each other are particularly important in the
unsettled society of *Epicoene,* where conventional roles are ques-
tioned at every turn. The gallants encourage, support, and teach each
other. Their education often takes the form of witty argument and
spirited disagreement, as in the famous discussion of cosmetics which
neatly crystallizes conflicting notions of art's relationship to nature.
Clerimont comes to accept Truewit's approval of artifice, and
Dauphine requests Truewit's instruction in wooing the Ladies
Collegiate. But the experienced Truewit also learns from his friends,
and at the end of the play he awards the garland of wit to Dauphine
and Clerimont. The youths' openness to new ideas and to revision of
old ones is a function of their urbanity.

Most of the other characters in *Epicoene* are flawed to varying degrees. Morose, for example, is seriously disturbed. His humor manifests itself in his unreasonable determination to make the world around him silent. But his full passion is broader in scope, as he reveals in his first speech: "all discourses, but mine owne, afflict mee, they seeme harsh, impertinent, and irksome" (II.i.4–5). His real desire is to be the complete and unquestioned master of his household. In fact, he wants to be obeyed far beyond his own domain. For his nephew's suspected disobedience, he vows to "thrust him out of my bloud like a stranger" (II.v.100–101). He tries to silence all noises of the street and the neighborhood; and when Cutbeard brings Epicoene for an interview with Morose, the old man requires the barber to answer questions in the same silent, ridiculous, but broadly comic manner demanded of the servant Mute. Furthermore, his passion for total obedience is tellingly betrayed in his initial examination of Epicoene, whose poverty pleases him, for it will make her "more loving, and obedient" (II.v.93). Morose attempts to trick the prospective bride into revealing an inclination for fine company and expensive clothes, as well as for talking. He determines to marry her only after her meek answers convince him that she will be completely submissive to him in all matters, including, but by no means limited to, silence.

The nature of Morose's humor and the seriousness of its consequences have often been misunderstood. Its statement in terms of physical ailment has afforded it sympathy, and it has been seen merely as a comic extension of the right of *pater familias.*[25] But Morose's passion, if realized, would result in an unconscionable dictatorship which could threaten the social fabric. Even the specific manifestation of total silence except for one lone, sullen voice is a symbolic denial of human communication. Many of the world's noises are as silly and annoying as the chatter of Daw and LaFoole and "The spitting, the coughing, the laughter, the [s]neesing, the farting" of the marriage banquet (IV.i.8–9), but an indiscriminate denial of all sound would also silence poets, teachers, musicians, and other conveyors of compassion, wisdom, delight, and inspiration.

The fate which Dauphine engineers for the old bridegroom fittingly punishes the excessiveness of his desire for dominance. Significantly, Dauphine does not take unfair advantage of the misanthrope's discomfort. He refuses to be "un-reasonable" when Morose offers him the entire estate (V.iv.176); he accepts only one-third of his uncle's income and the assurance that he will be named heir. Morose's real punishment is not the recognition of his legitimate obligations to his nephew, however, but his public admission of impotence. The announcement, "I am no man, ladies" (V.iv.44), is a surrender not only of dominance, but also of the symbol of maleness which conventionally justifies it.

That Morose's punishment is effected in sexual terms is particularly significant in a play entitled *Epicoene*. The word means androgynous, or having the characteristics of both sexes. Appropriately, the comedy abounds in sexual innuendo of all kinds.[26] The world of the play is a world in sexual flux, a society in which conventional sexual distinctions are reversed, blurred, or comically exaggerated. The bizarre cast of minor characters exemplifies this society's unsettled sexual attitudes. These characters are, in varying degrees, foolish, but the questions of sexual identity they raise and the assumptions they challenge are very real. The play treats the issues of sexuality with deft lightness, but it embodies an urbane vision of sexual accommodation which implicitly criticizes stereotyped wisdom about the relationships of the sexes.

Two of the play's most amusing minor characters are the pretentious fools, Sir John Daw and Sir Amorous LaFoole. Daw affects wit and poetry, but understands neither. Like Lady Wouldbe in *Volpone*, he passes weighty judgment on books he has not read. He even goes further than his fellow bird to insist that *Syntagma Juris civilis*, *Corpus Juris civilis*, and other titles are actually the names of authors. The *"Corpusses,"* he claims to have known personally; "they were very corpulent authors" (II.iii.88–89). The poetry he recites includes a trite, self-contradictory tribute to his "mistress" Epicoene which, as the true poet Clerimont comments, "chimes, and cries tinke i' the close" (II.iii.42). His companion, Sir Amorous, is an equally empty-headed fop with social pretensions. He is absurdly proud of his family and its coat of arms, not recognizing that the latter is the traditional motley of fools: "*Yellow*, or *Or*, checker'd *Azure*, and *Gules*, and some three or foure colours more, which is a very noted coate, and has, some-times, beene solemnely worne by divers nobilitie of our house" (I.iv.42–45). Similarly, his knowledge of polite society is so superficial that he misunderstands its etiquette, as Clerimont explains: "Hee is one of the *Braveries*, though he be none o' the *Wits*. He will salute a Judge upon the bench, and a Bishop in the pulpit, a Lawyer when hee is pleading at the barre, and a Lady when shee is dauncing in a masque, and put her out" (I.iii.29–33). He renders courtesy counterproductive.

Both Daw and LaFoole are pretenders to manliness as well. They wear swords, constantly seek the company of women, and boast of their sexual prowess. But they are actually cowards and neither knows how to court ladies successfully. Daw attempts to seduce Epicoene by praising her modesty and LaFoole uses banquets and sweetmeats "for a bait" (I.iii.41). Understandably, neither is success- ful. Women use them for amusement, not love. Their problem with women rests in their own effeminacy. Clerimont describes LaFoole as "a precious mannikin!" (I.iii.25), and the phrase fits Daw as well. Especially important in a comedy which plays upon the stereotype of women's loquaciousness, both chatter pointlessly. Truewit ironically defines Daw as "The onely talking sir i' th' towne!" (I.ii.66); and Clerimont scornfully exclaims of LaFoole, "Did you ever heare such a wind-fucker, as this?" (I.iv.79). The fools' constant noise often consists of gossiping and boasting of their (imagined) sexual exploits, slandering the women of their acquaintance in the process. This breach of decorum contradicts all the courtesies of polite society which they profess, and it violates the code of discretion upon which social arrangements are based.

Daw and LaFoole, like Morose, are punished in progressive stages. The gallants first trick the two knights into a farcical public demonstration of their cowardice, then manipulate them by means of their cowardice and egotism into swearing before the assembled company that they have enjoyed Epicoene's sexual favors. Mavis's outcry against them, "Now out upon 'hem, informers!" (V.iv.125), although uttered by one of the play's foolish characters, is fully warranted. Subsequently, the revelation of Epicoene's true sex also reveals Daw and LaFoole as ridiculous liars. Their indiscretion is their worst fault, and it is far more serious than their cowardice. Truewit dismisses them as "cuckowes. . . . You are they, that when no merit or fortune can make you hope to enjoy [ladies'] bodies, will yet lie with their reputations, and make their fame suffer. Away you common moths of these, and all ladies honors" (V.iv.236–40). Their punishment is fitting: banishment from the society whose code of decorum they have violated.

Morose's exaggerated desire for dominance has a comic foil next door in the household of Otter. Truewit may have the Otters in mind when, in his attempt to dissuade Morose from marriage, he warns that if the bride is rich, "you marry her dowry, not her; shee'll raigne in your house, as imperious as a widow" (II.ii.70–72). Mistress Otter's pride in her family—she is of "the LA-FOOLES of *London*" (I.iv.35)—is as ridiculous as her social climbing, but she has the

money, if not the wit, to support her pretensions. In both title and
status, she far outranks her husband. He may have been a captain at
sea, but on land he is an impoverished nobody and "She commands
all at home" (I.iv.29). Captain Otter, the *"animal amphibium"*
(I.iv.26), is even more fatuous than his wife. In Truewit's estimation,
he is "An excellent animal, equall with your DAW, or LA-FOOLE, if
not transcendent" (II.vi.52–53). While he affectedly spouts tags of
Latin, and does so marvelously in his impersonation of a learned
divine, his wit is so shallow that when he adopts a humor, he states it
in terms of his three drinking cups: "these things I am knowne to the
courtiers by. It is reported to them for my humor, and they receive it
so, and doe expect it. TOM OTTERS bull, beare, and horse is
knowne all over *England*, in *rerum natura*" (III.i.11–15).

The Otters' marriage reflects their sexual ambiguity. Truewit
describes the relationship succinctly, with a mixture of ridicule and
titillation: "hee is his wifes Subject, he calls her Princesse, and at such
times as these, followes her up and downe the house like a page, with
his hat off, partly for heate, partly for reverence" (II.vi.54–57). If the
Captain's position is undignified, at least it is of his own choosing. As
he explains it, he fell in love with his wife's "sixe thousand pound"
(IV.ii.78) and signed a marriage agreement acknowledging her right
to be "Princess" and rule the household. Their marriage has sometimes been described in moralistic terms as a reversal of the "natural
order."[27] But such a description assumes that the natural order allows
the husband dictatorial power, and the play uses the Otters to
question that common assumption. The comic shock afforded by their
marriage is only partly attributable to its reversal of traditional sex
roles. The greater jolt arises from the recognition that the relationship parodies—and thus exposes to ridicule—the domination men
ordinarily exert over women. When Mistress Otter asks, "Who gives
you your maintenance, I pray you? who allowes you your horse-meat,
and mans-meat? your three sutes of apparell a yeere? your foure paire
of stockings, one silke, three worsted? your cleane linnen, your
bands, and cuffes when I can get you to weare 'hem?" (III.i.38–43),
she unwittingly mocks the attitudes husbands often display toward
wives. Mistress Otter's domination of her husband is no more—and
no less—unnatural than the more common domination of women by
men. In fact, her treatment of Captain Otter is considerably more
humane than Morose's initial plans for the obedient, silent Epicoene
he thinks he is marrying. Interestingly, the Otters provide their own

punishment for each other in the play. Their foolishness should not obscure the seriousness of the issues they parody.

The characters who most directly challenge conventional sex roles are the Ladies Collegiate: Madame Haughty, Madame Centaure, and Mistress Mavis. Early in the play, Truewit describes them as "an order betweene courtiers, and country-madames, that live from their husbands; and give entertainement to all the *Wits,* and *Braveries* o' the time, as they call 'hem: crie downe, or up, what they like, or dislike in a braine, or a fashion, with most masculine, or rather *hermaphroditicall* authoritie" (I.i.75–80). Like men, they address each other by their surnames, and Haughty proudly announces that "CENTAURE has immortaliz'd her selfe, with taming of her wilde male" (IV.iii.27–28). As promiscuous as men, they entertain a "pluralitie of servants, and doe 'hem all graces" (IV.iii.31). Moreover, they control the rituals of courtship, as their active wooing of Dauphine demonstrates. This wonderfully comic scene reverses the conventional roles of sexual pursuit. Centaure and Mavis are frankly sensual in their praise of Dauphine's physical charms, and each invites him to a private rendezvous. Haughty, on the other hand, parodies the Petrarchan lover's idealism, masking her sensual appetite in the praise of higher things: "I assure you, sir DAUPHINE, it is the price and estimation of your vertue onely, that hath embarqu'd me to this adventure, and I could not but make out to tell you so; nor can I repent me of the act, since it is alwayes an argument of some vertue in our selves, that we love and affect it so in others" (V.ii.1–6). Although Haughty protests that "It is not the outward, but the inward man that I affect" (V.ii.17–18), her ends are the same as those of Mavis and Centaure. The comic reversal of sex roles in this scene brilliantly, and affectionately, parodies the conventional courtship ritual.

The independent Ladies Collegiate are undeniably comic, but they are not merely ridiculous. They are foolish enough to be manipulated by anyone who is even moderately clever; as Truewit explains, "all their actions are governed by crude opinion, without reason or cause; they know not why they doe any thing: but as they are inform'd, beleeve, judge, praise, condemne, love, hate, and in aemulation one of another, doe all these things alike" (IV.vi.64–69). They are silly enough to think that Daw and LaFoole are actually wits and to be impressed with the brave shows of wealth and status. Yet their rebellion against the restrictions placed on their sex is not in itself ridiculous. While presented in a comic context, their protest raises serious issues which cannot be jokingly dismissed as "hermaph-roditicall" or sneeringly denounced as unnatural.[28] In a society which freely allows promiscuity to men, for instance, their revolt against the double standard is reasonable. "Why should women denie their favours to men?" Haughty asks, "Are they the poorer, or the worse?" (IV.iii.32–33). Similarly, her justification of birth preventives is valid: "How should we maintayne our youth and beautie, else? Many births of a woman make her old, as many crops make the earth barren" (IV.iii.59–61). The ladies' practice of birth control is not evidence of the "sterility" of their lives, as one critic asserts.[29] Haughty's protest is not against childbearing itself, but against the numerous pregnancies expected of a woman.

The comic ambiguity of Jonson's presentation of the Ladies Collegiate is perfectly illustrated in their *carpe diem* arguments justifying promiscuity:

HAU. Besides, ladies should be mindfull of the approach of age, and let no time want his due use. The best of our daies passe first.

MAV. We are rivers, that cannot be call'd backe, madame: shee that now excludes her lovers, may live to lie a forsaken beldame, in a frozen bed.

CEN. 'Tis true, MAVIS; and who will wait on us to coach then? or write, or tell us the newes then? Make *anagrammes* of our names, and invite us to the cock-pit, and kisse our hands all the play-time, and draw their weapons for our honors? (IV.iii.40–50)

The shallowness of their values is obvious in their addiction to fashionable amusements and in their trivialization of a very serious issue. Still, there is melancholy truth in their perception that women face grim futures in the sexual arena as they age. That this reflects a double standard is obvious from Morose's easy arrangement of marriage to the youthful Epicoene. Moreover, the passage strikes to the heart of the play's exposure of the sexual dichotomy itself. To defend their promiscuity, the ladies use arguments traditionally employed by men to convince coy mistresses to grant sexual favors. This reversal of roles parodies the conventional male arguments by exposing the inequity on which they are based. The further irony is that the ladies' active pursuit of men must be expressed in passive terms: the females must appear to be the recipients of male courtship.

In his instruction of Dauphine in the art of seduction, Truewit observes that women "would sollicite us, but that they are afraid. Howsoever, they wish in their hearts we should sollicite them" (IV.i.77–78). The fear of which he speaks underlines the danger in the courtship ritual, and more particularly the risk women face in a brave new world of sexual etiquette. Their boldness may damage their reputations or may frighten men into retreat. The sophistication of their social circle can protect their honor, but only if its code of discretion is observed—hence Clerimont's admonition to Dauphine, "you must not tell" (V.ii.51), and the necessary ejection of Daw and LaFoole, who are too witless to understand the need for decorum. The risk of frightening away suitors may be ameliorated only if men are urbane enough to realize that the ladies' boldness is not emas-culating. Dauphine is unthreatened by the Ladies Collegiate, and he is eager to learn how to win their favors. With the aid of his friends, he succeeds in his quest. Although the Ladies Collegiate are essentially comic characters whose follies are exposed, their collective name implies not only that they are able to educate Dauphine in the art of love, but that they—unlike the other ridiculous characters—may themselves be educable.

Epicoene is a play of suggestion rather than of definitive statement. Jonson is fully aware of the profound mystery that surrounds human sexuality, and he does not presume to offer revolutionary formulas for society. But he does suggest that certain assumptions concerning the roles considered proper to the sexes are unreasonably confining; and in his exposure of the absurdities of the courtship ritual, he points toward a freedom for both sexes to express their desires. The final comment on the play's title character implies the possibility of sexual accommodation. As Epicoene stands revealed as a boy on the edge of puberty, Truewit commends him to the Ladies Collegiate in these words: "let it not trouble you that you have discover'd any mysteries to this yong gentleman. He is (a'most) of yeeres, & will make a good visitant within this twelve-month. In the meane time, we'll all undertake for his secrecie, that can speake so well of his silence" (V.iv.246–51). The word "mysteries" is resonant and suggestive. It refers to the code of discretion necessary to the society of the play; and in the name of all three gallants, Truewit pledges that Epicoene will observe that code. The deeper implication of "mysteries," here as in the reference to "The mysteries of manners, armes, and arts" (l. 98) in "To Penshurst" (*F.* 2), is intimate knowledge of the essence of things. Epicoene has been in a uniquely instructive position. His experience far transcends the assumption of a wig and female clothing. For a time he has been treated by women as one of themselves, sharing intimacies they would normally never reveal to men. The experience bodes well for both Epicoene and the ladies in his future. What he has learned from his experience will help make him a good lover when he is a man. The sexual accommodation Jonson envisions in the play is one to be achieved through education.

Epicoene is among Jonson's greatest comedies. Its plot, always controlled and completely integrated with theme, balances calculated plan with spontaneous action and reaction. The decision to withhold the full details of Dauphine's scheme from the other gallants was inspired. Enormously influential on the Restoration masters of the form, *Epicoene* is a model comedy of manners. It perfectly achieves the delicate balance demanded by the genre: equally criticizing the flaws of an imperfect, polite society and affirming its sophistication as sufficient remedy for those shortcomings. It places a high value on wit, yet humanely punishes only that witlessness which is dangerous to the social fabric. It explores serious issues, but with an urbanely light touch. It luxuriates in variety of character and language, yet unobtrusively observes decorum. Most of all, while it does not underrate the need for privacy and solitude, it joyously celebrates men and women as social beings.

IV   The Alchemist *(1610)*

Jonson's most famous comedy, *The Alchemist*, was written for the King's Men, who premiered it at the Globe near the middle of 1610 and included it in the repertory of their autumn tour. In it, the playwright turns from the restricted social milieus of *Volpone* and *Epicoene* to a canvas even broader than that of *Every Man in His Humour* to paint a detailed "Image of the times" with the deft strokes of a master at the height of his powers. Although its cast of characters includes representatives of all but the lowest and highest social strata, *The Alchemist* is the most concentrated of Jonson's comedies. All its events take place in one house and in the lane adjacent; the time it covers is at most seven hours; and all its parts add up to a single action. Yet the play is unforced, exciting, and provocative, suggesting the complexity of an entire city. Unmistakably a London comedy, it teems with her varied citizenry and visitors; it speaks with her particular range of accents; it breathes with her odoriferous air; and it bustles with her chief preoccupation, the acquisition of money. Furthermore, the play has a special sense of immediacy. Set in an autumn day of the year of its initial production, its events are presented in the context of the time's chief horror, the plague, and its subject is the "vices" bred in the "clime" and "age" of London, 1610 (Pro., ll. 7, 13, 14).

Using materials from such disparate sources as Plautus's *Mostellaria,* Erasmus's *De Alcumista,* alchemical and religious treatises, and the written and oral reports of contemporaneous quackery of all kinds, Jonson constructed a comedy of enormous vitality and freshness. To escape the plague's contagion, the prosperous London citizen Lovewit spends the summer months in his country hopfields. In his absence, Jeremy, the butler left in charge of his Blackfriars townhouse, forms an alliance with Subtle, a starving cheater, and his prostitute companion Dol Common. They set up a laboratory in the deserted house and fleece a variety of gulls with ruses that promise wealth and success through alchemy, astrology, and demonology, used alone or in various combinations. On the climactic day of the scheme, their alliance shows the strain of mutual suspicion and distrust, but the three rally together sufficiently to attend to the host of London citizens and visitors who flock to them almost begging to be cozened: a law clerk, a shop keeper, a separatist elder and his parson, a city knight, his skeptical gamester companion who later returns disguised as a Spanish grandee, and a young country squire and his rich widowed sister. To succeed in their schemes, the three tricksters contrive to keep the gulls separated from one another; and as the latter crowd in for return visits, the cozeners rise to extremes of improvisation. When the action reaches a frantic pace, Lovewit returns unexpectedly and the whole fabric of deceit crumbles. Subtle and Dol are forced to flee penniless; but by giving the ill-gotten wealth to his fun-loving master and arranging for him to marry the rich young widow, Jeremy saves himself.

Although its masterful plot is a series of replications of a single action, cozenage, *The Alchemist* is varied and complex. As the title suggests, the play focuses on transformation. The aspirations of the individual gulls differ, but each comes to the house used by Subtle, Face, and Dol hoping to escape the realities of self. Ironically, they only become more completely what they already are.[30] Even the three cozeners who offer the hope of metamorphosis effect for themselves only superficial and temporary transformations. Their identities are as false as the hopes they hold out to their gulls; and when faced with reality, they are as vulnerable as the most stupid of the victims. The play is vitalized by tensions—the tension between reality and desire in both the gulls and the tricksters, and the tension between the attractiveness of many of the desired transformations and the ugliness of the values which animate them. As an exposé of human fallibility, of man's capacity for deception and especially self-deception, of his false values and his cynical veneers of altruism and piety which mask greed and corruption, *The Alchemist* is a deadly serious play. Yet it wears its didacticism lightly, and the delight it takes in its rogues and fools reflects the characteristic ambiguity at the heart of the Jonsonian comic spirit. *The Alchemist* clearly reveals the flawed reality of the human condition, but its "wholesome remedies are sweet" (Pro., l. 15): the fair correctives of robust laughter.[31]

Most of the play's exposure of vice and folly is improvised by Subtle, Face, and Dol. The three tricksters are among Jonson's most triumphant inventions. Intelligent, resourceful, and accomplished in the arts of seduction, they are united in a tenuous alliance which threatens to fall apart at various points in the play. They manipulate the gulls with consummate skill, illustrating their insight into the nature of folly and greed. They even help the fools articulate repressed desires and unacknowledged aspirations. But they themselves forget their own realities as petty cheats and swindlers, and their attempts to transmute themselves are as doomed as Mammon's and Wholesome's hopes of the philosopher's stone. The rivalry of Face and Subtle, exacerbated by the trio's early success and by the opportunity for the main chance which Dame Pliant represents, is only barely held in check by the ministrations of Dol and by their mutual dependence on each other. The appearance of Lovewit merely hastens the inevitable collapse of the collaborators' uneasy truce. Because they are so adept at their confidence games and because their gulls are so ripe for cheating, Subtle, Face, and Dol command the audience's sympathetic interest. Like the three gallants in *Epicoene,* they function collectively to expose the folly of others, yet are highly individualized.

As befits the range of connotations in his name, Subtle is a complex figure. He is intelligent and knowledgeable. He knows the theory, the history, and the processes of alchemy, and he uses its terminology accurately.[32] He is acquainted with scholastic reasoning; he knows the vocabularies of palmistry, astrology, and demonology; and he is proficient even in the etiquette of quarreling.[33] He also knows something of the theology and practices of the separatist Anabaptists, and he is a quick and able casuist. But he uses his intelligence and knowledge merely to transform himself into appearances which temporarily disguise his reality. Ironically, however, the successes of his schemes in the Blackfriars house lead him to believe that he has actually become what he pretends to be, a man whose knowledge entitles him to dominion and respect. He boasts that it was his power which transformed the shabbily dressed menial Jeremy into the resplendently uniformed Captain Face. He demands of the erstwhile butler:

> Thou vermine, have I tane thee, out of dung,
>
> . . . . .
>
> Rais'd thee from broomes, and dust, and watring pots?
> *Sublim'd* thee, and *exalted* thee, and *fix'd* thee
> I' the *third region,* call'd our *state of grace*? (I.i.64, 67–69)

The process described is alchemical, and it is clear that Subtle believes himself a real alchemist, of men if not of metals, a transformer of base matter into a higher state. But the terms he uses are also theological, and the language reverberates with ironic blasphemy. In the questions that climax the tirade, "have I this for thanke? Doe you rebell?" (I.i.78), Subtle assumes the persona of God rebuking an unworthy creature whom he has favored with his ultimate blessing of grace. But in reality he is a petty cheat, one so unsuccessful that he was starving and homeless when Face first noticed him. The discrepancy between desire and reality renders his pretensions pathetic.

While the specific manifestations of his role vary as occasion demands, Subtle always presents himself as extraordinarily knowledgeable and his name remains constant. His male confederate, on the other hand, assumes different kinds of roles and is a man of many names: Jeremy, Face, Lungs, Ulenspiegel. Although used only rarely, Ulenspiegel is a key both to his dramatic genealogy and to his function as a person of multiple identities. Ulenspiegel is the merry prankster of German legend, a low character who uses his wit to trick his social betters. Thus the Face of *The Alchemist* betrays kinship to the vice of medieval drama. He is less learned than Subtle, but he has a keen knowledge of human nature. He quickly perceives each fool's hidden desire, and he exploits his insight to lure the prospective victim into cozenage. He is the chief possessor of the deceiving wit necessary to the triumvirate. In exercising his wit, he assumes the outward show, the face, of a number of roles. To those awed by the paraphernalia of science, he is Lungs, the conscientious laboratory assistant. To those impressed by swagger and worldliness, he is Captain Face, successful gambler and gallant about town. But, like Subtle, he confuses his appearance with his reality. Convinced by his own ego that the success of the collaborative venture is due much more to his cunning wit than to Subtle's knowledgeability, he demands priority in the trio. He angrily reminds Subtle that when all his "conjuring, cosning, and your dosen of trades" could not relieve his penniless condition, "I ga' you count'nance," "Built you a fornace, drew you customers, / Advanc'd all your black arts" (I.i.40, 43, 45–46). Subtle may be the master of knowledge, but as Face emphatically points out, "You must have stuffe, brought home to you, to worke on" (I.iii.104). His early success deludes him into the belief that he really is a master of men, yet the reality he can never escape is that of the subservient housekeeper Jeremy.

Dol Common is less complex than her two male associates, but she has comparable wit and intelligence. She functions largely as peacemaker between the quarreling Subtle and Face. She reminds them of the terms of their collaboration, stressing the "equalitie" of their roles and the agreement that no one should have "prioritie" (I.i.134, 136). Dol flatters the two men with titles that play to their conceptions of themselves. She addresses Subtle as "Soveraigne" and Face as "Generall," while referring to herself in the less exalted but equally telling term "your *republique*" (I.i.5, 110), a title which may pun on the Latin words *res publica,* or public thing, indicating both her profession and the claims her confederates make on her in and out of bed. But Subtle exalts her with the epithet "Royall DOL" (I.i.174), and as the comedy progresses she plays in turn a noble lady and the Queen of Faery. Like her collaborators, she too confuses her role-playing and her reality, as is evident when Subtle tries to coach her in the part she is to play with Mammon. When he reminds her that as "my lord WHATS'HUM'S sister, you must now / Beare your selfe *statelich*" (II.iv.6–7), she exclaims:

> I'll not forget my race, I warrant you.
> I'll keepe my distance, laugh, and talke aloud;
> Have all the tricks of a proud scirvy ladie. (II.iv.8–10)

She clearly relishes the disguise and hopes to be transformed into a genuine lady. But her reality as a slatternly whore mocks the transmutation she desires.

The individual threads of plot in *The Alchemist* are essentially variations of the same action, and all develop the same broad theme, but Jonson avoids any sense of mere repetition. The gulls are strikingly differentiated from one another. Spread widely across the social and occupational ranges of the middle class, they vary in levels of intelligence and sophistication. Thus they demand different strategems from the tricksters. Some are in the process of being cozened by slow degrees over a period of weeks, while others visit the Blackfriars house for the first time, so the various schemes are shown in different stages of maturity. What the gulls share in common is their capacity for self-deception, their overwhelming desire to avoid their own repugnant realities. They are, in effect, their own victims as well as the dupes of Subtle, Face, and Dol. By making them responsible for their own cozening, Jonson preserves the play's comic spirit and maintains sympathy for the mischievous triumvirate, who are themselves trapped in unacceptable realities.

The least sophisticated of the fools are Dapper and Drugger, both recruited by the dashing Captain Face, who offers to intercede for them with the necromancer Subtle. Dapper, a young law clerk who "Consorts with the small poets of the time," who can write "sixe faire hands," and who "can court / His mistris, out of OVID" (I.ii.52, 54, 57–58), desires transmutation into a successful gambler. Abel Drugger, a slow-witted young man just entering the livery of the Grocers Company and setting up his own tobacco shop, wants to know "by art," "by *necromancie*" how to arrange his premises and what sign to erect over the door in order to become a successful businessman (I.iii.10, 11). Exploiting Dapper's romantic sensibility, Subtle claims to recognize him as a favorite nephew of the Queen of Faery and promises that if he will endure "a world of ceremonies" (I.ii.144), his aunt will grant him a personal audience and present him a "Fly" which will guarantee him luck at gambling. Subtle satisfies Drugger's unimaginative simplicity with extemporaneous readings in astrology and palmistry, with authoritatively stated directions for ordering the tobacco shop, and with a "mystick" rebus on his name (II.vi.15). Though manipulated by the schemers, Dapper and Drugger are more truly victims of their own stupidity and inchoate greed.

The snappish Kastril and his sister Dame Pliant are unwittingly added to the list of gulls by Drugger. The brother is a rich country squire who has "come up / To learne to quarrell, and to live by his wits" like the "angrie Boyes" of London (II.vi.60–61, III.iv.22). The worldly-wise but scholarly Subtle impresses him with "the *Grammar*, and *Logick*, / And *Rhetorick* of quarrelling" (IV.ii.64–65). In some respects, Kastril is reminiscent of Stephen in *Every Man in His Humour*, but he has an ugly cast to his character. He bullies his sister, and he wants to learn city vices in order to be an ungenerous tyrant to his country tenants and neighbors alike. He too is a victim of his own stupid ambitions. Fortunately, he is as incapable of being transformed into his unlovely vision as all the other characters, and at the end of the play he remains the ridiculous, easily manipulable fool he is at the beginning. His sister is beautiful but unrelentingly stupid. A wealthy widow of nineteen, she has come to town "To learne the fashion," and she longs "to know her fortune" (II.vi.38, 39). The Subtle of palmistry and crystal balls forecasts "some great honour" for Dame Pliant (IV.ii.49). The honor he has in mind for her is her own prostitution and marriage to a cheat. But her vacuity victimizes her as much as the schemers do, and appropriately she becomes the prize Face offers to his master.

Considerably superior to these four simple creatures in cunning and imagination are Tribulation Wholesome and Sir Epicure Mammon. They are clever men, and while they are as selfish as their more foolish fellows, they use causes greater than themselves to mask the reality of their true desires. They can be cozened only by a Subtle who is a serious and learned alchemist. The tricksters have been working on these two gulls for several weeks, gradually bleeding them for the largest swindle of all, the promise of the philosopher's stone itself. As an emblem of Renaissance aspiration, the philosopher's stone symbolizes man's hope to control his own reality, including the reality of nature. In *The Alchemist*, however, Jonson insists that self-knowledge is the *sine qua non* of any attempt to cope successfully with the reality of an imperfect world. Thus the gullibility of Sir Epicure Mammon and Tribulation Wholesome is a function of their self-delusion.

Pastor of a congregation of exiled English Anabaptists in Amsterdam, Tribulation Wholesome is a hypocrite who conceals his lust for power beneath the cloak of a holy cause. He defends the Separatists' scandalous exploitation of others as effective "Wayes, that the *godly Brethren* have invented, / For propagation of the *glorious cause*" (III.ii.98–99). The specific end he seeks is "the restoring of the *silenc'd Saints*" to the pulpits of England (III.i.38). But his real desire is to be transformed into a man of power. As a source of gold, the philosopher's stone, Subtle assures him, can be used for "hiring forces" to fight the enemies of their church (III.ii.22). As a medicine and restorative, it can be doled out to the infirm and aged among persons of influence to "make you a faction, / And party in the realm" (III.ii.25–26). With great satisfaction, Wholesome contemplates an England in which he and his brethren may be "temporall lords, our

selves" as well as spiritual leaders (III.ii.52). Since the Separatists
have complained of the time involved in the production of the
philosopher's stone, Subtle offers a more immediate temptation. If
the "holy purse" is low and "the *Saints* / Doe need a present summe,"
the alchemist proposes counterfeiting "as good *Dutch* dollers, / As
any are in *Holland*" (III.ii.140, 141–42, 144–45). When Tribulation
worries that coining might be considered unlawful by the brethren,
Subtle bests him at his own hypocritical game by speciously distinguishing between coining and casting, assuring him that the process
would be casting. Wholesome, though obliged to "make a question of
it, to the *Brethren*" (III.ii.157), is clearly tempted; and Ananias's later
report to Face comes as no surprise:

> the Holy *Synode*
> Have beene in prayer, and meditation, for it.
> And 'tis reveal'd no lesse, to them, then me,
> That casting of money is most lawfull. (IV.vii.75–78)

The distance between Tribulation's image of himself as a holy
Christian and his reality as a hypocritical crook is a measure of his
self-delusion.

Unlike Tribulation Wholesome, Sir Epicure Mammon has wealth
and a respected social position; furthermore, if Surly can be believed,
the knight was at one time considered wise. Mammon is the most
intelligent of the gulls and by far the most imaginative. His is the most
audacious dream of all. He will use the philosopher's stone to rectify
all the shortcomings of nature. In effect, he will use it to transform
himself into a god who will "turne the age, to gold" (I.iv.29). He will
eliminate all disease, even the plague; restore youth and vigor to the
aged; and enrich the poor. But most of all, he will indulge himself in a
life of unparalleled luxury. He will have "a list of wives, and
concubines, / Equall with SALOMON," and he will make his back as
tough as Hercules's "to encounter fiftie a night" in his seraglio
(II.ii.35–36, 39). He will eat only the most exotic foods, dress only in
the finest raiment, enjoy the most exquisite pornography—in short,
do all the things that Volpone would do, but with the added power to
escape the Venetian's limitations by maintaining eternal youth and
health, "And so enjoy a perpetuitie / Of life, and lust" (IV.i.165–66).
Subtle realizes that Mammon's fantasy and lust are so great and so
unfettered by either rationality or decorum as to be self-delusive. The
cozener brilliantly feeds the knight's selfish dreams not by direct

encouragement, but by frequent reminders that the stone cannot provide what Mammon really wants. Such cautions not only strengthen Mammon's faith in Subtle as an "honest wretch, / A notable, superstitious, good soule" (II.ii.101–102), but they also confirm the knight's assumption that he knows better than the unworldly alchemist, that he really can have all he desires. Mammon's combination of selfishness and heroic magnanimity makes him far more affecting than any other character in the play. Indeed, he is one of Jonson's greatest creations. The defeat of his Faustian vision does in fact make the commonwealth poorer, yet his egocentrism blinds him to the reality of his own absurdity.

The secondary cheating of Sir Epicure that the tricksters initiate— the introduction of Dol Common as a noble lady driven mad by biblical studies—not only cozens Mammon of additional money, but also strikingly demonstrates and exploits his self-delusion. Refusing to identify the lady because reports of her madness would greatly embarrass her illustrious family, Face and Subtle present her to Sir Epicure, who immediately professes to see "the *Austriack* princes" in her eyes, lips, and chin; "The house of *Valois*" in her nose; and "the *Medici* / Of *Florence*" in her forehead (IV.i.56, 58, 59–60). Mammon determines to make the common prostitute his consort in a perpetual life of luxury, as though she were ennobled by his desire to see nobility in her. Like all the other gulls, Mammon cozens himself.

Wholesome is frequently accompanied by his elder Ananias, Mammon by his friend Pertinax Surly. Though Ananias and Surly are less important than the men they attend, both are used to significant effect in the play. Ananias is a zealous but ignorant Separatist, Surly a cheating gambler and pimp. Both are hypocrites and both feel smugly superior to Subtle and Face. Although their motives differ, both are skeptical of the philosopher's stone, and each tries to dissuade his companion from its pursuit. Ironically, the objections they raise spur their friends onward. They are ineffective spokesmen for truth because they know themselves insufficiently and they confuse the roles they assume with the realities in which they are imprisoned. Ananias is not gifted with the divine revelation he claims, and Surly is not the honest reformer he pretends to be.

Surly boasts that he will not "willingly be gull'd" (II.i.78). When he enters the Blackfriars house, hears Subtle's learned disquisitions, sees Dol Common, and is handed a message from "Captain Face," he recognizes his own kind. He perceives in Subtle's speeches the cant of the cozener and sees in alchemy "a pretty kind of game, /

Somewhat like tricks o'the cards, to cheat a man, / With charming"
(II.iii.180–82). He accurately labels the three inhabitants of the house
"confederate knaves, and bawdes, and whores" (II.iii.248). But
Surly's "foolish vice of honestie" (V.v.84) is itself only a scam designed
to gain Dame Pliant for himself and to dupe his fellow schemers.
Significantly, however, when Surly reveals the truth, only Dame
Pliant will believe him, and—as her name suggests—she believes
anything that anyone tells her. Face convinces the other gulls present
that Surly is an enemy, and because they prefer to believe their
illusions rather than to accept their realities, they force the would-be
reformer from the house. Surly's ill-fated attempt to expose the
cheaters illustrates the ineffectuality of direct instruction of fools.

The only other character who will not be tricked is Lovewit, the
master of the house whose unexpected return brings about the play's
catastrophe. When Face, necessarily reverting to his role as Jeremy
the butler, tries his self-vaunted cleverness on Lovewit in an attempt
to salvage as much of the situation as possible, the man who is his
social superior proves to be his intellectual master as well. Since the
neighbors contradict each other in their tales of comings and goings
over the past several weeks, Lovewit is prepared to credit Face's
claim that they are mistaken. But the master will not believe that
Dapper's plaintive cries from the privy are "Illusions, some spirit
o'the aire" (V.iii.66), and he sternly demands of his servant, "No more
o' your tricks, good JEREMIE, / The truth, the shortest way"
(V.iii.73–74). Lovewit's commitment to the truth protects him from
the deceptions of cheats and from self-deception as well. He loves a
"teeming wit" (V.i.16), but he does not share Face's unbounded
confidence in the power of cleverness to transform him into some-
thing he is not. Indeed, while he can appreciate the warming of his
bed and the enlarging of his fortune by an alliance with Dame Pliant,
he does not want to be transmuted or to escape his own reality.
Unlike the other characters in the play, he possesses self-knowledge.

Combining as he does both a sense of humor and a sense of
perspective, Lovewit functions as a *deus ex machina* to restore order
to the confused world of the play. He is sometimes described as an
ironic character, "A Falsewit rather than a Truewit,"[34] but actually he
embodies the play's urbane attitude toward foolishness and vice in a
society rife with both.[35] The justice he metes out is perfectly
appropriate and altogether consonant with the play's comic spirit.
The tricksters who improvise the action have hardly preyed on
innocents as did Volpone and Mosca, and they do not deserve the

harsh sentences passed on the earlier villains. Subtle and Dol Common thus escape external punishment for their misdeeds, but they suffer confinement to their own unacceptable realities. The man who would be a great sovereign and the woman who would be a great lady become once more the cheat and whore they have always been. Jeremy's wit advances him slightly in his master's tolerant eyes, but the price is his acknowledgment of a reality far below the delusions of importance he had entertained as Captain Face. The gulls must also accept the realities their ambitions attempted to deny. Lovewit offers to return the confiscated goods if Mammon "can bring certificate, that you were gull'd of 'hem" (V.v.68). The knight's response, "I'll rather loose 'hem" (V.v.71), indicates the fools' continuing reluctance to recognize themselves as they actually are. True reform must begin with self-knowledge, but if the play's comic justice cannot guarantee reform, it does enforce order. Tribulation Wholesome, who would be a temporal lord, is awed into nervous patience by the threat of cudgelling; and the would-be pampered lord of a golden globe resolves to "goe mount a turnep-cart, and preach / The end o'the world, within these two months" (V.v.81–82), a touching but altogether characteristic extravagance.

The Alchemist is one of the greatest comedies in the language. Masterfully crafted with a plot which Samuel Taylor Coleridge considered one of the three best in literature[36] and with a sure grasp of time and place, the play transcends calendar and geography to speak to enduring questions of human nature itself. Man's capacity for self-delusion is an enormously important subject, one with serious consequences on both the individual and the social levels. Jonson never forgets the serious purpose of his depiction of human foolishness and vice, but his "faire correctives" (Pro., l. 18) permit genuine laughter as well as scorn. Perhaps Jonson's greatest single achievement in the theater, the play is neither a simple gallery of idiocy nor a bitterly satiric diatribe but an incredibly vital comedy. Combining a robust enjoyment of eccentric characters and colorful language, accelerated action and moral insight, *The Alchemist* is a work of mature genius.

V   Bartholomew Fair *(1614) and* The Devil Is an Ass *(1616)*

After writing *The Alchemist,* Jonson took a second leave of absence from the comic stage, this sabbatical lasting four years. He returned to comedy in 1614 with the production of *Batholomew Fair* and followed that play two years later with *The Devil Is an Ass*. *Batholomew Fair* is among Jonson's comic triumphs, and *The Devil Is an Ass* is an interesting example of topical Jacobean city comedy. The plays lack the obvious unity of *Volpone, Epicoene,* and *The Alchemist,* recalling more vividly the structural sprawl of *Every Man in His Humour* and the frank theatricality of the comical satires. In these plays, however, Jonson's theatricality is in the service of comic realism, and he avoids the overt moralizing and static commentary of *Every Man out of His Humour* and *Cynthia's Revels.* Like *Every Man in His Humour* and *The Alchemist,* the new plays are firmly rooted in London.

Batholomew Fair was premiered by the Lady Elizabeth's Men in their new theater, The Hope, on Halloween 1614, and was presented at court the following day. A play of great and exciting extremes, extraordinarily crowded, noisy, and episodic, it provides a panoramic view of London low life. It hosts a large gallery of bawdy characters given to broad humor and rowdy action, and its setting at a great civic festival allows the inclusion of these robust outlaws without a breach of decorum. *Bartholomew Fair* exposes folly and vice as serious as that presented in *The Alchemist* or even *Volpone,* yet its perspective is significantly different. The play presents life in all its squalor and vulgarity, its foul smells and natural functions, but reserves its censure for those who would pretend to be aloof from the common humanity represented by the denizens of the fair. If *The Alchemist* illustrates man's capacity for self-deception, *Bartholomew Fair* repeats the lesson in a new guise. It insists upon the commonality which unites human beings: the prerequisite for self-knowledge is acceptance of the fact that human nature is so flawed as to make judgment tentative at best. Although this recognition of human limitations may seem grim and pessimistic in the abstract, the comedy realizes its theme through playful action which celebrates the human potential for laughter.

Although specific incidents in the play may have been suggested to Jonson in the course of his reading, the plot of *Bartholomew Fair* is of his own devising, and it owes its complex fascination to his firsthand knowledge of London's underworld. The plot consists of a large number of events loosely connected by personal relationships among its characters. Two family groups go out from London to nearby Smithfield to attend the St. Bartholomew's Day Fair. Through most of the day they meet and interact with the crowd of low characters who provide the fair's food, drink, trinkets, and assorted amusements. For a time the members of each family separate from their fellows and have various adventures, some of which center on the marriage arrangements of the wealthy widow Dame Purecraft and the young ward Grace Wellborn. In the late afternoon, all come together at a puppet play.[37] Toward nightfall, after some regrouping of personal alliances, they retire to supper at the home of a London Justice of the Peace, whose own investigations into the "enormities" of the fair have been hilariously ineffectual. The characters who set themselves up as censurers of others must acknowledge their own limitations, but the play ends with a feast from which no one is excluded.

Bartholomew Fair opens with an induction which self-consciously calls attention to the comedy's artifice. The Stage-Keeper complains that what is to be presented "is like to be a very conceited scurvy [play], in plaine English. When 't comes to the *Fayre*, once: you were e'en as good goe to *Virginia*, for any thing there is of *Smith-field*" (Ind., ll. 9–11). He is driven away by the Book-Holder and the Scrivener who present "Articles of Agreement" between the spectators and the author. In return for the audience's commitment to "remaine in the places, their money or friends have put them in, with patience," Jonson promises "a new sufficient Play . . . merry, and as full of noise, as sport: made to delight all, and to offend none. Provided they have either, the wit, or the honesty to thinke well of themselves" (Ind., ll. 77–79, 81–84). The promise of a decorous, inoffensive comedy is disingenuous, but it enlists the audience's engagement as understanding judges. Rather than distancing the spectators from the events presented on stage, the framing device invites them to test the play's artifice against their own realities and, by extension, to match their own judgments against those of the play's characters. Moreover, the provision that the spectators have "either, the wit, or the honesty to thinke well of themselves" sets the terms of the comedy's examination of human folly. As L. A. Beaurline comments, "If they are conscious of their worth and think well of their potential good, they can relish whatever fare is put before them, without offense."[38] More pointedly, the provision enunciates a nexus between self-knowledge and good judgment. Wit and honesty are necessary to self-knowledge, and self-knowledge is essential to good judgment and ought to preclude facile judgment of others.

The issue of judgment is faced squarely in the opening act, set in Littlewit's London house, where most of the middle-class characters who presume to judge the denizens of the fair are introduced. *Bartholomew Fair* is in some respects similar to Shakespeare's festive comedies;[39] and as the first act of *As You Like It,* for instance, establishes the "envious court" (II.i.4) which contrasts with the "liberty" of the Forest of Arden (I.iii.138), so the middle-class setting of the opening act of *Bartholomew Fair* functions as a foil to the holiday world of Smithfield where inhibitions are relaxed. For most of the middle-class characters, the fair beckons as an escape from everyday restrictions to freedom and even license. That the delights of Smithfield are sordid and ordinarily forbidden only increases its attractiveness as a temporary respite from the pressures of polite society. But some of the characters attempt to deny their need for the holiday spirit and they go to Smithfield in search of "enormities," as in the case of Justice Overdo, or they disguise their pleasure-seeking as an opportunity to "be religious in midst of the prophane" (I.vi.73), as in the case of Zeal-of-the-Land Busy. The irony of the play, however, is that while the enormities and the profanity of the fair are indeed exposed, the greater satire is directed against the middle-class characters, and particularly against those who would peremptorily or self-righteously judge others. As Brian Gibbons remarks, "The main satiric force is directed towards Puritanical attitudes to art and life: the didactic purpose of Jonson is to demonstrate that here, in 1614, these attitudes are more of a threat to the Commonwealth than even the crassest stupidity, fashion-following, or pretentiousness. . . ."[40]

Most of the play's middle-class characters are variations of types already familiar in the Jonson canon. John Littlewit, a proctor of an ecclesiastical court, is a would-be wit and poet. His wife, Win-the-Fight Littlewit, is—despite her imposing Puritan name—an empty-headed, pretty little woman easily impressed with the outward show of things. Dame Purecraft, her mother, is a widow of apparently sober Puritan rectitude; and her suitor of the moment, Zeal-of-the-Land Busy, is a former baker of Banbury, now a purifying prophet and self-appointed arbiter of morals in the Littlewit household. Also attached to the Littlewit group, if only tenuously, is Ned Winwife, a gentleman of real wit whose courtship of Dame Purecraft has been eclipsed by the arrival of Busy. Accompanying Winwife is his clever friend Tom Quarlous, a gambler given to drink and foolery.

The other group of visitors to the fair is the entourage of Bartholomew Cokes, a rich but exceedingly foolish young country squire. This eager and resolute ninny is accompanied by Humphrey Wasp, a self-important, testy old servant who tries, unsuccessfully, to control the idiocies of his young master. An unwilling member of the group is Grace Wellborn, Cokes's scornful young fiancée, the ward of Justice

Adam Overdo. Serving as Grace's chaperone is Dame Overdo, the Justice's wife and Bartholomew Cokes's sister. A social climber of proud dignity, she constantly reminds everyone of her own importance. Also present at the fair, but arriving separately and disguised, is Justice Overdo himself. And haunting the festival is Trouble-All, a man driven mad by the severe judgment Overdo rendered against him, who now insists on having Overdo's written warrant for any action he takes.

The fair itself is crowded with still a third group—low characters, some there to provide its wares and services, others to prey on its customers by the more direct means of thievery. These are among the most colorful people Jonson ever invented. Their very names, Joan Trash, Lantern Leatherhead, Ezekiel Edgeworth, Jordan Knockhum, Nightingale, Punk Alice, Captain Whit, Mooncalf, and Ursula the pig woman, indicate their earthiness. Much of the play's vitality stems from its depiction of the moral and physical depravity of these prostitutes, pimps, and petty criminals; and they provide the comedy with its pungent air of humanity at its basest and most basic levels. These characters share goodnatured contempt for the pretensions of their social betters, an honesty with themselves regarding their own shortcomings, an accurate perception of the world about them, a facility for trickery, and a jovial spirit of camaraderie with their fellow rogues. Collectively, they test the characters and wits of their middle-class customers.

The more foolish customers are easy prey for the rogues. Assured by her imperceptive husband that the men he leaves her with, the horsetrader Jordan Knockhum and the pimp Captain Whit, are "honest Gentlemen . . . they'll use you very civilly" (IV.v.8–10), Win Littlewit succumbs to the offer of fine clothes and the promise that she will be worshiped as a lady and thereby unwittingly becomes part of Whit's merchandise. The proud Dame Overdo, having overindulged in drink and neglected her chaperonage of Grace, confesses drunkenly that she admires "Men of warre, and the Sonnes of the sword" (IV.iv.228), and she too is added to the Captain's stable. The temptations of the fair prove over and over again Bat Cokes's fundamental foolishness, as he delightedly goes from one attraction to another. He buys the entire stock of Lantern Leatherhead's toys to serve as his wedding masque and the lot of Joan Trash's gingerbread men to furnish his nuptial banquet, and then leaves his purchases behind, trusting the dishonest vendors to deliver them at a later date. He persists in disregarding the advice of Wasp and keeps company with men who twice rob him of his purse and eventually steal his hat and cloak as well. He is thoroughly impressed by the absurd puppet play and becomes so engrossed with the puppets that he treats them like real people. The most naive character in the play, he cannot distinguish between surface and substance in either objects or people. John Littlewit, tempted by the occasion of the fair to display his wit and poetic skill, arranges for Leatherhead's puppet theater to present a play he has written. The drama, in halting poulter's measure, combines the myths of Hero and Leander and Damon and Pythias and absurdly trivializes them.

The foolishness of these four characters may have serious consequences for themselves, but it is of little danger to society as a whole. Four other characters are in positions where their foolishness can affect the lives of others, however, and the fair provokes the public discovery of their more serious folly. Humphrey Wasp not only has charge of Bat Cokes, but he defiantly assumes leadership of the whole group that accompanies the young man to the fair. Although basically honest and intelligent, Wasp is constantly angry, and his expression of testiness toward everyone he presumes to correct—his favorite phrase is "turd i' your teeth" (I.iv.53)—makes his admonitions offensive and thereby ineffectual. Moreover, his indiscriminate indignation blinds him to worth where it does exist and prohibits an accurate assessment of the situations in which he finds himself. His loss of Coke's marriage license, the immediate cause of his ultimate humiliation, is only the most tangible reflection of the serious flaws in Wasp's perception.

Dame Purecraft, matron and ruler of the Littlewits as well as an officer in her Puritan congregation, reveals in response to the temptations offered by the fair both the shallowness of her faith and the serious crimes she has committed while hypocritically clothing herself in precisionist self-righteousness. The fair offers Purecraft, in the person of Quarlous disguised as Trouble-All, the madman of gentle birth that a fortune-teller has prophesied she should marry. To get him, she must overcome his prejudice against Puritan hypocrisy, and the "truth" she tells him about herself is a chilling confession of venality: "These seven yeeres, I have beene a wilfull holy widdow, onely to draw feasts, and gifts from my intangled suitors: I am also by office, an assisting *sister* of the *Deacons*, and a devourer, in stead of a distributer of the alms" (V.ii.53–56). Fortunately for her, the man to whom she proposes is just as fond of money as she is; and he responds favorably to her invitation to "enjoy all my deceits together" (V.ii.72).

Zeal-of-the-Land Busy, who for the three days of his visit has assumed moral leadership in the Littlewit household, is drawn to the fair by his gluttony. But once there, he is tempted to use his divinely inspired zeal for the correction of the whole community of the ungodly at the Smithfield celebration: "I was mov'd in spirit, to bee here, this day, in this *Faire*, this wicked, and foule *Faire;* and fitter may it be called a foule, then a *Faire:* To protest against the abuses of it, the foule abuses of it, in regard of the afflicted Saints, that are troubled, very much troubled, exceedingly troubled, with the opening of the merchandize of *Babylon* againe, & the peeping of *Popery* upon the stals, here, here, in the high places" (III. vi. 86–93). His attempt to overturn the tents of Baal causes him to be confined in the stocks for disturbing the peace, and his railing at the presentation of the play results in exposing the ignorance which underlies his fanaticism. Although he calls upon his zeal to "fill me, fill me, that is, make me full" (V. v. 45–46), he is bested in a theological argument by a puppet manipulated by a low character.

The occasion of the fair tempts Justice Overdo to don "the habit of a foole" to discover firsthand the "enormities" perpetrated there (II. i. 9, 45). Like the elder Knowell in *Every Man in His Humour*, he is well intentioned and basically good. His reasoning is sound: judges too often "heare with other mens eares; wee see with other mens eyes; a foolish Constable, or a sleepy Watchman, is all our information" (II. i. 29–31). His cause is admirable: "in Justice name, and the Kings; and for the Commonwealth" (II. i. 48–49). But he exaggerates his importance and the seriousness of the "enormities" he seeks to expose. Most significantly, however, his perception is sadly deficient. Lacking a quick wit, Overdo is beaten and placed in the stocks; and he consistently misinterprets what he observes. Thinking Ezekiel Edgworth "has a good Clerks looke with him" (II. iv. 33), Overdo mistakes the cutpurse for a "proper young man" who needs to be rescued from his "debaucht company" (III. v. 2, 3) and protected from a dangerous tendency toward poetry. His attempt to pass judgment at day's end begins in bombast: "looke upon mee, O *London!* and see mee, O *Smithfield;* The *example of Justice,* and *Mirror of Magistrates:* the true top of formality, and scourge of enormity. Harken unto my *labours,* and but observe my *discoveries*" (V. vi. 33–37). Yet all his judgments are mistaken, and the play ends with his exposure. Although Justice Overdo is foolish, he has the capacity to learn from his experience, and his late realization that he needs to be more gentle when he returns to his official role as judge is a direct result of his firsthand contact with common humanity at the fair.

The characters in *Bartholomew Fair* who come nearest to a normative balance of wit and self-knowledge are Ned Winwife, Tom Quarlous, and Grace Wellborn. Like the witty gallants of other Jonsonian comedies, Winwife and Quarlous are perceptive and intelligent, and they enjoy sporting with fools. But as their names suggest, one is preoccupied with winning a rich wife and the other is inclined to quarreling. Furthermore, when the fair offers each the possibility of wedding the young and wealthy Grace, their first instinct is not to aid each other, but to settle the question by swordplay. And when chance awards Grace to Winwife, Quarlous, who has often scorned old wives and hypocritical Puritans, all too easily yields to the proposal of Dame Purecraft, with her "sixe thousand pound . . . and a good trade too" (V.ii.76–77). But this marriage itself signifies Quarlous's recognition of human imperfections, including his own. Thus it is fitting that Quarlous should untangle the plot complications at the end of the play and propose that Overdo invite everyone home to supper: "There you and I will compare our *discoveries;* and drowne the memory of all enormity in your bigg'st bowle at home" (V.vi.99–100).

Grace Wellborn is "discrete, and as sober as shee is handsome" (I.v.55–56). Justifiably scornful of the foolish young man her guardian expects her to marry, she scorns the fair as well: "there's none goes thither of any quality or fashion" (I.v.131–32). But when it offers her the opportunity to escape Cokes by marrying either Winwife or Quarlous, both "reasonable creatures" with "understanding, and discourse" (IV.iii.35–36), she seizes the occasion. After protesting that she cannot make "a choyse, without knowing you more" (IV.iii.32), she devises a plan to have the next passerby pick her husband, an impetuous and irrational action. That the man who makes the actual decision is the mad Trouble-All underscores the irrationality of the marriage lottery and may validate her opinion that "*Destiny* has a high hand in businesse of this nature" (IV.iii.51–52). Certainly her trust that "if fate send me an understanding husband, I have no feare at all, but mine owne manners shall make him a good one" (IV.iii.36–38) seems justified in her union with Winwife. If the marriage of the two young people seems unsentimental, it is nevertheless a perfectly suitable match.

Although *Bartholomew Fair* contains some of Jonson's most serious examinations of folly and vice, its didacticism is conveyed in some of his most robustly comic characters and situations. Ursula, the fat and foul-mouthed purveyor of roast pig, who sweats so profusely that she waters the ground "like a great Garden-pot" (II.ii.52), may in her frank gluttony serve as a foil to Busy, but she is a magnificent creature in her own right. Busy, though an arch hypocrite and a danger to the state, has a memorable comic presence. The ridiculousness of the way in which his lack of wit is exposed—by a puppet talking him into a corner and then raising its skirt to show that it has no sex—is howlingly funny. Wasp may be thoroughly disagreeable, but his cleverness in escaping the stocks earns him the respect of delighted laughter. Though in the strictest sense undeserved, the whipping Punk Alice administers to the proud Dame Overdo when she mistakes the drunken matron for a "privy rich" whore who steals trade from "poore common whores" (IV.v.70,69) is comically appropriate to Dame Overdo's folly. Trouble-All, potentially the grimmest reminder of the serious consequences of justice without mercy and whose plight convinces Overdo that "compassion may become a *Justice*" (IV.i.82–83), is comic in his exaggerated obsession. Even the puppet play, embodying all the faults Jonson saw in Jacobean drama, is not without positive charm. When Hero, transformed by Littlewit into a Bankside maiden, first sees Leander, a dyer of Puddle Wharf, she notes his "naked legge, and goodly calfe," and casts on him an affecting "Sheepes eye, and a halfe" (V.iv.124, 125).

With such good humor throughout, there is no compulsion to enforce strict justice at the end of the play. All of its characters are in some way compromised; and Overdo's final words, a quotation from Horace, perfectly suits the mood in which they have been tested: "*Ad correctionem, non ad destructionem; Ad aedificandum, non ad diruendum*" [for correction, not for destruction; for building up, not for tearing down] (V.vi.112–13). Wasp's comment, "He that will correct another, must want fault in himselfe" (V.iv.99–100), crystallizes the play's attitude toward those who would too easily judge others. The most serious offenders, those who have held themselves aloof from common humanity, have all been shamed in the course of the play. Certainly Justice Overdo has gained a new awareness of his limitations and, consequently, of his possibilities. His justice will be more compassionate and more constructive in the future.

Bartholomew Fair is one of Jonson's most fascinating plays. Alternatingly "indignant and compassionate, farcical and serious,"[41] it embraces a tolerant view of human nature while never suppressing unpleasant aspects of human experience. Devastatingly anti-Puritan, the play nevertheless refuses to banish even Zeal-of-the-Land Busy from the feast which includes rich and poor, witty and witless, justice and cutpurse, ladies and whores alike. As a celebration of humanity in all its diversity, and as an affirmation of the holiday spirit, it teaches all to "remember you are but *Adam*, Flesh, and blood! you have your frailty" (V.vi.96–97). Zestful and exuberant, earthy and vital, *Bartholomew Fair* is one of the most energetic plays in English literature.

While far less complex and crowded than *Bartholomew Fair*, *The Devil Is an Ass* shares the earlier comedy's theatricality. First presented by the King's Men at Blackfriars Theater late in 1616, *The Devil Is an Ass* is framed by infernal scenes which are unique in the Jonsonian canon. A realistic, topical city comedy on the subject handled so brilliantly in *The Alchemist*, cozenage, the play uses its framing device to set its comic depiction of man's foolishness within a witty allegorical context. The human characteristics of pretentiousness and gullibility are exposed with particular reference to a serious economic and social abuse of the day, the granting of monopolies.[42] In addition, the play satirizes some of Jonson's favorite targets: people who are ruled by fashion, affected travelers, social climbers, emptyheaded playgoers who visit the theater only to be seen, and Puritans.

A minor devil, Pug, wheedles permission from a reluctant Satan to work evil on earth for a single day. Set down in London in the young and handsome body of a just-executed cutpurse, Pug attaches himself as serving man to a foolish, pretentious, and guillible squire from Norfolk, Fabian Fitzdottrel. Through the events of the day, especially his attendance at a "school" where women are taught to be fashionable, Pug makes two related discoveries. He finds that humans are more sophisticated in evil than devils. "You talke of a *University!*" he exclaims, "why, *Hell* is / A Grammar-schoole to this!" (IV.iv.170–71). The corollary discovery is that hell has a lesser array of torments than does London society. Having disgraced his calling by letting "men know their strength, / And that they are able to out-doe a *divel*" (V.vi.57–58), Pug is carried back to hell on the broad shoulders of old-fashioned Iniquity.

The play contains three familiar Jonsonian types among its human characters: a greedy cozener; foolish gulls who deserve to be cozened; and witty gallants who see through the tricksters as well as the gulls and who manipulate both groups, initially "for the mirth" inherent in the game (III.iv.26) and eventually to effect justice. The cozener is Meercraft, a "projector" of monopolistic schemes. He is clever and quick-witted, but as his name implies, he can be bested by someone who relies on a higher, more humane intelligence. Unlike Jonson's other cozening plays, however, *The Devil Is an Ass* focuses not on the trickster, but on the victim; and though several people are gulled in the play, Fitzdottrel is always the center of attention. Meercraft proposes many projects to make the squire rich, the distillation of wine from raisins and the manufacture of fine gloves from dog skins, for example; but the scheme that most excites Fitzdottrel is the draining of fenlands to make them arable, a project which will not only enrich him but will be of such value to the kingdom that he can expect a dukedom for his efforts.

The gallant Wittipol, assisted by his friend Manly, engineers two of the best schemes in the play. Knowing Fitzdottrel's passion for fine clothes, Wittipol trades a rich cloak for the foolish squire's permission to speak to Mistress Fitzdottrel, whereupon he proceeds to woo the young woman in the presence of her husband, who—according to the terms of the agreement—must remain silent or forfeit the cloak (I.vi). Later, in a scene replete with characteristic Jonsonian catalogues and high-sounding doubletalk, Wittipol, disguised as a young English widow lately come from Spain, holds a "school" for fashionable ladies at Lady Tailbush's house, instructing them in exotic manners and elaborate cosmetic concoctions (IV.iii–iv). The ultimate and serious action of the gallants, however, is to trick Fitzdottrel into giving his power of attorney to his sensible young wife before he can waste his entire fortune on the toys of fashion and on Meercraft's impossible schemes.

The Devil Is an Ass contains the most passionate and fully realized courtship in all of Jonson's dramatic canon. In professing his love for Mistress Fitzdottrel, Wittipol uses most of the devices available to seventeenth-century lovers. Courting her in the presence of her foolish husband, he invokes the arguments of suitability and of *carpe diem* (I.vi.122–32). In a later scene, alone with the young woman, Wittipol runs his hands over her body and describes her charms in the conventions of the sonneteer's *blason*, while at the same time arguing the "naturalness" of their love (II.vi.71–87). One of the most sympathetically drawn women in Jonsonian comedy, Mistress Fitzdottrel is sensible, beautiful, intelligent, and much aggrieved in being yoked to an extraordinarily foolish husband. Wittipol is a handsome, sound young man of wit who truly loves her. He would make a far more appropriate mate for her than the witless man to whom she is wed. She is undoubtedly tempted by Wittipol's advances, and the expectation is raised that somehow, by the end of the play, the two lovers will be united. But Mistress Fitzdottrel is irrevocably married, and Jonson resists the easy solution of romantic comedy in favor of realism. In the last scene, Manly assures Fitzdottrel that his wife has remained "chaste, and vertuous" (V.viii.151). Wittipol, an "honest" man (V.viii.152), respects the woman he loves; although he would prefer things to be otherwise, he contents himself with being her Platonic admirer: "Lady, I can love *goodnes* in you, more/Then I did *Beauty*" (IV.vi.37–38).

The Devil Is an Ass is not a profoundly moving comedy. It fails to strike below the surface of cleverness and comic incident. Fitzdottrel's dream to become Duke of Drown'd-Land and to cut a gallant swath through London society is superficial. It does not touch the deep, secret longings in the human psyche which Volpone's and Mammon's voluptuous fantasies excite. Similarly, the cozener Meercraft, while extraordinarily clever, is basically simple. Motivated entirely by greed, he possesses none of the self-delusive complexity that makes Subtle such an interesting character. Moreover, the form that his cozenage takes, the projection of monopolistic schemes, lacks the imaginative appeal of alchemy, with its mystical promise of perfecting all creation. But *The Devil Is an Ass* is a sophisticated, witty comedy. Its topicality may render it inaccessible for many readers, but the play dwells enough on the universal follies of mankind to merit a respectable place in the history of Jacobean comedy. Although it cannot be ranked among Jonson's greatest plays, *The Devil Is an Ass* is exhilarating and inventive.[43]

VI *The Late Comedies (1626–1632)*

Jonson's third leave of absence from comedy lasted almost ten years. When he returned to the genre, he produced a festive and topical city comedy, *The Staple of News* (1626); a much misunderstood romantic comedy, *The New Inn* (1629); and a farewell humor comedy, *The Magnetic Lady* (1632). While the last two, and sometimes all three, of these plays have often been referred to as Jonson's "dotages," they do not show any decline in his inventiveness. While none is a masterpiece, all break new ground, and all reflect the playwright's abiding concern with educating his audience in the purpose and theory of comedy.

The Staple of News was first presented by the King's Men at Blackfriars Theater shortly before the beginning of Lent in 1626, with a court performance following, probably on Shrove Tuesday. Like

Bartholomew Fair, it is a festive comedy.[44] Its holiday tone is set by Gossip Mirth, "the daughter of *Christmas*, and spirit of *Shrovetide*" (Ind., ll. 11–12), and her three companions—Gossips Tattle, Expectation, and Censure—who interrupt the prologue, demand seats on the stage, and proceed throughout the play to "interpret" everything they see. The play itself, though it does not contain supernatural materials, shares with *The Devil Is an Ass* an allegorical significance. Its central plot is a variation of the ancient motif of the prodigal son, and its theme is the equally venerable ideal of "The golden meane" (V.vi.64). Also like *The Devil Is an Ass*, *The Staple of News* comically dramatizes the abuses possible in a current London phenomenon, in this case the fledgling journalism of the early period of the Thirty Years War. The Staple of the play's title is an office where news is not only collected but also manufactured out of rumor and even out of thin air, then categorized, packaged, and sold to an eager and gullible public at prices based on bulk.

The play's focal character, Penniboy Junior, has recently been told by an old vagabond—whom he subsequently adopts into his retinue as Penniboy Canter—that his father has died, leaving him heir to a fortune. The young man spends the day he comes of age in prodigal misuse of that wealth. He buys elaborate new clothes at exorbitant prices; he purchases a position on the Staple for his barber, a man who, by profession, is a natural peddler of "news"; and he courts, at considerable expense, the city's most eligible and sought-after young heiress, Lady Aurelia Clara Pecunia Do-All. This "princess" of Cornish tin and copper, grandly referred to as "Infanta of the Mines," is, with allegorical aptness, the closely guarded ward of young Penniboy's miserly uncle, Richer Penniboy. When Penniboy Canter has seen enough to be thoroughly disgusted with Penniboy Junior's behavior, he reveals himself to be the young man's father and explains his disguise and the report of his own death as a test of his son's ability to manage money. The young man is left in disgrace, but when his father is threatened with ruin at the hands of the dishonest lawyer Picklock, Penniboy Junior summons the wit to thwart the attempted fleecing and thereby redeems himself in his father's eyes and wins the hand of Pecunia.

The subjects of money and news come together at the exact center of the play. In an effort to impress Pecunia, Penniboy Junior takes her to the Staple of News, whereupon the master of the establishment, Cymbal, tries to steal her away from the young prodigal, correctly perceiving that her patronage of his place of business will draw

customers. When he calls her the "*State*, and wonder, / Of these our
times" and bids her "dazle the vulgar eyes, / And strike the people
blind with admiration" (III.ii.238–40), Penniboy Canter, who embodies the play's "humane scheme of values,"[45] exclaims:

> Why, that's the end of wealth! thrust riches outward,
> And remaine beggers within: contemplate nothing
> But the vile sordid things of time, place, money,
> And let the noble, and the precious goe,
> Vertue and honesty; hang 'hem; poore thinne membranes
> Of honour; who respects them? O, the *Fates!*
> How hath all just, true reputation fall'n,
> Since money, this base money 'gan to have any! (III.ii.241–48)

The Staple of News does not suggest that money should be despised,
only that it should be kept in proper perspective and used wisely. The
Staple fails because it caters to the worship of money. Richer
Penniboy goes mad when his desire to enslave money is thwarted.
Penniboy Junior, who almost loses Pecunia when he prostitutes her
to the Staple, succeeds in his courtship of her only when he finally
realizes that he should "use her like a friend, not like a slave, / Or like
an *Idoll*" (V.vi.22–23).

Since much of its comedy is based on the ridiculousness of the
"news" offered by the Staple, this play is even less accessible to the
modern reader than *The Devil Is an Ass*. It presupposes fairly
detailed knowledge of the background and the events of the early part
of the Thirty Years War; the complex religious situation in Europe;
the state of science and technology in 1626; the era's exploration and
exploitation of the non-European world; and even something of the
infancy of the English "newspaper." In addition, many of the
characters in *The Staple of News* are so flatly representative of
abstractions and types that they fail to engage more than superficial
interest as individuals. In enough passages to make the play rewarding, however, the topical is tied recognizably to the universal; and the
comic overrides the particular. And while many of the characters are
flat, the dialogue is sparkling and varied, ranging from sophisticated
barb to crude scatology. Moreover, the play is perfectly suited to the
occasion of its Shrove Tuesday production. Through festive comedy,
The Staple of News sets the house of flesh in order, an appropriate
prelude to the otherworldly contemplations of Ash Wednesday and
the Lenten season which it inaugurates.

Jonson's next comedy, *The New Inn. Or, The Light Heart*, received its first and, for almost three hundred years, its only performance by the King's Men at Blackfriars Theater early in 1629. In materials appended to the first printing of the play (1631), Jonson blamed its poor reception on bad acting and on the insensitivity and boorishness of the spectators. But even given a good performance, the play demands extraordinary sophistication from its audience to see behind its facade. In some ways, *The New Inn* is the most daring experiment that the constantly experimental Jonson ever attempted. It is a comedy about decorum and role-playing; and, indeed, the whole may be seen as a dramatization of many of Jonson's theories concerning drama.[46] Its points are made by such indirect means that they can easily be missed, however. The prologue and epilogue give little hint as to how the play is to be viewed; and there are no audience pointers such as Jonson provides in the inductions and intermeans of several other comedies. What is presented in *The New Inn* is a presumably straightforward play that is extremely indecorous and excessively flawed by the compounded absurdities of the worst examples of romantic comedy. But the play's breaches of decorum serve to comment, by indirection, on appropriate conduct in several interrelated spheres of human affairs: love and courtship, social position, and responsibility toward others. Moreover, the plot of *The New Inn*, also by indirection, makes three points. On the simplest level, it criticizes by exaggeration the romantic comedy that it imitates. On another level, it graphically illustrates the illusory nature of much that human beings experience and think they understand. And on still another level, it demonstrates the truth that can emerge through theatrical feigning. *The New Inn* concerns discovery of the self in the maze of conscious and unconscious role-playing.

A frivolous but virtuous young noblewoman, Lady Frances Frampul, accompanied by her waiting maid Prudence and a brace of young gallants, Lords Latimer and Beaufort, determines to sport for a day in a country inn near London, The Light Heart. Unknown to her, that particular hostelry, presided over by a determinedly jovial host, Goodstock, is the refuge of Lovel, a middle-aged gentleman who loves her but who has promised a dying friend, old Lord Beaufort, that he will look after the welfare of that nobleman's son, now coincidentally Lady Frampul's chief suitor. To fool young Latimer and Beaufort, Pru suggests that the innkeeper's adopted son, a pretty lad sold to him by a drunken old woman now employed as a nurse and char at the inn, be dressed as a girl and introduced to the company as a relative of Lady Frampul's. As the main entertainment of the day,

Lady Frances, assisted by the Host, decides to tease the melancholy Lovel by having him pay suit to her in a formal court of love presided over by Prudence. With long set speeches on the nature of love and honor, paraphrased from popular neoplatonic literature, Lovel rather improbably sobers the flippant young lady and wins her love. In the meantime, Latimer falls in love with Prudence; and Beaufort succumbs to the charms of the host's disguised son and, much to the delight of the company, marries "her" in a hastily arranged ceremony in the stables. Intermingled with these events, the servants and other low characters banter, drink, and quarrel below stairs. Finally, in an unmasking scene going beyond that of the most outrageous of romantic comedies, the innkeeper announces that he is the long-lost Lord Frampul; the drunken charwoman proclaims herself the equally long-lost Lady Frampul; and the Host's adopted son is revealed to be his real younger daughter Laetitia. Lady Frances, who for many years has thought herself an orphan, thus suddenly has her entire family restored to her; and the play ends in the happy pairing of Lovel and Frances, Latimer and Prudence, Beaufort and Laetitia, and the reunited Lord and Lady Frampul.

In *The New Inn*, characters and situations are both not what they seem and more than what they seem. The inn itself is a theater, recalling the genesis of the Elizabethan playhouse, and the Host its appreciative audience:

> I imagine all the world's a Play;
> The state, and mens affaires, all passages
> Of life, to spring new *scenes*, come in, goe out,
> And shift, and vanish; and if I have got
> A seat, to sit at ease here, i' mine Inne,
> To see the *Comedy*; and laugh, and chuck
> At the variety, and throng of humors,
> And dispositions, that come justling in,
> And out still. (I.iii.128–36)

The Host is also a character; and most of the characters in the play, like actors, have assumed identities not their own, or else they attempt to do so. Some, with indecorous presumption, try to rise above their abilities and worth. The servant Fly assumes the dignities of "Deacon," "Doctor," "Captaine," "Lieutenant," and "Professor" (II.iv.33–34; V.i.2). The tailor's wife, Pinnacia Stuff, dons the clothes that her husband makes for great ladies, assuming a dignity she does not have for purposes of erotic stimulation. Some of the characters assume roles to evade responsibilities. Lord Frampul, having spent years in the company of "Pipers, Fidlers, Rushers, Puppet-masters, / Juglers, and Gipseys" (V.v.96–97), presides over an inn rather than over his family. Even more grotesquely, his wife has deserted one of her daughters, reared the other as a boy, and lives in the inn as the drunken widow of a Welsh herald.

In some cases, however, the assumption of a false identity points toward a character's true self. The innkeeper's adopted son, dressed as a girl and presented as a kinswoman of Lady Frances, is actually that noblewoman's sister. The Host, who recognizes virtues beneath Lovel's melancholy inertia and assists in forcing the lovesick man to woo Frances, is the lady's father; and even though he has for a long time evaded his responsibilities toward his daughter, he is brought to an indirect performance of his fatherly function. Lovel is made to assume openly the role of suitor to Frances, realizing, though unwillingly, his secret wish.

The character in whom all the elements of the play come together is Prudence, the chambermaid. She recognizes the importance of decorum, she questions the validity of appearances, and she carefully distinguishes between role-playing and real life. When Frances forces her to be queen of the court of love, Pru protests, calling attention to the unsuitability of such a role: "To be translated thus, 'bove all the bound / Of fitnesse, or *decorum*" (II.i.54–55). But her conduct in that assumed role proves that in wit and good sense she is suited to a high station; and, without presuming to think herself worthy of it, she wins the love of Lord Latimer. Judged by the Host to be the "best deserving / Of all that are i' the house, or i' my Heart" (V.v.130–31) and by Latimer to be "all-sufficient in her vertue and manners" (V.v.144), Prudence is raised above her allotted place in society. She is a unique creation in the Jonsonian comic canon, an indirect though eloquent plea that human beings be judged on their merits and behavior, rather than on the accidents of birth.

The New Inn is an intriguing play, one whose riches are still being explored with sympathetic understanding.[47] Perhaps it can never be successful in production. The prolonged antics of its low characters and the lengthy disquisitions of Lovel, while making important statements, are tedious; and both hobble the dramatic flow. Similarly, the improbabilities of the play have a force which almost overpowers the serious intent; and most of the play's subtleties reveal themselves only through diligent study and quiet reflection. But the lessons of *The New Inn* are both valid and humane, and the play deserves the attention it is now receiving.

The Magnetic Lady: or, Humours Reconciled was presented by the King's Men at Blackfriars Theater in the autumn of 1632. Apparently it had three public performances, all unsuccessful; and it may have been presented at court. Although Jonson revised *A Tale of a Tub* extensively for a new production in 1633 and in the last years of his life may have worked on *The Sad Shepherd*, a pastoral romance left unfinished, *The Magnetic Lady* is his last wholly new play; and both its subtitle and the tone of its induction and choral intermeans indicate that the playwright thought of it as the final effort of his dramatic career, rounding off thirty-four years of mature production. As the Boy of the House explains:

The *Author*, beginning his studies of this kind, with *every man in his Humour*; and after, *every man out of his Humour*: and since, continuing in all his *Playes*, especially those of the *Comick* thred, whereof the *New-Inne* was the last, some recent humours still, or manners of men, that went along with the times, finding himselfe now neare the close, or shutting up of his Circle, hath phant'sied to himselfe, in *Idaea*, this *Magnetick Mistres*. A Lady, a brave bountifull House-keeper, and a vertuous Widow: who having a young Neice, ripe for a man and marriageable, hee makes that his Center attractive, to draw thither a diversity of Guests, all persons of different humours to make up his *Perimeter*. And this hee hath call'd *Humors reconcil'd*. (Ind., ll. 99–111)

The play places its humor characters, most of them pretentious and greedy, in a situation appropriate to romantic comedy. It introduces characters not seen before in Jonsonian plays, and it modifies significantly some familiar types.

A group of people gather in the house of Lady Loadstone, most of them attracted, as the Boy notes, by the presence of the lady's wealthy young niece, Placentia Steel, an orphan who has reached the marriageable age of fourteen. During an altercation at dinner, the young girl goes into labor and gives birth. Although there are desperate attempts to hide what has happened, the girl's miserly uncle who has charge of her fortune, Sir Moth Interest, discovers the truth and delightedly takes his niece's immorality as an excuse to keep her property. Compass, the focal character of the play, discovers that Placentia's nurse, Mistress Polish, substituted her own daughter, Pleasance, for the heiress when the two were infants, whereupon he marries the false Pleasance, whom he has loved for some time; reveals her true identity to the company; and demands her dowry. The false Placentia is given to Lady Loadstone's steward Needle, the father of her illegitimate child; and Lady Loadstone offers herself to Compass's adopted brother, Captain Ironside, who accepts her hand and her fortune.

The Magnetic Lady presents, with modifications, some familiar humor characters, including a miser, Sir Moth Interest; a foppish and cowardly courtier, Sir Diaphanous Silkworm; and an unscrupulous lawyer, Mr. Practice. Among the play's characters, however, are some types new to Jonson, among them a hedonistic Anglican priest, Parson Palate; a greedy and subornable physician, Doctor Rut; and a devious politician, Mr. Bias. One of the liveliest characters in the play, also new, is Mistress Polish, the loquacious, scheming, and wholly unrepentant "she-Parasite" who advances her child at another's expense. But one of the most interesting aspects of the play is what Jonson does with the witty gallants. Compass, who sports with folly and manipulates fools, and Captain Ironside, who exposes Silkworm's cowardice, are not young. Like Lovewit in The Alchemist, they are experienced men of maturity and achievement; and the whole comedy has an aura of worldly wisdom which tempers exuberance.

The allegorical intent of The Magnetic Lady seems imperfectly realized. Lady Loadstone is shadowy almost to the point of passing unnoticed; and her niece attracts the company to the house, not the lady. In addition, while Jonson's personal device—a broken compass, its circle left incomplete—is no doubt the source of the major character's name, the Compass of the play is at times the needle drawn to a magnet, a very different instrument altogether; and the relationship between his two functions remains unclear. Moreover, Compass and Ironside expose the follies of many of the play's fools, but exposure is not synonymous with reconciliation, and neither the Boy's remark in the induction nor Lady Loadstone's comment near the end of the play—"Well, wee are all now reconcil'd to truth" (V.x.126)—is wholly satisfying as an explanation of the comedy's subtitle. But the plot of The Magnetic Lady is carefully constructed; its induction and intermeans provide a systematic and useful statement of Jonson's comedic intent and practice; and many passages in the play are witty and pointed. This last of Jonson's comedies may lack the spark of his greatest achievements in the genre, but it should not be dismissed out of hand as a dotage.[48]

Jonson's last three comedies are not great, but they are far from negligible. *The Staple of News* is energetic, robust, and witty. *The New Inn* deserves respect for what it attempts. And while *The Magnetic Lady,* the last of Jonson's long line of humor comedies, may not rank with the best of its fellows, it betrays no real decline in Jonson's inventive powers. All three of these plays are urbane and humane. All three are much concerned with drama as a meaningful art form and with educating their audiences to a full appreciation of what they experience in the theater. The career that they complete, while often interrupted and not uniformly successful, never wavered in vision or in aim; and the circle that they close has a just and true shape.

Ben Jonson must be ranked in the very forefront of English comic dramatists. He contributed five plays to the permanent repertory of English comedy, and his other experiments in the *"Comick* thred" (*M. L.*, Ind., l. 102) repay interest as well. More than any other of his contemporaries, he took seriously the writing of comedy and gave to his craft a sense of dignity. He imposed discipline and structure on the disorderly comedy of his age, while preserving its boisterous vitality. He ridiculed the vices and follies of his era, portraying the men and manners of seventeenth-century England in images of grossness, vulgarity, and disease. But he never abandoned an abiding vision of human possibilities and a sophisticated stance which accepted the flaws of human nature even as he derided them. Indeed, the impetus for his scorn was always a social ideal which the reality of his gilt age mocked. Perhaps his greatest achievement was to articulate a comic spirit which could be simultaneously didactic and delightful, serious and earthy, scornful and genial, satiric and celebratory.

CHAPTER 3

The Tragedies

Ben Jonson's two surviving tragedies were conspicuous failures on the Jacobean stage, and while he was defiantly proud of them, they are not likely ever to win general approval.[1] Their failures as popular drama may be attributable to the bleakness of their themes and to their lack of interest in individual psychology and motivation. They are bitter indictments of social disease, and they deliberately avoid exploring individual predicaments. Since they fail to engage much interest in their characters as human beings and since they provide little hope of heroic action, they seem oppressively didactic. Nevertheless, Jonson's tragedies constitute an important aspect of his career as a social poet, and they merit our attention. Jacobean intellectuals hailed *Catiline* as the supreme dramatic achievement of their age, and *Sejanus* is a notable accomplishment.

The relative failure of Jonson's tragedies has sometimes been explained as the result of their alleged neoclassicism. In fact, however, the plays are rooted far more securely in English dramatic tradition than in either classical theory or practice.[2] Indeed, they adhere to the classical unities far less strictly than do most of Jonson's comedies. Their action is clearly influenced by the Machiavellian intrigue of the Elizabethan revenge tragedy, and their occasional mixture of the farcical and the tragic recalls Christopher Marlowe and William Shakespeare more vividly than it does classical models. The didactic spirit and pessimistic vision of the plays owe far more to the influence of George Chapman than to Aristotle. The plays do, however, embody a tragic dignity which might be described as classical, and they incorporate superb classical scholarship.

Sejanus and *Catiline* are based on carefully documented history. Jonson does, of course, alter some historical facts for dramatic purposes, and he interprets for thematic point some events of the past which were unverifiable, as, for example, his indictment of Julius Caesar for complicity in the conspiracy of Catiline. The thoroughness of Jonson's humanistic scholarship in these plays convinces the reader of their "truth of Argument" (*Sej.*, To the Readers, ll. 18–19), their faithfulness as representations of actual events.[3] But Jonson did not recreate the past for its own sake or merely as an academic exercise. For him, as for most Renaissance historians, history was primarily important as a source of lessons valuable to the present.[4] In his tragedies, Jonson depicts ancient Rome in order to cast light on the England of his own and future days. The lessons he derives from the corrupt imperial Rome of *Sejanus* and the beleaguered republican Rome of *Catiline* are lessons of social irresponsibility. The plays recreate the past to warn the present of the dangers of social decay. Their moral urgency stems directly from their faith in the continuing relevance of history.

As recreations of ancient Rome, Jonson's tragedies are brilliant successes. Yet they suffer dramatically, for the inevitability of their action robs their characters of spontaneity. Jonson's bleak view of the periods of Roman history which he depicts allows very little opportunity for heroic action. His deterministic interpretation of history emphasizes broad social currents rather than individuals. Thus the would-be Tamburlaine, Sejanus, is finally understood as merely a consequence of social decadence; and the success of the courageous Cicero is placed within an historical context which renders his victory hollow. The tragedies generally present flatly drawn characters, types rather than individuals, embodiments of vice or virtue rather than believable human beings. Jonson was certainly capable of creating memorably realistic serious characters, as his portrait of Tiberius—a masterpiece of dramatic subtlety—illustrates. But he deliberately chose not to write tragedies which pivot on individual action or inaction. The choice, which doomed the plays on the popular stage, may have been fatally mistaken. But it was a choice consistent with the role Jonson adopted for himself as public poet, as counselor to his age. His tragedies are profoundly political. They are concerned not with the dilemmas of particular politicians but with the intimate connection between the health of a society and the quality of its political life. The plays achieve tragic intensity by the fierceness of their indignation and tragic scope by the breadth of their concern.

Their tragic dignity results largely from their didactic purpose, but it also stems from their weighty diction. The language and tone of Jonson's tragedies are not of a single piece. In *Catiline*, the conspirators speak quite distinctly, and the comic scene between Fulvia and Sempronia features colloquial speech. In *Sejanus*, Tiberius's evasive manner of communication perfectly mirrors his Machiavellian character. But the speeches in both tragedies tend to be tediously long, and too often the characters speak at the same oratorical pitch. Although it is too unvaried to be dramatically satisfying, the diction of the tragic characters is poetically pleasing: a grave, deliberative, carefully balanced language. Often there is a disparity between the bombastic content of a speech and the solid blank verse in which it is delivered. For instance, when Sejanus exultantly recapitulates his evil and dares his destiny shortly before his fall, there is a marvelous tension between the horrors he rehearses and the dignified language he uses:

> Fortune, I see thy worst: Let doubtfull states,
> And things uncertaine hang upon thy will:
> . . . . .
> I, that did helpe
> To fell the loftie Cedar of the world,
> GERMANICUS; that, at one stroke, cut downe
> DRUSUS, that upright Elme; wither'd his vine;
> Laid SILIUS, and SABINUS, two strong Okes,
> Flat on the earth; besides, those other shrubs,
> CORDUS, and SOSIA, CLAUDIA PULCHRA,
> FURNIUS, and GALLUS, which I have grub'd up;
> And since, have set my axe so strong, and deepe
> Into the roote of speading AGGRIPPINE;
> Lopt off, and scatter'd her proud branches, NERO,
> DRUSUS, and CAIUS too, although re-planted;
> If you will, destinies, that, after all,
> I faint, now, ere I touch my period;
> You are but cruell. . . . (Sej., V.236–37, 241–55)

The poetry here, as throughout the tragedies, rescues the play from the melodrama implicit in the events recounted. The clarity, balance, and solidity of the expression counter the excesses which the plays depict, and so give the tragedies an air of classical dignity.

I   Sejanus (1603)

Sejanus His Fall was premiered by the King's Men in 1603, with Burbage, Shakespeare, Heminges, and Condell in the cast. The acted version included scenes written by a collaborator, probably Chapman; but when the play was issued in quarto two years later, Jonson substituted passages of his own for those written by the "second Pen" (To the Readers, l. 45). *Sejanus* aims for and achieves "truth of Argument, dignity of Persons, gravity and height of Elocution, fulnesse and frequencie of Sentence" (To the Readers, ll. 19–20). Its picture of a corrupt age, with values so distorted that an emperor and his favorite cynically practice evil while an indecisive and fawning senate acquiesces, is chillingly grim. Yet the play offers only superficial motives for the actions of its vicious characters, it depicts their natures unrelieved by any elements of nobility, and it makes no positive suggestions as to desirable conduct in so debased an era.

In constructing *Sejanus*, Jonson relied most heavily on Tacitus's *Annals*, but he also incorporated materials from Dion Cassius's *Roman History*, Suetonius's anecdotal "Life of Tiberius," Seneca's "On Tranquility," and Juvenal's tenth satire. The action is set in Rome and covers approximately eight years. Sejanus, a Roman of obscure background, manipulates himself into the favor of the emperor Tiberius. By being both an encourager of the ruler's licentious nature and a tool through which Tiberius can, without soiling his own hands, carry out vicious acts against those who threaten him or oppose his desires, Sejanus rises to a position which "wanted nothing, but the name, to make him a copartner of the Empire" (The Argument, ll. 5–6). He seduces Livia, the wife of Tiberius's son Drusus, and with her aid poisons the prince. That hindrance removed, he feeds Tiberius's fears that the virtuous widow and popular children of the noble Germanicus are a threat to the imperial throne. Tiberius gives his favorite permission to destroy them and their followers, but Sejanus, thinking the emperor a manipulable fool, betrays the extent of his personal ambition by asking for permission to marry Livia. A sly man who only pretends to indecision and dotage, Tiberius determines to check his favorite. In secret, the emperor solicits another ambitious man, Macro, to spy on Sejanus. At the suggestion of the unsuspecting favorite, Tiberius retires to a life of luxury and lust on Capri. But from his retreat, the emperor sends letters to important Romans which alternate between praise and condemnation of Sejanus and create confusion among the sycophants. When the time is right, Tiberius calls an extraordinary session of the senate, ostensibly to honor Sejanus; but the imperial letter which is read to the senators after much vacillation ultimately blames the powerful favorite for excesses and hints that he may be guilty of treason. Macro, who has gained control of the Praetorian guard, arrives to accuse Sejanus in person and is acclaimed savior of

Rome by the foolish senators. The senate, without according him a
trial, sentences Sejanus to death; the mob that witnesses his execution tears his body to shreds; and Macro delivers the dead traitor's
innocent young children to rape and strangulation.

The play revolves around two characters, Sejanus and Tiberius; as
the drama progresses, emphasis gradually moves from the former to
the latter. Despite his importance as the title character, however,
Sejanus is sketchily drawn. He is a proud and ambitious man, but
apparently seeks power only to commit "A race of wicked acts" which
will be a wonder to the world (II.151). The face which Tiberius
presents to him, that of indecisive servility, causes him to despise the
emperor and to underestimate him. As honor piles upon honor, until
Sejanus is worshiped as a god in the temples of Rome alongside
Tiberius, the favorite's pride outdistances his wit even further, and
he rashly comes to believe that he has completely mastered fortune.
As is the case with many of Jonson's comic characters, Sejanus is
actually manipulated and brought low not by the *de casibus* turn of
fortune's wheel, but by his own self-delusion and by the wit of a
greater Machiavellian than himself.

The true master of fortune is Tiberius. The emperor is personally
corrupt and, like Sejanus, evinces no concern at all for the commonwealth. But he has the wit and the deviousness to survive. In private
sessions with his advisor, he pretends to be indecisive and oblivious
to political reality, but he, rather than Sejanus, actually manipulates
the events of the play. Tiberius carefully transfers the odium of
unjustly persecuting his greatest rivals—the family of Germanicus
and their supporters—onto his favorite. On public occasions, he
allows Sejanus to reveal himself as a vicious zealot, while he strives to
seem magnanimous and merciful. He recognizes that Sejanus's own
ambition soars as high as the throne itself, and he carefully plots the
downfall of the favorite even as he uses him. Tiberius also knows how
to manipulate the senate for his own purposes. Realizing that its
members fear his spies and want only to be left to their lives of ease,
he confuses them with contradictory letters until they are ready to
accede to anything. Tiberius is totally unprincipled, but he prevails
by dint of his own cunning statecraft.

The foils to these selfish schemers are the aristocratic partisans of
the Germanicus family, notable among them Silius, Cordus, Sabinus,
and Arruntius. All upright men, they bemoan the age they live in,
complaining that the commonwealth has been degraded and
enslaved by "one mans lusts" (I.63), that the senate has abdicated its

responsibility to the people, and that civic morality is a thing of the past, an "old vertue" which died with Germanicus (I.119). Their disgust is well founded, yet their inability to counter the evil around them is itself a source of the disease which corrupts their society. They congratulate themselves that they are morally superior to Tiberius and Sejanus, but they retreat into detached self-examination and accomplish nothing constructive. Arruntius's public complaints against the emperor and his favorite are so ineffectual that Sejanus recommends that he be permitted freedom of speech in order to lull other malcontents into a false sense of security. Silius's dramatic suicide in the senate is equally futile, a mere gesture which removes him from an unpleasant situation and furthers Sejanus's ends. That the Germanicans are aristocrats only underlines their failure of responsibility. The conditions of which they so frequently and justly complain are the result of their abdication of leadership, of their refusal to oppose actively the evil that they recognize around them. Marvin L. Vawter comments pointedly, "As always in Jonson's plays, the health and strength of a society is, or should be, most clearly reflected in its nobility. When the nobility ceases to be actively virtuous, when the 'seedes of the old vertue' no longer bear fruit, the entire garden decays and becomes overgrown with the weeds of evil."[5]

The world of Sejanus is the amoral world of political terror. One outrage succeeds another. Individuals are murdered with impunity; political dissidents are peremptorily convicted of crimes against the state; history is ordered rewritten and books burned; surveillance is constant, and freedom only a memory. Hypocrisy, ambition, and brute force pervade all aspects of human life. Jonson depicts this degenerate police state with remarkable clarity, and he offers no consolation that the excesses of Sejanus are merely temporary aberrations. The fall of Sejanus, the play's central event, changes nothing except the cast of characters; one villain is replaced by another. "The wittily, and strangely-cruel MACRO" (V.851) is as frightening a product of imperial Rome's civic disease as Sejanus himself. His triumph is anything but comforting.

Sejanus is a bitter satire which achieves tragic scope by the relentless singlemindedness of its vision. The tragedy it depicts is that of an entire society. It has no heroes and it offers no hope for happy endings. Even the traditional private consolations of "plaine, and passive fortitude" (IV.294) ring hollow in *Sejanus*, for they are indicted as failures of leadership. A grim warning to Jonson's own and future ages, the tragedy depicts the moral and political bestiality of individuals like Tiberius, Sejanus, and Macro as reflections of a debased age and as inevitable consequences of social degeneration. Its lack of interest in individual motivation and its severity may limit its popular appeal, yet its determined and sophisticated exposure of corruption gives *Sejanus* continuing interest. As J. W. Lever remarks, "Without stage horrors or sensational effects, Jonson's play depicts with timeless relevance a society in the grip of state terror."[6] By locating the sources of that terror in the degenerate values of the society itself, Jonson translates what might have been the stuff of historical melodrama into an incisive statement of social tragedy.

II   Catiline *(1611)*

Catiline His Conspiracy was presented by the King's Men in 1611 and published in quarto the same year. Like its predecessor *Sejanus*, and for many of the same reasons, the play was unsuccessful on the stage. Although Jonson severely criticized the audience for liking the first two acts, the "worst" part of the play (To the Reader in Ordinarie, l. 7), and for disliking Cicero's long oration in the fourth, it is difficult not to sympathize with the audience's judgment. The first two acts, despite their faults of Senecan melodrama and boudoir farce, contain interesting actions and move at a satisfying pace. Much of the fourth act is static, almost 300 of its 842 lines devoted to a single speech that is seldom, and then only briefly, interrupted. In some respects more "classical" than *Sejanus*—it employs a chorus and the action is reduced to a shorter span—*Catiline* is less unified in tone and singleminded in purpose than the earlier tragedy. Nonetheless, it is an interesting reenactment of an episode in Roman history which would have been very well known to its original audience. Jonson's interpretation of that event places the familiar incident in an unexpected light.

The principal sources of *Catiline* are Sallust's *Bellum Catilinae* and Cicero's *In Catilinum,* with materials added from other Ciceronian orations, Dion Cassius's *Roman History,* Plutarch, and the Renaissance jurist-historian Constanzo Felice. Jonson compresses the events of several months into three days and sets the play in Rome with two brief scenes in the country near Fesulae. Inspired by the ghost of Sulla, the impoverished patrician Catiline determines to overthrow the Roman republic and draws into his conspiracy several malcontents, notable among them the outcast senators Curius and

Lentullus and the rash and cruel Cethegus. The first step in Catiline's plan is to be elected to one of the two consulships. Although he is supported by such powerful people as Julius Caesar, Catiline is not chosen: the people elect the nonentity Antonius and the "new man" Cicero, the latter favored by the wise Cato. Catiline furiously determines to subject the city to a bloodbath, beginning with the murder of Cicero; and Caesar advises him in his plans, but does not actually join the conspiracy. Fulvia, a dissolute young woman, gets details of the conspiracy from the braggart Curius. Jealous of one of Catiline's partisans, the learned and proud older woman Sempronia, she reveals the plan to Cicero. The new consul protects himself from assassination by surrounding himself with friends and impartial observers, and the next morning he delivers an oration against Catiline in the senate. Catiline threatens revenge on both Cicero and the senate and rushes to join his army at Fesulae. Cato warns Cicero of Caesar's secret support of Catiline, but the consul decides against an open break with the powerful man. Instead, he sets about gathering incriminating evidence against Catiline. When this is presented to them, the senators, against the advice of Caesar, condemn Catiline and his known cohorts to death. After the execution of some of the conspirators, a leader of the Roman army arrives from the field to report Catiline's defeat and death; and Cicero, honored by the senate, gives thanks to the gods for the rescue of Rome.

As he had done with Sejanus, Jonson simplifies the character of Catiline. The conspirator is given two motives for his attempted overthrow of the state. One is the need to achieve power to protect himself from prosecution for his past crimes—incest, murder, rape, parricide, and a previous, unsuccessful conspiracy against the senate. His other motive, and the one on which he most dwells, is a conviction that Rome has used him badly, turning him down when he "stood *Candidate*, / To be commander in the *Pontick* warre" (I.89–90). His defeat in the race for the consulship feeds this grievance and makes him more determined than ever to avenge the slights. Catiline is a good manipulator of men less intelligent than himself. He urges his fellow conspirators to desperate action by asserting strongly what they want to believe, that the "giants of the state" have enslaved them (I.348). And like demagogues in all ages, he cloaks selfishness in a glorious ideal: "We doe redeeme our selves to libertie, / And break the yron yoke, forg'd for our necks" (I.344–45). Catiline carefully masks the disappointment that he feels over his defeat for the consulship; but when provoked, he acts rashly. Disregarding Caesar's advice to "Be resolute" (III.491), he does not calmly deny Cicero's charges against him in the senate, which are for the most part unprovable at that point. Instead, he flares out at the impertinence of the upstart Cicero and betrays himself publicly, allowing the state sufficient time to arm itself against his plot.

Cicero is much more subtly drawn. Proud and altogether too self-satisfied, he is nevertheless an unselfish patriot. He even gives the rich province of Macedonia, conferred on him by the senate, to his fellow consul Antonius to make the latter "that which he is not borne, / A friend unto the publique" (III.475–76). Always conscious of the fact that he is a "new man" (III.19) and that most of Rome's aristocrats scorn him, he moves carefully through the maze of political intrigue. While he shares the ideals and the perception of Cato, he is more realistic than the great, but short-sighted "conscience of Rome." He knows that his allegations against Catiline will not be persuasive without unimpeachable evidence, and he gets proof any way that he can, even stooping to meanness of conduct. He flatters Fulvia and Curius, the one "a base / And common strumpet" (III.450–51), the other a selfish turncoat. Like Cato, Cicero is certain that Caesar is somehow involved with the conspiracy. Unlike Cato, however, he realizes that Caesar, a much more powerful and intelligent man than Catiline, has hidden his involvement well and is virtually impervious to attack, and he refuses to press the point. "If there were proofe 'gainst CAESAR," he declares, "or who ever, / To speake him guiltie, I would so declare him" (V.89–90). The allegations of Vectius and Curius, without strong documentary substantiation, are not enough to convict Caesar, and Cicero contents himself with watching him closely.

Jonson's portrayal of Caesar conveys much of the tragedy's social theme. Caesar was an ambiguous figure to the Renaissance: on the one hand, he was sometimes depicted as among the most heroic figures of the ancient world; on the other hand, he was frequently attacked as an ambitious and unscrupulous politician. Jonson abandons his primary source, Sallust, and goes beyond a secondary source, Plutarch, to make Caesar unquestionably a partisan of Catiline.[7] He pictures him as an unprincipled man totally committed to Machiavellian intrigue. Caesar makes pious and patriotic comments in the senate, while at the same time he advises Catiline in the overthrow of the republic. The play suggests that the more complex and subtler Caesar uses the simpler Catiline as a stalking horse to test the possibility of seizing control of the commonwealth himself.[8] What is most tragic in *Catiline* is what is to occur beyond the time of the play. The drama ends with thanksgiving to the gods that Rome has been preserved from Catiline's bloody designs, but Jonson's original audience would have known that Caesar, in little more than a dozen years, will put an end to the effectiveness of the republican institutions of Rome.

The most important aspect of *Catiline* is its interpretation of the historical event that it chronicles. Jonson chooses a less bleak period for this tragedy than he did for *Sejanus*. Republican Rome is at the height of her powers, and her institutions—the consuls and the senate—are still capable of effective action. But her worldly success has in it the seeds of the subsequent depravity which *Sejanus* depicts. As the Chorus complains, Rome "doth joy / So much in plentie, wealth, and ease, / As, now, th'excesse is her disease" (I.548–50). She is beginning to fall prey to avarice and riot, her offices and laws can be bought and sold, and her senators can be bribed:

> Such ruine of her manners *Rome*
> Doth suffer now, as shee's become
>
> . . . . .
> Both her owne spoiler, and owne prey. (I.583–84, 586)

It is still possible for a good man to effect good public ends, and Cicero does; but the price he must pay is discouraging and his success is limited. Catiline is destroyed, but a far more intelligent and subtle threat to the state must be left untouched because he is "mightie" (IV.531). Although the degeneracy it exposes is not as advanced as it is in *Sejanus*, *Catiline* is equally a tragedy of social decay. Inasmuch as the events Jonson depicts in *Catiline* parallel some aspects of the infamous Gunpowder Plot of 1605, in which a small band of Roman Catholics planned to blow up parliament and the King, the play may have had particular topical significance as a warning to its original audience.[9]

Jonson's two tragedies are not great plays, but they merit respect as profoundly serious experiments. It may be that Jonson's satiric cast of mind prevented his depiction of heroic action or that his dramatic genius was comic rather than tragic. But such easy explanations of the relative failures of the tragedies beg the essential question of Jonson's actual achievement in them. As accurate reenactments of ancient eras and as chilling reminders of the consequences of social decay, the plays are of enduring value. *Sejanus*, particularly, is among the finest social tragedies of the age. The two plays are also important as evidence of Jonson's lifelong commitment to public poetry, a vocation he fulfilled less obviously in the comedies and most successfully in the masques and the nondramatic poetry. The failure of his tragedies on the stage puzzled and frustrated Jonson, but in the "apologeticall Dialogue" appended to *Poetaster* (To the Reader, l. 3), which announced his intention to pursue the tragic muse, he expressed his characteristic scorn for the popular audience. He hoped only to "prove the pleasure but of one, / So he judicious be; He shall b'alone / A Theatre unto me" To the Reader, ll. 226–28). Appreciation of Jonson's tragedies will always be confined to a judicious minority. As he prophesied they would, these plays remain "high, and aloofe, / Safe from the wolves black jaw, and the dull asses hoofe" (To the Reader, ll. 238–39).

CHAPTER 4

The Masques

BEN Jonson probably earned more money and received more advantageous contemporary recognition from his masques and other courtly entertainments than from even his most successful plays. His career as court poet is a long one, beginning at least as early as 1603, when he wrote The Entertainment at Althorp to welcome the new royal family to England. It embraces the glittering Christmas-season celebrations he and such collaborators as the architect and scene designer Inigo Jones, the composer Alphonso Ferrabosco, and the choreographer Thomas Giles prepared for the court of King James; and it concludes with masques and entertainments written for King Charles near the end of Jonson's life. The access to court which this employment afforded him is particularly important, for it may have helped to foster Jonson's entire conception of himself as a public poet and it provided him opportunity to study at close hand the ruling class whom he undertook to counsel in his poetry. But the masques, although they are difficult for a modern reader to comprehend and to appreciate fully, are important in and of themselves. They "eyther have bene, or ought to be the mirrors of mans life" (*L. T.*, ll. 3–4), Jonson declared, metaphorically crystallizing their ability to reflect profound truth about human activity.

I The Masques and the Court

Developing from several native and foreign traditions of mummers' pageants, triumphs, and dances, the masque combines music, choreography, spectacle, and poetry into a theatrical presentation which largely excludes the conflict and tension of the popular drama. Lavishly produced and featuring illusionistic stage settings animated by spectacular machinery, the masque celebrates the seventeenth-century court hierarchy, ritualizing social and political realities into

an idealistic vision of harmony and order. Essential to its very
conception is the royal presence and the court setting. The king is
always the center of the masque, seated strategically and addressed
directly or indirectly. Professional actors and singers perform the
speaking parts, but the masquers are noble ladies and gentlemen
whose very presence provides the impetus for the idealized fictions of
the usually slight plot. The masque culminates in a dance in which the
courtly spectators join the masquers in a self-congratulatory celebration of aristocratic community.[1]

It is easy to dismiss masques as ephemeral and expensive
entertainments, occasional, extravagant, and wasteful spectacles
characterized by unrealistic and shameful flattery. Indeed, they were
often attacked on precisely these grounds in the seventeenth century. But the masques in general, and Jonson's in particular, were
more serious than such easy dismissals allow. Jonson considered
them important enough to publish his texts, even though he knew
that the bare text of a masque might seem hardly more than a scenario
which needs to be fleshed out by scenic invention, musical accompaniment, and choreographic art. He believed the poet's vision to be the
soul of the masque, capable of existing independently of the immediate circumstances of production. By publishing the texts, often
accompanied by detailed descriptions of his collaborators' contributions, he sought to counter the ephemerality of performance, to
"borrow a life of posteritie" for them (*M. Bl.*, l. 5).

In the introduction of *Hymenaei*, Jonson proclaims the essential
seriousness of his intention and justifies publication: "This it is hath
made the most royall *Princes*, and greatest *persons* (who are commonly the *personaters* of these *actions*) not onely studious of riches,
and magnificence in the outward celebration, or shew; (which rightly
becomes them) but curious after the most high, and heartie *inventions*, to furnish the inward parts: (and those grounded upon *antiquitie*, and solide *learnings*) which, though their *voyce* be taught to
sound to present occasions, their *sense*, or doth, or should alwayes lay
hold on more remov'd *mysteries*" (ll. 10–19). The "more remov'd
mysteries" of the poet's vision enable the masque to survive the
occasional nature of production, just as the soul of man survives the
death of his body. Jonson's conception of poetic meaning as more
important than the choreographic, musical, and scenic elements led
to a bitter and protracted controversy with Inigo Jones.[2]

The enormous expense devoted by the Jacobean and Caroline
courts to the production of masques can best be understood as

displays of liberality and magnanimity. Renaissance ideals, and *Realpolitik* theory as well, held that princes should give the appearance of magnificence. These ideals, and this theory, were especially congenial to the Stuart monarchs and their evolving pursuit of the divine right of kingship. The sumptuous show, the outward form of the masque, Jonson remarks, "rightly becomes" princes and other great persons. In addition, the productions justify their staggering cost by elevating the court, if only for a moment, beyond the petty concerns of transient politics, by reminding the king and his courtiers of the duties and opportunities resulting from their positions, and by providing them a glimpse of individual and civic possibilities.

Modern readers are apt to recoil from praise which appears to be fulsome, as, for example, the hymn to Pan in *Pan's Anniversary*, where Jonson describes King James as "our All, by him we breath, wee live,/Wee move, we are" (ll. 191–92). But the praise in these works is not mere flattery; rather, it is a function of the masque's intrinsic didacticism. Jonson held that masques and entertainments "ought alwayes to carry a mixture of profit, with them, no lesse then delight" (*L. T.*, ll. 6–7). This profit is often conveyed by means of *laudando praecipere*, a kind of praise Sir Francis Bacon describes as "a Forme due in Civilitie to Kings, and Great Persons . . . When by telling Men, what they are, they represent to them, what they should be."[3] Jonson acknowledges this principle in "An Epistle to Master *John Selden*" (*U.* 14), where he admits that he has sometimes praised undeserving individuals, but adds " 'twas with purpose to have made them such" (l. 22). The praise in the masques, as in the poems, is fundamentally a kind of counsel. As Stephen Orgel observes, the masque "is the opposite of satire; it educates by praising, by creating heroic roles for the leaders of society to fill."[4]

Jonson's intention, then, is not simply to flatter the king and his court, but to create in his "most high, and heartie *inventions*" an ideal society, founded on ancient principles and nurtured by a wise, divinely anointed monarch. Jonson was a notably independent individual who respected achievement and virtue more than title or position. He knew that the monarchs and courtiers who participated in his masques were not in reality gods and superhuman heroes and that seventeenth-century England did not in fact represent the restoration of a Golden Age. He wrote many satiric epigrams attacking courtiers and in "To Sir Robert Wroth" (*F.* 3) he specifically indicts masquing, "the short braverie of the night" (l. 10), for its wasteful expense and vanity. But the exalted depiction of king and court in the masques is intrinsic to the ceremonial form. In his masques, Jonson ritualizes experience and transforms the literal and mundane into the symbolic and eternal. If the realities of life at court seem far removed from the ideals of order and harmony, love and virtue which the masques celebrate, the transcendent vision which could perceive an English Golden Age among rather sordid circumstances is not on that count ignoble or dishonest. The gap between the realities of court life and the ideals of the masque may be directly proportional to the need for such ideals. "To the extent that the actuality falls short of the ideal," Jonas Barish remarks, "the masque may be taken as a kind of mimetic magic on a sophisticated level, the attempt to secure social health and tranquility for the realm by miming it in front of its chief figure."[5]

As a form of mimetic magic, the masque is a highly complex ritual. It is essentially nondramatic, for its ceremonial mode allows no room for tension or conflict or character development. It is assertive and dogmatic rather than argumentative or tentative, and its characters are symbolic rather than realistic. Drama is possible only within the *antimasque* which Jonson developed as a "foyle, or false-*Masque*" (*M. Q.*, 1, 13) and incorporated as an important structural feature of his masques from *The Masque of Queens* onward. Performed by professional actors, the antimasque is a grotesque world of vice or comic disorder which is subdued or displaced by the courtly masque. The tension between the two is purely artificial for there is never any question that the harmonious masque will supersede its unruly foil. Nevertheless, the juxtaposition of masque and antimasque is an essential structural development since it makes possible an important basis of contrast and provides needed lightness and variety.

Much of the complexity of the masque form stems from its need simultaneously to represent and to transcend the realities of the court. The masques frequently allude to political controversies and occasionally offer rather daring though indirect advice concerning specific political issues.[6] Moreover, the masquers themselves add topical significance to a production by their very presence. As well as participating as symbolic characters in the "more remov'd *mysteries*" of the poet's invention, the courtiers remain themselves. Indeed, they are selected to be masquers precisely because of who they are and the positions they command in the court hierarchy.

Yet if the topical realities of the court can never be totally obliterated in a masque production, the masque itself is never merely topical. Its whole purpose is to elevate the temporal realities of power and politics by subsuming mundane concerns into allegorical representations of absolute and eternal harmony. This process of elevation is the most interesting challenge confronting the masque writer. Jonson accomplishes it by grounding his poetic fictions upon *"antiquitie*, and solide learnings" (*Hym.*, l. 16). He links his fanciful actions to classical and native mythology and to Renaissance philosophical and iconographical traditions.[7] By making his lavish and occasional entertainments the mirrors of enduring ideals, Jonson invests the superficial glitter of the Jacobean and Caroline courts with transcendental meaning and creates a ceremonial and humanistic literature of continuing relevance.

II *The Early Masques:* The Masque of Queens *(1609)*

Jonson probably came to the attention of the court as a result of the entertainments he provided early in the reign of King James: the welcome at Althorp in June 1603; the King's coronation in March 1604; and the royal visit to Sir William Cornwallis's home at Highgate in May 1604. These slight entertainments combine classical and native lore, dignified and weighty counsel, and arcane and learned symbolism. His first masque was commissioned by Queen Anne for performance on Twelfth Night 1605. "It was her Majesties will," Jonson writes in the introduction to *The Masque of Blackness*, "to have [the masquers] *Black-mores* at first" (ll. 21–22). From this royal direction, Jonson derived a graceful fable adapted from the legend of Phoebus and Phaeton. *The Masque of Blackness* was notably successful at court and led to other commissions, including a companion piece, *The Masque of Beauty*, which was not performed until January 1608. The wedding masque *Hymenaei*, produced on Twelfth Night 1606, added to the grace of its predecessor more severe learning and more recondite symbolism. Jonson's masque for Lord Haddington's wedding, sometimes given the title *The Hue and Cry after Cupid*, performed in February 1608, contains an antic dance of boys. This embryonic form of the antimasque adds a gently comic spirit to the solemnity of the whole. But the Jonsonian masque did not reach full maturity until the performance of *The Masque of Queens* in February 1609.

The Masque of Queens is the earliest truly ensemble production in which the disparate elements of scenic and costume design, stage machinery, music, choreography, and poetry all are functional parts of a unified whole; and it contains the first fully developed antimasque.

Jonson accompanies his text with copious annotations and detailed descriptions of the performance. The annotations, requested by King James, give a sense of the form's seriousness and provide evidence of the poet's learning. In describing the performance, Jonson announces that "it was my first, and speciall reguard, to see that the Nobilyty of the Invention should be answerable to the dignity of theyr persons. For which reason, I chose the Argument, to be, *A Celebration of honorable, & true Fame, bred out of Vertue:* observing that rule of the best *Artist,* to suffer no object of delight to passe without his mixture of profit, & example" (ll. 3–9). The masque, then, combines Horatian didacticism with careful observation of social decorum. Its earnest moral is simple and easily comprehensible, but especially appropriate for the court, which needs to be particularly sensitive to the relationship of fame and virtue; and it is buttressed by enormous literary and iconographical learning.

Jonson attributes the development of the antimasque to Queen Anne's suggestion. "And because her Majestie (best knowing, that a principall part of life in these *Spectacles* lay in theyr variety) had commaunded mee to think on some *Daunce,* or shew, that might praecede hers, and have the place of a foyle, or false-*Masque"* (ll. 10–13). In response, the poet devised a grotesque company of twelve witches, "sustayning the persons of *Ignorance, Suspicion, Credulity,* &c. the opposites to good *Fame"* (ll. 17–19). This antimasque is a "spectacle of strangenesse, producing multiplicity of Gesture, and not unaptly sorting with the current, and whole fall of the Devise" (ll. 20–22). The antimasque adds variety to the production, but it also plays an important thematic function, serving as a foil which sets off the main masque.

The production begins with the courtly spectators in their assigned places, awaiting the spectacle prepared by Inigo Jones and the allegorical fiction devised by Jonson. "First, then, his Majestie being set, and the whole Company in full expectation, that which presented it selfe was an ougly *Hell.* . . . These Witches, with a kind of hollow and infernall musique, came forth from thence" (ll. 23–30). Jonson describes the scene and costumes in great detail, justifying the most minute representations by reference to classical and iconographical lore.[8] He gives full credit to his collaborators, but he subordinates all the individual elements of design, stage machinery, costuming, and choreography to the unifying moral vision of the poet's fiction.

In the antimasque, that moral vision is presented by means of antithesis. The eleven hags and their Dame are defined solely in terms of their impossible mission: "And come We, fraught with spight, / To overthrow the glory of this night" (ll. 111–12). They are "faythfull Opposites / To *Fame*, & *Glory*" (ll. 132–33). By antithesis, their chaotic evil defines the harmonious virtue to be represented in the main masque and assumed to be present in the courtly audience presided over by King James. The hags hate "to see these fruicts of a soft peace, / And curse the piety gives it such increase" (ll. 144–45), thus indirectly but unmistakably alluding to the pacific king. The spells and incantations of the witches culminate in a frenzied but futile moment of parodic revelry, characterized by dissonant sound and boisterous movement: "with a strange and sodayne Musique, they fell into a *magicall Daunce*, full of praeposterous change, and gesticulation" (ll. 344–46).

In the midst of the grotesque dance, however, the antimasque is suddenly ended, subdued by the appearance of the real masquers: "on the sodayne, was heard a sound of loud Musique, as if many Instruments had given one blast" (ll. 354–56). The hags and their hell vanish; the attempt to forestall the appearance of virtue has failed. The scene alters to reveal "a glorious and magnificent Building, figuring the *House of Fame*, in the upper part of which were discovered the twelve *Masquers* sitting upon a Throne triumphall, erected in forme of a *Pyramide*, and circled with all store of light" (ll. 359–63).

The conception of a House of Fame Jonson owes to Chaucer, but it is Inigo Jones's genuis which effects the triumphant transformation scene. Jones's building was adorned with statues, visually announcing a crucial relationship between poetry and fame. On the lower tier are "the most excellent *Poets*, as *Homer*, *Virgil*, *Lucan*, &c. as beeing the substantiall supporters of *Fame*" (ll. 684–86); on the upper are "*Achilles*, *Aeneas*, *Caesar*, and those great *Heroes*, which those *Poets* had celebrated" (ll. 686–88). The design thus functions to further the humanist vision which finds inextricable links between poetry and heroism and between fame and virtue.

Heroique Virtue comes forth to explain the transformation which has taken place: "at FAMES loud Sound, and VERTUES sight / All poore, and envious Witchcraft fly the light" (ll. 367–68). He reveals that he is the father of Fame and her strength. He points to his daughter's house and describes it as "Built all of sounding brasse, whose Columnes bee / Men-making *Poets*" (ll. 385–86), emphasizing poetry's immortalizing power. He introduces the mythological and quasi-historical queens, culminating with Bel-anna, Queen of the

Ocean, who "alone, / Possess all vertues" (ll. 416–17) and who was represented by Queen Anne herself. Heroique Virtue addresses King James directly, complimenting him and explaining the benefits of fame based on virtue, as exemplified in the masquers. Fame herself comes forward to the accompaniment of music and directs the procession of Queens. The masquers descend from their pyramidal throne and mount chariots which are drawn across the stage by appropriate "Birds, & Beasts" (l. 465) and by the vanquished hags of the antimasque.

The performance concludes with lovely, self-consciously formal songs and graceful dances which starkly contrast with the ugly incantations and unnatural contortions of the antimasque. One of the dances in the main masque is "*graphically* dispos'd into *letters,* and honoring the Name of the most sweete, and ingenious *Prince, Charles, Duke of Yorke*" (ll. 750–52). Choreographed by Thomas Giles, this dance was so graceful that "if *Mathematicians* had lost *proportion,* they might there have found it" (ll. 754–56). The final song specifically denies any necessary connection between the queens' military glory and their fame:

> Force Greatnesse, all the glorious wayes
> You can, it soon decayes;
> But so *good Fame* shall, never:
> Her triumphs, as theyr Causes, are for ever. (ll. 770–73)[9]

Jonson offers as epilogue a simple list of the masquers, revealingly indicating the intimate relationship between the poet's fiction and the court's reality.

III   *The Later Masques*

The Masque of Queens marks a pivotal point in the development of the Jonsonian masque, but it does not mark a final point. In the years following 1609, the masque developed further. It remained preoccupied with broad ethical issues and it continued to envision almost limitless social possibilities, reminding the courtly audience of responsibilities as well as blessings. In the later masques, Jonson returns again and again to the myth of the Golden Age, evoking classical and mythological glories with affecting nostalgia and fervid optimism in such works as *The Golden Age Restored* (1616) and *Time Vindicated* (1623). He continues to concern himself with the questions which dominate the early works, exploring issues of love and beauty, virtue and reason in masques like *Love Restored* (1612) and *Lovers Made Men* (1617) and informing his explorations with the same kind of erudition and philosophical seriousness which mark *The Masque of Queens*. But in the later years, the masque becomes a more subtle and more complex species of poetry.

Although the famous quarrel between Jonson and Jones reflected their profound disagreement about the relative importance of the verbal and non-verbal elements of the masque, Jones's eventual triumph did not lead, as some have supposed, to an increasing emphasis on spectacle.[10] Indeed, the movement is in the other direction. Jonson's settings become less spectacular in the years following *The Masque of Queens*, including those settings designed by Inigo Jones. They come to have less of an independent existence and to function more effectively as media for dramatic and poetic action, merging the stage's illusion with the court's reality. The very absence in the later masques of the kind of detailed descriptions of the performance, the scene designs, and the stage machinery which are so prominent in *The Masque of Queens* indicates the form's developing literary integrity and its capacity to sustain an imaginative existence separate from the circumstances of production. Although not true of *Love's Triumph through Callipolis* and *Chloridia* (both 1631), the later masques generally rely more on poetry to effect their various transformations than on spectacular stage machinery.

In the later works, the antimasque develops into a more supple device. It continues to provide variety and contrast, but tends to rely less on simple antithesis. The worlds of antimasque and masque become less rigidly separated, and the antimasque is sometimes subsumed positively into the world of the revels, as in *Oberon* (1611) where the satyrs of the antimasque are converted to the service of Prince Henry.[11] Most significantly, the antimasque comes more often to represent comic disorder rather than abstract vice, as in *Mercury Vindicated* (1615), *The Gypsies Metamorphosed* (1621), and *Neptune's Triumph* (1623). It grows more worldly and its values become less obviously evil. Indeed, the antimasque and main masque, rather than contrasting absolute representations of vice and virtue, occasionally contrast a lesser good with a higher one.

Poetry and song more completely dominate the main masques of the later works than they do in *The Masque of Queens*. *Lovers Made Men* has some claim to be considered the earliest English opera, since the entire masque was sung in recitative "after the Italian manner" (ll.

26–27); and *The Golden Age Restored* is a sequence of lyric poems, its resolution accomplished by the invocation of English poets, Geoffrey Chaucer, John Gower, John Lydgate, and Edmund Spenser. Jonson uses the songs of the later masques to effect scenes of transformation, as in *Neptune's Triumph,* where the presentation of the masquers is accomplished by means of music and song as well as by elaborate machinery.[12] Apollo and a Grand Chorus sing as the scene is transformed from an almost bare stage, which served as the backdrop for the antimasque, into the island of Delos: "some *Muses,* & the Goddesse *Harmony,* make the musique, the while the Iland moves forward, *Proteus* sitting below, and APOLLO sings" (ll. 334–39). This integration of song and music with action marks a considerable advance in fusing the disparate elements of the masque. Similarly, songs rather than prose or spoken poetry come regularly to persuade the dancers to dance and to interpret the significance of the dances. In *Pleasure Reconciled to Virtue* (1618), for example, Daedalus invites the masquers to dance in a lovely song which both instructs the dancers and explains the thematic relevance of the dance:

> Come on, come on; and where you goe,
>   so enter-weave the curious knot,
> as ev'n th'observer scarce may know
>   which lines are Pleasures, and which not.
>
>   .   .   .
>
> Then, as all actions of mankind
>   are but a Laborinth, or maze,
>   so let your Daunces be entwin'd,
>   yet not perplex men, unto gaze.
> But measur'd, and so numerous too,
>   as men may read each act you doo.
> And when they see the Graces meet,
>   admire the wisdom of your feet. (ll. 253–56, 261–68)

This song, with its emphasis on the hieroglyphic nature of dance, is more than ornamental: it gracefully explicates the masque's theme of the reconciliation of pleasure and virtue, and it helpfully interprets the significance of dance in realizing that theme.

The songs admirably crystallize the ideas more fully developed in the blank verse and the non-verbal elements in which they are embedded. Simple, brief, elegant, and characterized by brilliant stanzaic variations, they reveal numerous aspects of Jonson's talent. A song like "The faery beame uppon you," from *The Gypsies*

Metamorphosed, demonstrates his gift of delicate grace; while the Satyrs' catch from *Oberon,* "Buz, quoth the blue Flie," illustrates his comic spirit; and the song for Comus in *Pleasure Reconciled to Virtue,* "Roome, roome, make roome for the bouncing belly," indicates his ability to use poetry and music to reveal character. Jonson often creates unusual effects in his songs by alternating solo and choral passages, a technique used brilliantly throughout *Neptune's Triumph.* Most significantly, however, in the later works the songs become an integral part of the masque, used for various purposes, but always central to the form itself.

Perhaps the most important development in the later masques is the progressive movement away from moral absolutism, already noted in reference to the antimasques. This development is reflected in the evolution of the characters in the masques: those of the main masques remain symbolic, but less singularly so than in the early works; they become less static and more capable of action. Increasingly, they are faced with decisions and internal conflicts. They function more as exemplars than as abstractions. For instance, in *Pleasure Reconciled to Virtue,* Hercules enters the antimasque world of excess and rejects it in favor of the masque's world of higher pleasures, illustrating the human obligation to make moral choices. While he may have made his choice long before the masque begins, Hercules functions as an allegorical type of the hero "who can enter the world of misrule, assess it, and lead us from it into the masque."[13]

Pleasure Reconciled to Virtue is an especially important masque, for it epitomizes the tendency of the later works to reconcile apparent opposites rather than merely to contrast them through antithesis. Pleasure in the masque is finally revealed as only ostensibly opposed to virtue. Comus, the lord of misrule, is exposed as a god of base sensuality and of tired excess rather than of true pleasure. The masque transforms the court into the innocently pleasurable garden of Hesperus; tellingly, entrance to the garden is dependent on virtue. The masquers are called forth in a song which stresses the relationship of pleasure and virtue:

> Descend,
> descend,
> though pleasure lead,
> feare not to follow:
> they who are bred
> within the hill

> of skill,
>   may safely tread
>   what path they will:
> no ground of good, is hollow. (ll. 226–35)

Pleasure, thus, can lead to wisdom, and those wise in the "*hill* of
knowledge" (l. 204) are able to enjoy pleasure safely and innocently. As a result of a "roial education" (l. 223), which combines
pleasure and virtue, Prince Charles qualifies as chief "of the bright
race of *Hesperus*" (l. 205). Presided over by King James as Hesperus,
the Hesperidean garden reconciles pleasure and virtue by subor-
dinating the former to the latter and by defending pleasure as an
impetus to virtue.

Not surprisingly, *Pleasure Reconciled to Virtue* influenced John
Milton's "A Masque Presented at Ludlow Castle" (1634), and in more
significant ways than simply providing Milton with the name of his
antagonist Comus.[14] Both masques pivot on questions of choice and
create highly ritualized worlds which are nevertheless grounded in
human experience. *Pleasure Reconciled to Virtue* and "A Masque
Presented at Ludlow Castle" both depict the conflict of virtue and
license without simplifying the attractions of either. Jonson's later
masques are not truly dramatic any more than Milton's magnificent
achievement in the genre is dramatic, but Jonson's work develops in
that direction to the extent that it comes more and more to admit of
human conflict and moral complexity.

The masque, though it did not survive the era which produced it,
greatly influenced the development of the illusionistic stage, and on
that count alone merits sympathetic consideration in the history of
English theater. But the masque is a form of literature as well as
theater, and Ben Jonson more than anyone else made it so. He was
the greatest masque writer of his age. In his hands, the form became a
medium for the presentation of a humanist vision which perceives
connections between the world of experience and the world of ideals
and which interprets these connections as faithful mirrors of human
potential. He invested the masque with dignity, learning, and ethical
force. In his sumptuous shows, he mixed profit with delight and
attempted to translate the mundane into the transcendent.

CHAPTER 5

The Poetry

TODAY casual readers probably know Ben Jonson best as a comic playwright, but in the seventeenth century his nondramatic work was thought to be his more secure claim to fame. In fact, he was the most honored poet of his age. When King James awarded him a pension in 1616, he became unofficially Poet Laureate of England. The pension was probably in recognition of Jonson's court poetry, verse not regarded very highly today, yet the position of poet laureate is peculiarly appropriate for him. He is preeminently a social poet who "can faine a *Common-wealth* . . . can governe it with *Counsels*, strengthen it with *Lawes*, correct it with *Judgements*, informe it with *Religion*, and *Morals*" (*Disc.*, ll. 1035–37). The commonwealth metaphor is more than fanciful: it enunciates a nexus between poet and society which is crucial to appreciating Jonson's achievement.

Jonson's role as social poet, and the consequences of that role, help distinguish him from his great contemporary John Donne. Born within two years of each other, the two men helped create a new kind of poetry in the early seventeenth century, and they share as many similarities as they exhibit differences.[1] What they have in common are a proclivity for the "plain style" of strong lines, colloquial language, natural rhythms, and economy of expression; a disdain for the sensuous ornateness and pictorial diffuseness of their Elizabethan predecessors and neo-Spenserian contemporaries; a willingness to explore individual sensibilities; and a dedication to philosophical truth and moral principle. Both created distinct and personal voices. Their poetry is an intellectual, tough-minded verse in which the formal properties of rhythm and meter emphasize meaning; and individual poems are organic, each part governed by a prior conception of the final form and growing into a highly structured, untransposeable whole. For both men, poetry is a means of "expressing the life of man in fit measure, numbers, and harmony" (*Disc.*, ll. 2349–50).

One can easily exaggerate the differences between the two, so it is worthwhile to remember that each occasionally wrote the kind of poetry most often associated with the other. They differ chiefly and most clearly in that Donne is more often a private poet than Jonson. Introverted and sometimes eccentrically, unclassically individual, Donne is more intent on fashioning realms of private emotion than on creating a poetic commonwealth. Consequently, his poetry is more arcane and more often inaccessible than Jonson's, and he writes more frequently of extremely private subjects, of sex and religion. He characteristically devises elaborate and extended conceits, self-consciously affecting wit and worrying minute points of logic and learning in order to startle his readers into recognition and acquiescence. Jonson, while capable of the imaginative perceptions of Donne, is not as interested in discovering unexpected resemblances between unlike phenomena. While he is a far better love poet than is generally conceded, love is not his foremost poetic subject, and only once does he approach a religious question with an intensity comparable to Donne's. Even when he is at his most personal—mourning his children, for instance—Jonson is never eccentrically private, and he rarely attempts to capture the kind of emotional ecstasy Donne achieves in his verse.

Jonson's role as social poet is a function of his classicism.[2] He boasted to William Drummond of Hawthornden that "he was better Versed & knew more in Greek and Latin, than all the Poets in England" (*Conv.*, ll. 622–23). He had a profound admiration for classical literature, but tellingly he regarded ancient authors "as Guides, not Commanders" (*Disc.*, ll. 138–39). The classical qualities of Jonson's poetry may be located in a number of specific manifestations. Certainly the urbanity, simplicity, and decorum of his lyrics are the products of a classical sensibility. Jonson frequently alludes to and even translates or paraphrases Greek and (more often) Roman authors, and he self-consciously identifies with poets like Martial and Horace. He adopts as his own the classical ideals of balance and stoic self-sufficiency, incorporating for himself and his age an ethical code or moral philosophy derived from, or at least paralleled in, the works of great Roman writers, especially Horace, Cicero, and Seneca. The weighty statement and broad generality of his verse, often employing vividly concrete detail only to illustrate received wisdom, are classical qualities. In addition, Jonson revives classical forms such as the epigram, the epitaph, the ode, and the verse epistle, and he does so with a scholar's knowledge of the origins and conventions of each genre. But the most fundamental reflection of his classicism is the social and public nature of his poetry, his vision of an ordered society in which the poet plays an indispensable role as arbiter of civilized values.[3]

Jonson's poetry is, for the most part, didactic. It counsels the ruling class on how best to achieve a good society, praising in order to inspire and ridiculing in order to shame. Jonson is sometimes the convivial drinking companion singing the pleasures of love and friendship; frequently he is the energetic satirist echoing the Ciceronian lament *O tempora! O mores!* Nearly always, he is the self-nominated maker of a moral vision of the integrated life. In satiric verses, he exposes the vice, disorder, and exploitation he observes around him. But in his poetic commonwealth, he also creates a positive ideal of the harmonious society, one founded on enduring notions about the good life. He sees the great and virtuous men and women of his age as mirrors of old and still vital truths and frequently as anachronistic reincarnations of ancient grace. That this positive ideal and these exemplary individuals are often defined by contrasting them with the negative and the flawed is a measure of Jonson's realism and of the perceived vulnerability of his values in a time of change and peril. The poet's personal emblem was the broken compass; he entertained no illusions about the possibility of perfection in the real world. But he never forsook the ideal as an individual and public goal, and his verse is supremely a poetics of human possibilities. If the possibilities Jonson envisions are in real life achieved only infrequently, and in the artifice of verse realized only in fragmentary and nostalgic glimpses of an older and increasingly threatened civilization, the integrity of the vision is none the less for that. The functional aspect of Jonson's classicism is his faith in the continuity of ethical principles and in the living relevance of timeless questions about the nature of the good life.

To say that Jonson is a social poet is not to imply a lack of personal engagement and to call him didactic is not to deny him subtlety. Indeed, few poets have ever displayed in their work so complete and so assertive a personality as does Jonson and still fewer have permitted large preconceptions to inform individual poems so naturally and so easily. His poetry is sustained by moral vision and energy, but it is almost never moralistic in any narrow or self-righteous way. Poems which celebrate occasions and persons now long forgotten can still excite interest precisely because of the poet's engagement. Moreover, the large scope and continuing relevance of his moral concerns help make even the most topical and time-rooted of his poems more than simply documents of a culture now lost.

Jonson's appeal may be more clearly intellectual than emotional. He is seldom ecstatic and rarely does he create poems of private sensation. Nevertheless, there is a great deal of emotion in his verse, although it has been too little appreciated. He expresses anger and joy, grief and gratitude, dejection and exhilaration, passion and love, and manipulates his poems so that they stir these emotions in his readers as well. He is capable of conveying fine shades of feeling and of orchestrating delicate shifts of tone. From poem to poem, he assumes a variety of dramatic poses, each of them true to one or another facet of his personality and all of them invested with individualized emotion. He is tactful advisor, respectful admirer, proud poet, grieving father, courteous host, affectionate parodist, enraged satirist, amused observer, witty commentator, loving friend, loyal subject, unhandsome lover. Most often his persona is characterized by enormous dignity and fierce independence, and sometimes he exposes himself as affectingly vulnerable.

The variety of voices Jonson adopts, or more accurately, the number of facets of a single personality he reveals, usefully reminds us that he is a great dramatic poet. Each voice is decorously suited to the situation of the individual poem. The dramatic qualities of the poetry help place in perspective Jonson's penchant for weighty statement and broad generality. The vivid dramatic situations rescue the poems from any potential for dullness or banality. Although the poetry is frequently motivated by a didactic impulse and its concerns are with ethical commonplaces, this didacticism and these concerns are presented in highly particularized situations of masterfully controlled drama. The drama is sometimes suggested rather than stated, as in the lovely lyrics "Drinke to me, onely, with thine eyes" (*F.* 9) and "Oh doe not wanton with those eyes" (*U.* 4). At other times, as in "An Elegie On the Lady Jane Pawlet" (*U.* 83), it is self-consciously exaggerated and theatrical. But whether implied or explicit, Jonson's articulation of dramatic context is at the heart of his illumination of human experience in the poetry.

At first glance, the bulk of Jonson's verse may seem somewhat prosaic in its lack of startling imagery, its sparseness, and apparent lack of ambiguity. As he remarked, "Pure and neat Language I love, yet plaine and customary" (*Disc.*, ll. 1870–71). On his schoolmaster's instruction, he composed his poetry by first writing it out in prose and then turning it into verse. Moreover, he gives highest priority in poetry to "matter." The poet, he says, "must first thinke, and excogitate his matter; then choose his words, and examine the weight of either" (*Disc.*, 11. 1701–02). Jonson aims for clarity and artful shapeliness. As Drummond remarks, "his inventions are smooth and easie" (*Conv.*, 11. 693–94). But the appearance of placidity and conventionality is often simply an appearance, a calm surface which makes possible surprising and resonant reverberations. Jonson's poetry is active, animated by verbs rather than adjectives; it is fresh, vital, symmetrical; it typically reinvigorates tired conventions and exhausted traditions; it is sometimes inventive, playful, and imaginative; and it is nearly always carefully controlled and neatly unified.[4]

Perhaps the most consistent tool Jonson uses to impart expansive meaning unobtrusively is his careful diction. His use of words is always precise, although he is sometimes thought not to be evocative. Actually, he often gains richness of implication by choosing a single word or phrase which echoes with meaning. For instance, near the end of his famous tribute to the Sidney family, "To Penshurst" (*F.* 2), he remarks that the Sidney children, by observing their parents, may learn "The mysteries of manners, armes, and arts" (l. 98). The word "mysteries" here gives transcendence to what might appear merely a conventional compliment. Suggesting as it does a whole wealth of meaning, from secret social rites to the Christian religion itself, the word infuses powerful implication into the rest of the line and into the work as a whole. Similarly, at the end of this poem, Jonson contrasts the owners of ostentatious, new country homes with the owner of Penshurst: "their lords have built, but thy lord dwells" (l. 102). Deriving naturally from all that has come before in the poem, this simple but precise opposition of building and dwelling implies a wealth of meaning, much of it nonparaphrasable, but all of it appropriate to the central distinction between the imposing "heaps" (l. 101) erected for the sake of vanity and the organic, living embodiment of civilized values which is Penshurst. A final example of Jonson's subtle but imaginative diction may be cited from "A Hymne On the Nativitie of my Saviour" (*U.* l, iii). Depicting Christ as Theantropos, the Word of God become man, Jonson writes of the nativity, "The Word was now made Flesh indeed" (l. 17). There is a marvelous suggestiveness in the word "indeed." It exclaims Christ as the perfection of man and it also coolly states a fact: by assuming man's nature God became flesh in deed. By this simple, seriously witty device, Jonson effectively locates Christ's birth as an active fulfillment of ancient prophecy, a pivotal moment in human history.

Semantic play abounds in Jonson's poetry, enriching the texture of the seemingly smooth poetic surfaces. But perhaps even more important than the verbal and linguistic skill of the poet is the tension he generates through the balancing of various oppositions throughout his work. He sometimes depicts idealized landscapes only to intrude realistic figures upon them, allowing experience to impinge upon innocence and realism to temper idealism. In "An Elegie" (U. 22), for instance, idealistic assumptions about love are placed in a realistic perspective which adds deep and surprising poignancy to the poet's celebration of neoplatonic virtue. Sometimes Jonson will force attention upon the artifice of his poetry in order to emphasize the reality which animates it. Often he juxtaposes one emotion with another, as in "My Picture left in Scotland" (U. 9), where playful wit balances and then intensifies pathos. Sometimes contradictory attitudes are placed in opposition and the poet refuses to reconcile them. "On My First Daughter" (E. 22), for example, gains great power by never reconciling its oppositions of soul and body, heaven and earth, allowing them to coexist as discrete elements in the paradox of human love. And perhaps equally miraculous is Jonson's ability to mingle seemingly opposed emotions without ever permitting them to develop into oppositions, as in the "Epitaph on S[alomon] P[avy]" (E. 120), where he is at once witty and sincere, playful and earnest.

When one generalizes about Jonson, it is easy to forget the great variety of his poetry. As social poet, he frequently employs public modes of expression, the ode, the verse epistle, the epigram, revitalizing these public forms with refreshing intimacy and confident familiarity. But he also incorporates into his poetic commonwealth a space for the private and the personal, mastering the less philosophical forms such as the love elegy, the song, and even—though rarely—the sonnet. Jonson's various art can best be illustrated by discussion of the individual poems, among which are some of the best-crafted works in the English language.

I   Epigrams (1616)

Jonson seems to have prepared his *Epigrams* for publication in 1612, when it was entered in the Stationers' Register. Apparently, however, the collection was not printed until its inclusion in the 1616 *Works*. Dedicating them to William Herbert, Earl of Pembroke, Jonson refers to his epigrams as "the ripest of my studies," distinguishes them from the scurrilous lampoons which had come to be synonymous with the term *epigram,* and extends to Herbert "the honor of leading forth so many good, and great names (as my verses mention on the better part) to their remembrance with posteritie" (ll. 4, 18–21). This preface indicates both the seriousness with which Jonson regards his collection and the consciousness of his departure from the practice of such contemporary epigrammatists as John Davis of Hereford and John Weever, from whom he dissociates himself in *Epigram* 18.

For Jonson, the epigram is not merely a satiric mode; it is also a medium for the praise of "good, and great names." He does not desire "with lewd, prophane, and beastly phrase, / To catch the worlds loose laughter, or vaine gaze" (*E.* 2, ll. 11–12). By conceiving the epigram as a vehicle for praise as well as blame, he realizes that many of his readers may be startled, as he admits in "To My Meere English Censurer" (*E.* 18): "To thee, my way in *Epigrammes* seemes new, / When both it is the old way, and the true" (ll. 1–2). As T. K. Whipple has shown, Jonson finds "the old way, and the true" in the classical form of the epigram, particularly as perfected by Martial.[5]

The epigram may best be defined as a brief poem, generally no more than twenty lines long and usually shorter, which points toward a witty, ingenious, or surprising conclusion or turn of thought. The qualities most appropriate to an epigram are conciseness and wit. Jonson especially prizes subtlety, irony, and implication in preference to the obviousness and the direct abuse he found in the work of his contemporaries. The style of his epigrams is colloquial, the tone familiar and conversational. The poems benefit from being read aloud, and the heavy punctuation seems calculated to help the reader in this regard. Following Martial, Jonson thought of the epigram as a form admitting of wide variety of subject and feeling. In theory, no theme is too exalted and no feeling too intense to be conveyed in an epigram; in practice, Jonson rarely treats explicitly religious subjects, and the collection contains no love poems. He most often uses the genre to satirize the foibles of his fellows, to celebrate his king, to compliment the worthy, to perform the various rites of friendship, and to commemorate the loss of loved ones. And in his collection, Jonson mingles forms other than the epigram, including the epistolary "Inviting a Friend to Supper" (*E.* 101) and the burlesque epic "On the Famous Voyage" (*E.* 133).

For all the variety of subjects, *Epigrams* gains unity by the coherence of its vision and the mastery of its expression. In this collection, satiric and panegyric, comic and serious poems occur almost randomly, but what emerges from the whole is an individual sensibility, one which both sees the follies of the age and celebrates its ideals. Since these ideals are only rarely realized in "the sloth of this our time" (E. 66, l. 5), they are all the more to be prized. Jonson is not rigidly moralistic in the *Epigrams*. His common sense and his appreciation of the comic are too pervasive to permit his verse to become oppressively didactic. But he is concerned with moral questions and social issues, and these concerns are never sacrificed to the demands of wit. The persona of these poems is the poet *par excellence:* a good man armed with moral authority, exercising his responsibility to expose and to extol by means of *"Poesy,* a dulcet, and gentle *Philosophy,* which leades on, and guides us by the hand to Action, with a ravishing delight, and incredible Sweetnes" (*Disc.,* ll. 2398–2400). By exposing types of vice and foolishness, and by extolling particular exemplars of virtue and achievement, Jonson's book aspires to what he saw as the end of all true poetry. It becomes a collection the study of which "(if wee will trust *Aristotle*) offers to mankinde a certaine rule, and Patterne of living well, and happily; disposing us to all Civill offices of Society" (*Disc.,* ll. 2386–88).[6]

The seriousness with which Jonson regards his epigrams can best be measured by the large number of poems which comment on his book, as he addresses the book itself, its readers, its critics, and its seller. The very first poem instructs the reader:

> Pray thee, take care, that tak'st my booke in hand,
> To reade it well: that is, to understand. (E. l)

This epigram states a recurrent theme, the need for a fit audience. In its stress on the final word, it illustrates in a minor way Jonson's technique of allowing a single precise, low-keyed but expansive phrase or word to infuse the understated whole with unexpected force. The importance Jonson attaches to readers who "understand," in all senses of that word, can scarcely be overestimated: not only must the reader be capable, he must be an active participant in the poetry. Jonson makes a similar point in *Epigram* 17, where he addresses "the Learned Critick" (title), as opposed to the mere English censurer of the poem which immediately follows. From the learned critic alone comes "a legitimate fame" (l. 3). The poet expresses honest ambition for the praise of intelligent and educated readers: "a sprigge of bayes, given by thee, / Shall out-live gyrlands, stolne from the chast tree" (ll. 5–6). This brief poem, with its concentrated energy, careful diction, and unified imagery based on various forms of "legitimacy," clarifies Jonson's desire for discerning readers from whom he can demand much and to whom he can look for poetic immortality. He realizes that lasting poetic laurels cannot be stolen; they must be freely given by a learned audience. By submitting his work to understanding critics, he seeks, in the words of one of his epigrams to fellow poet John Donne, "great glorie, and not broad" (*E.* 96, l. 12).

Jonson's confessed ambitions for his work are nicely tempered by humor in "To My Booke-seller" (*E.* 3), where his self-regard is leavened by his ability to laugh at himself without sacrificing his dignity. It begins with the poet acquiescing in the profit motive of his bookseller, although from a position of implied superiority:

> Thou, that mak'st gaine thy end, and wisely well,
>   Call'st a booke good, or bad, as it doth sell,
> Use mine so, too: I give thee leave. (ll. 1–3)

The poet does, however, insist that the bookseller not pander his work by advertising it in undignified ways to unworthy or incapable readers. But, in the conclusion, the poem reverses itself to a comic close: "If, without these vile arts, it will not sell,/Send it to *Bucklers-bury*, there 'twill, well" (ll. 11–12). Bucklersbury was a commercial street lined with grocery and apothecary shops; there the leaves of the book would be used as wrapping paper, a fate which haunted several classical writers who worried about the popularity of their books. Horace himself declined "to be praised in verses ill-wrought, lest I have to blush at the stupid gift, and then along with my poet, outstretched in a closed chest, be carried into the street where they sell frankincense and perfumes and pepper and everything else that is wrapped in sheets of useless paper" (*Epistles*, II. l. 265–70). By ironically alluding to Horace's observations on the fate of poor poetry, Jonson draws a significant distinction between Augustan Rome and Jacobean England. In his own age, it is not poor verse but good poetry which is neglected. Jonson's poem satirizes the bookseller's greed, the undiscriminating readers of his time, and the failure of the general public to appreciate the true utility of serious poetry. But the humor and gentle mockery of the ingenious conclusion precludes bitterness. Jonson's tone here, as in many of the epigrams, is that of a good natured observer of the human condition, one aware of the flaws in his society but able to be amused as well as occasionally enraged by them.

Not surprisingly, Jonson is most aware of the flaws of his society in the satiric epigrams. In these poems, which dominate the first half of the book but recede in the second, the poet presents a wide panorama of foibles. Affected courtiers and plagiarists receive much of Jonson's attention, but he satirizes almost all elements of his society from pretenders to learning, unscrupulous professionals, and phony intelligence-mongers to vainglorious captains, jaded voluptuaries, and country bumpkins. The subjects of these epigrams are not identified in such a way as to be readily recognizable in the real world. Jonson is more interested in exposing foibles and vices common throughout his society than in attacking particular individuals who possess these characteristics. Nevertheless, the real genius of these epigrams is that they are unusually vivid. By the careful selection and accumulation of concrete details, the poet makes his gallery of contemporary types seem individualized in spite of their generic names and the wide application of the satire.

What distinguishes the satiric epigrams is their quality of wit and their verbal dexterity. These characteristics often take the form of puns and other kinds of wordplay, irony, and aphoristic ingenuity, and they are often achieved by masterful control of syntax and meter. The ironic wit of "To Alchymists" (*E.* 6) is achieved through reticence. It rests on our awareness of the alchemical attempt to turn base metals into gold:

> If all you boast of your great art be true;
> Sure, willing povertie lives most in you.

Similarly, "To Pertinax Cob" (*E.* 69) depends for its wit on our knowledge that one meaning of the Latin *pertinax* is "stiff." This squib on sexual exploitation is not a great poem, but it honestly achieves the epigram's aim of concision, subtlety, and wit:

> COB, thou nor souldier, thiefe, nor fencer art,
> Yet by thy weapon liv'st! Th'hast one good part.

Central to this small poem is Jonson's extraordinary sense of comic timing, as the exclamatory "Yet by thy weapon liv'st!" yields to the understatement of the punch line. The incongruous name which yokes a Latin adjective to a vernacular noun focuses attention on the comic juxtapositions within the poem. Cob's "sword" is not a martial weapon, but an erect penis; his is not an art of war but an art of love. To make this poem a bitterly satirical and narrowly moralistic attack, as one critic does, is to miss the comic tone of Jonson's wit.[7]

In several of the finest satiric epigrams, Jonson manipulates refrains to great comic effect, unifying colorful details and establishing comic patterns which the turns of the final couplets elaborate or refute. In "On Lieutenant Shift" (*E.* 12), for instance, the shifty lieutenant welshes on his debts "with this charme, god payes" (l. 4), repeated throughout the poem as Shift's invariable excuse in all circumstances. But in the conclusion, his attempts to defraud his whore lead to his own syphilitic retribution:

> Not his poore cocatrice but he betrayes
>> Thus: and for his letcherie, scores, god payes.
> But see! th'old baud hath serv'd him in his trim,
>> Lent him a pockie whore. Shee hath paid him. (ll. 21–24)

The refrain in "On Giles and Jone" (*E.* 42) is not a repeated word or phrase but a recurring sentiment, a kind of discordant *concordia concors*. It begins with the question, "Who sayes that GILES and JONE at discord be?" (l. 1), and proceeds to demonstrate their complete agreement: each is equally ill-disposed toward the other.

Several of the epigrams concern courtiers, and these tend to be among the most satiric of all. Jonson often attacks the hangers-on at court by depicting them as dehumanized poseurs. The title of "On Some-thing, That Walkes Some-where" (*E.* 11) points toward its subject's lack of humanity. The poem itself is beautifully constructed, all of its parts carefully arranged into a whole of unexpected force and taut power. The poet's contempt is perfectly conveyed in the dehumanizing pronouns applied to the courtier and in the account of his ineffectuality. Although the lord thinks he is an otherworldly creature trapped in a fleshly existence, in actuality he is less than human because he has betrayed the possibilities—and the responsibilities—of his position. Like the English monsieur of *Epigram* 88 and the rapacious court-worm of *Epigram* 15, this lord is a mere mannequin of fashion, too concerned with appearances and too dead to real life to accomplish anything, either good or ill. If the final pronouncement, "Good Lord, walke dead still" (l. 8), at first reading seems a little flat, one must notice how it echoes "buried" in line 5 and "grave" in line 2: death in life is its own punishment. In fact, the echoes and parallelism throughout this brief, carefully balanced poem are remarkable, particularly since it remains colloquial and dramatic despite its formality of construction.

The poems which satirize courtiers and other highly placed individuals such as Lord Ignorant (*E.* 10), Sir Cod (*E.* 19, 20, 50), Sir Voluptuous Beast (*E.* 25, 26), and Fine Lady Would-Be (*E.* 62) help preserve the independence of Jonson's persona in the *Epigrams* as a whole. It is a central fact of Jonson's personality and of his integrity as a poet that he is impressed by virtue and achievement rather than by title or position. He told Drummond that "He never esteemed of a man for the name of a Lord" (*Conv.,* l. 337), and in *Epigram* 9 he asserts, "I a *Poet* here, no *Herald* am" (l. 4). His emphasis on achievement is deeply felt and probably reflects religious conviction. As he says in one of the two overtly religious poems in the volume, "The ports of death are sinnes; of life, good deeds:/Through which, our merit leads us to our meeds" (*E.* 80, ll. 1–2).

Jonson's hierarchy is one of worth and achievement. He is not a democrat, but his position is not unlike that of Robert Burton, when the latter asks, "What man thinks better of any person for his nobility? . . . we are all born from one ancestor, Adam's sons, conceived all and born in sin, &c. We are by nature all as one, all alike, if you see us naked."[8] Undoubtedly, Jonson's independence, all the more striking in light of his political conservatism, reflects his awareness of his own rise from humble origins. He pays tribute to Sir Henry Nevil (*E.* 109) by establishing criteria for poetry which transcend those of birth. And in "To Sir William Jephson" (*E.* 116), he makes clear that merit and title are not synonymous. Jonson's integrity functions in many ways throughout all of his poems, but it is especially important in the complimentary epigrams, where it insulates him from any suspicion of sycophancy.

If Jonson finds the court corrupt and noblemen often contemptible, this is not to say that he rejects the political hierarchy of seventeenth-century England. He praises King James in several poems, and in *Epigram* 4 he addresses James as both king and poet. In *Epigram* 36, Jonson specifically contrasts his own position with that of his classical model Martial, who shamelessly flattered the despotic Emperor Domitian, while James "cannot flatter'd bee" (l. 4). In "On the Union" (*E.* 5), he celebrates James's "marriage" of England and Scotland in an elaborate and imaginative conceit which may have been suggested by the king himself:

> When was there contract better driven by *Fate?*
> Or celebrated with more truth of state?
> The world the temple was, the priest a king,
> The spoused paire two realmes, the sea the ring.

The first two lines announce a riddle whose solution is indicated in the title and explicated in the final couplet.[9] The poem easily integrates the natural and the artificial, the fated and the contrived. The ocean which surrounds England and Scotland, and separates the two from other geopolitical entities, becomes a natural wedding ring, symbolizing the inevitability of the union. The artificial linking of the two realms by a shared crown is celebrated as a fated event, preordained by God and contrived by the priestly King James. A graceful compliment, the poem is a serious political comment as well. By equating a political union with a holy sacrament and envisioning King James as an anointed agent of fate, Jonson reveals his conservatism. He embraces in the poem the conventional religious claims of the Stuart monarchy. Jonson's royalism in "On the Union" is not an isolated or opportunistic political attitude. It reflects a deep-seated philosophical commitment. This commitment is expressed most clearly in *Discoveries*: "*After God*, nothing is to be lov'd of man like the Prince: He violates nature, that doth it not with his whole heart. For when hee hath put on the care of the publike good, and common safety; I am a wretch, and put of[f] man, if I doe not reverence, and honour him: in whose charge all things *divine* and *humane* are plac'd" (*Disc.*, ll. 986–91).

The obligations of being a poet weigh heavily on Jonson in the complimentary poems. As he states in the Dedication, he wants to lead forth the "many good, and great names" of his time, but he also worries that he may indiscriminately praise the undeserving. In "To My Muse" (*E.* 65), he admits to just such an indiscretion, but remembers "Who e're is rais'd, / For worth he has not, He is tax'd, not prais'd" (ll. 15–16); and later in an *Underwood* poem, he will admit that he has sometimes praised too much, explaining " 'twas with purpose to have made them such" (*U.* 14, l. 22). But if there is danger of "smelling parasite" (*E.* 65, l. 14), there is equally peril in overlooking the virtuous. Jonson's fine tribute to the famous actor Edward Alleyn, *Epigram* 89, capitalizes on the poet's sense of obligation in this regard. "How can so great example dye in mee, / That, ALLEN, I should pause to publish thee?" (ll. 7–8), he asks, and neatly closes:

" 'Tis just, that who did give/So many *Poets* life, by one should live"
(ll. 13–14). To fail to celebrate deserving individuals is to injure the
poet, the subjects, and the age. By naming illustrious individuals in
his poems, and thus preserving them for the remembrance of
posterity, the poet helps create what Edward Partridge describes in a
Wordsworthian phrase as "one great society of the noble living and
the noble dead."[10]

Jonson is acutely conscious of the power of poetry and its potential
to bestow immortality on both the poet and his subject. Yet he is also
aware that the relationship between poet and subject is reciprocal. In
Epigram 43, he constructs an elaborate compliment by modifying the
conventional relationship and asking Robert Cecil, Earl of Salisbury,
"What need hast thou of me? or of my *Muse*? / Whose actions so
themselves doe celebrate" (ll. 1–2). He explains that while the poet
cannot add to the statesman's fame, yet the reverse may be true.
Similarly, in celebrating Lord Monteagle's role in foiling the infamous Gunpowder Plot, Jonson boasts that his own work will "out-last
common deeds," but adds that Monteagle's work "much exceeds" the
poet's craft (*E*. 60, ll. 6, 8). In praising these dissimilar men of action
at the expense of his own art, Jonson gracefully compliments them
and courteously effaces himself. His modesty makes his compliments
the greater precisely because he did care deeply for his work. If "to
write [is] lesser then to doo," writing "is the next deed, and a great
one too" (*E*. 95, ll. 25–26). Tellingly, Jonson praises Clement
Edmonds in *Epigram* 110 for translating Caesar's *Commentaries*; by
virtue of the translator's "learned hand, and true *Promethean* art" (l.
17), Caesar "can dye no more" (l. 22). Jonson most prizes the capacity
of poetry to recreate the past and to preserve the present for the
future. If he respects men of virtuous action, and occasionally assigns
them places of honor higher than those given to poets and scholars, he
never forgets the enduring power of art.

Whereas the subjects of the satirical epigrams are given imaginary
or generic names, the subjects of the complimentary poems are
identified as real people existing in actual situations outside the
artifice of the poems. They function as exemplars of ideals seriously
threatened in the real world of Jonson's society. Sir Henry Cary's
valor upbraids "the sloth of this our time" (*E*. 66, l. 5). William
Herbert, Earl of Pembroke's life is such that all who "hope to see/The
common-wealth still safe, must studie thee" (*E*. 102, ll. 19–20). Of
Susan, Countess of Montgomery, the poet asks, "Were you advanced, past those times [of former ages], to be / The light, and marke

unto posteritie?" (*E*. 104, ll. 11–12). Sir Thomas Overbury "mak'st life understood" (*E*. 113, l. 3). Even Sir Henry Goodyere's hawk "doth instruct men by her gallant flight" (*E*. 85, l. 5). Jonson's exemplary heroes are particular men and women whose lives and deeds are emblems of good conduct which need to be preserved for emulation by others both in his own and in future ages.

The celebration of exemplars is a public ceremony and fills a public need. But the poet's personal engagement can add deep feeling to such celebrations, giving them emotional as well as intellectual force. The best of the commendatory epigrams are at once public and private. Among the most affecting of such poems is "To William Camden" (*E*. 14), where the poet's personal attachment enriches his celebration of his subject's public achievement. An antiquarian and historian, Camden had been Jonson's schoolmaster at Westminster School and became his friend and mentor. The poem opens with a very personal acknowledgment: "CAMDEN, most reverend head, to whom I owe / All that I am in arts, all that I know" (ll. 1–2). It then moves outward from a private debt to a public one, acknowledging the country's obligation to Camden for his works *Britannia* (1586) and *Remaines of a Greater Worke Concerning Britaine* (1605). The center of the poem celebrates the scholar as humanist hero:

> Then thee the age sees not that thing more grave,
>   More high, more holy, that shee more would crave.
> What name, what skill, what faith hast thou in things!
>   What sight in searching the most antique springs!
> What weight, and what authoritie in thy speech!
>   Man scarse can make that doubt, but thou canst teach. (ll. 5–10)

These carefully balanced and dignified lines, the first half of each couplet centering on Camden, the second on the world around him, beautifully sum the antiquarian's commitment to discovering and disseminating knowledge. The poem then contracts, turning inward to acknowledge Camden's own modesty and to conclude with Jonson's courteous self-effacement and personal devotion: "Many of thine this better could, then I, / But for their powers, accept my pietie" (ll. 13–14). The word *pietie* in the final line recalls the opening couplet of the tribute to Francis Beaumont ("How I doe love thee BEAUMONT, and thy *Muse*, / That unto me dost such religion use" [*E*. 55, ll. 1–2]), and it illustrates Jonson's keen attention to diction. Quite simply, "pietie" perfectly expresses the poet's devotion to the

"reverend head" who is "more grave, / More high, more holy" than
the age could desire and who has such faith in things. The poem,
moving in a circular direction from the poet's own testimony and back
again, is simultaneously a personal tribute to a much admired friend
and a general celebration of the scholarly endeavor.

"To William Roe" (*E.* 128) also illustrates well the complexity of
Jonson's successful integration of public and private qualities. A
poem of surpassing beauty, it pivots on the assumption that private
virtues are prerequisite to public ones. A couplet-sonnet with a
significant octet-sestet division, the initial eight lines bid the adven-
turous traveler farewell and culminate in a striking circle image,
while the final six lines look forward to his safe return. A poem of
leave-taking, it is firmly rooted in the particular circumstances of its
occasion and it exploits the emotion potential to that occasion. The
sweetness of its tone invests the whole with intensely personal
feeling. Roe is a "joy" to name (l. 1); Jonson wishes him "windes as soft
as breath of kissing friends" (l. 5); "blest" with his return (l. 9), "We
each to other may this voyce enspire" (l. 11). The extraordinary
courtesy and tenderness here convince of the poet's engagement and
suggest his determined effort to restrain emotion even as he expresses
it. A marvelous tension emerges from the poet's gentle well-wishing
in the octet and his acknowledgment of danger in the sestet.

But the private emotions which Jonson feels are integrated into
public concerns, and William Roe is understood finally to be not
simply an individual friend of the poet but also a type of Aeneas whose
anticipated trials will strengthen his essential integrity and provide a
pattern for his friends (and others) to emulate. Moreover, since the
opening of the poem echoes the *Odyssey's* description of a voyage to
"The cities of a world of nations, / With all their manners, mindes, and
fashions,"[11] Roe is also a kind of Ulysses whose return will be a
blessed homecoming. The classical allusions are purposeful. In the
Odyssey, Ulysses is characterized chiefly in terms of his longing for
home, his suffering, and his endurance. Thus the opening lines which
sing the adventure of Roe's travels also subtly acknowledge the
hardship he must experience, although such trials are not made
explicit until the sestet. Aeneas in the *Aeneid* literally passes
"through fire, / Through seas, stormes, tempests" (ll. 12–13). He was
known in the Renaissance primarily for his piety and his faithfulness
to the old traditions of Troy. Paradoxically, this piety and devotion to
an old order qualify Aeneas to found a new and greater order, the
Roman empire.[12] Like Aeneas, Roe will be enriched and enlarged by

his travels, but he will remain true to his "first thoughts" (l. 10). It is significant that the subtle allusion to Ulysses in the octet is abandoned for an explicit evocation of Aeneas in the sestet. This movement parallels the progress in the poem from seeing Roe as an individual whose voyage ends in a simple homecoming to envisioning him explicitly as an epic type of the faithful traveler whose labors give birth to a new maturity.

Central to the poem is an implicit tension between internal and external worlds. Roe will digest and incorporate within himself the best of all he finds in the exotic places he visits. But he will come back essentially unchanged, enriched but not corrupted by the dangers he faces and the tests of fire and water he passes. The beautiful center of the poem, lines 4–8, introduces one of Jonson's favorite images—the circle—and it epitomizes the tension between the internal and the external. The circle is an emblem of perfection, a symbol of harmony and completeness. By hoping for Roe that his ends and beginnings "prove purely sweet, / And perfect in a circle alwayes meet" (ll. 7–8), Jonson simply wishes the traveler well in a beautiful metaphor of perfect harmony borrowed from classical thought. Roe's circle is meet in the sense of being "true" or "perfect," and it is also meet in the witty sense that in completing a circle a line literally meets itself, in effect returning home to its beginnings. But what should not be overlooked is that the image also places Roe as the unchanging center of a circle which circumscribes hell and all the trials of Aeneas. Thus the interior strength of Roe, his personal character, is measured by the external dangers to which he may be subjected. In another poem, Jonson writes, "He that is round within himselfe, and streight, / Need seeke no other strength, no other height" (*E.* 98, ll. 3–4). Roe is thus celebrated as a public example of private integrity; his inner strength in the outer world earns him the epithet, "This man hath travail'd well" (l. 14), in which the penultimate word punningly suggests both internal and external endurance. Concluding with a vision of homecoming, the poem completes its own circular pattern.

A number of the complimentary epigrams are addressed to accomplished women. These are important both because they are of very high quality and because they qualify Jonson's overstated reputation as a misogynist. In fact, Jonson is only rarely cynical in his attitude toward women, and the idealized portraits of noblewomen function as powerful antidotes to the unfavorable generalizations of a few satiric epigrams. The celebrations of women are among Jonson's liveliest and most satisfying poems, and they illustrate well some of his characteristic techniques, particularly the balance of idealism and experience to inform each other and his ability to freshen convention and invigorate tradition. In "To His Lady, Then Mrs. Cary" (E. 126), for instance, he self-consciously connects the contemporary and the classical. This playful and graceful integration of the idealized and the localized is not without irony:

> Retyr'd, with purpose your faire worth to praise,
> 'Mongst *Hampton* shades, and PHOEBUS grove of bayes,
> I pluck'd a branch; the jealous god did frowne,
> And bad me lay th' unsurped laurell downe:
> Said I wrong'd him, and (which was more) his love.
> I answer'd, DAPHNE now no paine can prove.
> PHOEBUS replyed. Bold head, it is not shee:
> CARY my love is, DAPHNE but my tree.

Clearly, the poet's placing of Mrs. Cary within a mythic framework compliments her. Moreover, the intrusion of an actual place and a real person into the timelessness of mythology revitalizes the myth and testifies to the continuity of human experience. By integrating the idealized classical past and the realistic contemporary present, Jonson imparts surprise and resonance to a poem which might otherwise be tired and conventional.[13] But this technique also creates a peculiar kind of irony which simultaneously undercuts the compliment and deepens it. The title, which pointedly emphasizes the past tense of the poet's attachment to Mrs. Cary, and the very violation of the Daphne-Apollo myth itself, ironically (and playfully) question the possibility of the ideal and call attention to the artificiality of its celebration. Thus the poet's ingenious praise of Mrs. Cary is wittily undercut by the same technique used to compliment her. Paradoxically, however, the praise is also the greater for being more realistic and less idealized.

Three other poems addressed to women need to be singled out for their remarkable vitality: "On Lucy Countesse of Bedford" (E. 76), "To Susan Countesse of Montgomery" (E. 104), and "To Mary Lady Wroth" (E. 105). All three poems portray their subjects as ideals existing within a temporal world. Mary, Lady Wroth, restores in herself all the lost treasure of past ages. Playing tactfully with the biblical story of Susanna and the elders, Jonson asks in the poem on the Countesse of Montgomery, "Were they that nam'd you, prophets?

Did they see, / Even in the dew of grace, what you would bee?" (ll. 1–2). The idealized portrait of Lucy, Countess of Bedford emerges from the poet's graceful participation in a knowing fiction. He enumerates the qualities he would have in the "creature I could most desire, / To honor, serve, and love; as *Poets* use" (ll. 3–4). This paragon of his imagination should be fair, free, wise, "more good then great" (l. 6), courteous, sweet, "Hating that solemne vice of greatnesse, pride" (l. 10). But most of all, she should be independent and self-assured, combining in her traditionally "feminine" pursuits "masculine" qualities so as to become the embodiment of an androgynous ideal:

> Onely a learned, and a manly soule
>   I purpos'd her; that should, with even powers,
> The rock, the spindle, and the sheares controule
>   Of destinie, and spin her owne free houres. (ll. 13–16)

In these lines Jonson brilliantly domesticates the emblems of the Fates, attributing to his paragon believable control over her own free hours. The poem ends with the muse bidding "*Bedford* write, and that was shee" (l. 18). The poem is thus a shared fiction in which the imagined ideal is finally revealed as an actual person. It self-consciously, with knowing and playful insinuation, adopts artificial conventions to strain them, to shape them to its own purposes, gently mocking but never rejecting them. What is most interesting about these idealized portraits of women is the way Jonson integrates in them fact and fiction, past and present. Although he addresses the ladies familiarly and even playfully, the women become embodiments of grace and virtue associated with the past. The poems celebrate enduring values in a living present.

Epigrams includes eight brief epitaphs which have often been praised. Among these are three poems which mourn the death of a friend, the minor poet and adventurer Sir John Roe, who died in Jonson's arms (*E*. 27, 32, 33); an acrostic commemoration of Margaret Ratcliffe, maid of honor to Queen Elizabeth (*E*. 40); an imaginative tribute to a child actor (*E*. 120); a curious epitaph on the elusive Elizabeth L. H., whose last name Jonson lets "sleepe with death" (*E*. 124, l. 10); and moving farewells to two of his own children (*E*. 22, 45). The best of these, the epitaphs for Salomon Pavy, the child actor, and for the poet's own children, are among the finest brief poems of the seventeenth century; and all eight are carefully executed. They

contain pithy and memorable lines, as, for example, "Under-neath
this stone doth lye/As much beautie, as could dye" (*E*. 124, ll. 3–4),
and they exhibit extraordinary metrical skill. They also demonstrate
well two aspects of Jonson's poetry which are often slighted: his
capacity for deep feeling and his religious faith.

Only two poems in *Epigrams* are overtly religious, but they both
establish attitudes mirrored in the epitaphs. In "Of Life, and Death"
(*E*. 80), Jonson contrasts earthly and heavenly life:

> This world deaths region is, the other lifes:
>   And here, it should be one of our first strifes,
> So to front death, as men might judge us past it.
>   For good men but see death, the wicked tast it. (ll. 5–8)

The Christian stoicism and the faith in resurrection indicated here is
restated in the aphoristic "Of Death" (*E*. 34):

> He that feares death, or mournes it, in the just,
> Shewes of the resurrection little trust.

The spiritual confidence of these abstract musings on death finds
occasion for testing in the poems which mourn the loss of loved ones.
Jonson's resolution in the face of death is characteristic of his
intellectual attitude in the epitaphs, but it is often countered by an
emotional response which complicates the intellectual acceptance of
death and gives to the best of the epitaphs great depth and power.

The power of the poems occasioned by the deaths of his children
stems directly from this conflict between Jonson's emotional response
to personal loss and his intellectual, religious acceptance of death.
"On My First Daughter" (*E*. 22) mourns the death of a six-month-old
infant. The first couplet, "Here lyes to each her parents ruth,/
MARY, the daughter of their youth," is quietly but profoundly
moving. The precision of the word *ruth* restrains the sentimentality
inherent in the occasion, while the private loss the parents feel is
evoked by the gentle nostalgia of the second line. By focusing on the
parents' loss and by finding in the daughter's death evidence of their
vulnerability—the passing of their daughter represents also the
passing of their youth and reminds them of their own mortality—the
opening couplet prepares for the religious consolation which forms
the center of the poem. Significantly, the daughter's reception into a
Christian afterlife comforts each of the parents in a particular way. By

submitting himself to God's will, "all heavens gifts, being heavens due" (l. 3), the father's grief is lessened. The baby's glory in joining the "virgin-traine" (l. 9) of "heavens Queene, (whose name shee beares)" (l. 7) assuages "her mothers teares" (l. 8). This individualizing of the grief each parent feels and the comfort each finds helps personalize and make intimate what might easily be a conventional response to the death of an infant.

After finding religious consolation in the safety of the child's soul, Jonson turns to his daughter's small body. The "fleshly birth" (l. 11), until it is reunited with her soul at the Resurrection, will remain in a grave, "Which," he pleads in the final line, "cover lightly, gentle earth" (l. 12). This hope that the earth not weigh heavily upon a dead body is a persistent motif in classical epitaphs.[14] But Jonson is not simply accommodating a classical tradition within a Christian poem. His concern with his daughter's "fleshly birth" betrays his human grief even in the midst of sincerely felt religious consolation. The understated but strong tension between his acceptance of God's will and his feeling of personal loss is developed in the poem's oppositions of heaven and earth, soul and flesh. These oppositions finally yield to a larger opposition, unreconciled in the poem and indicated by implication rather than direct statement, between the poet's intellectual assurance of his daughter's ultimate resurrection and his irrational, emotional concern for her little body. Precisely because it recognizes these conflicting emotions, "On My First Daughter" is a deeply affecting and honest account of the grief occasioned by the loss of an infant.

"On My First Sonne" (*E.* 45) also recognizes conflicting impulses in the response to loss. Again, there is tension between intellectual and emotional reactions. Jonson asks, "why / Will man lament the state he should envie?" (ll. 5–6). His son has escaped through death all the miseries of life. The father knows that God is just, that his son was only lent to him, that the boy has been "Exacted by thy fate, on the just day" (l. 4). But all this knowledge is at variance with his emotional response to the loss of his seven-year-old "lov'd boy" (l. 2). "O, could I loose all father, now" (l. 5), he exclaims, as his natural grief bursts the bonds of the intellectual restraint.

At the heart of the poem is the relationship of father and son, and, more specifically, the reconciliation of a father to the loss of a son. This relationship is strikingly underlined by allusions, witty in their subtlety but never indecorous. The first line, "Farewell, thou child of my right hand, and joy," alludes to the meaning of the boy's name,

Benjamin, in Hebrew, son of the right hand. This meaning of the name is particularly touching because of the further allusion submerged in it to the account in Genesis 35:16–20 of the naming of Benjamin. The biblical child is given two contrasting names: his mother Rachel, dying in childbirth, calls him Ben-oni, child of sorrow; his father Jacob names him Benjamin. The contrast between child of sorrow and "child of my right hand, and joy" is important. In addition, the name Benjamin also carries such connotations as one on whom the father expects to count heavily for support and comfort. In this allusive and etymological context, Jonson's first line has enormous power and implication, and the borrowing and repaying metaphor of the third line is thereby given an Old Testament locus of legalistic justice. By emphasizing the happy relationship he had with his son, a child of joy, the father attempts to restrain his sorrow, to balance his present grief by memory of former happiness and by placing his son's death in a transcendental context of Christian history. What happens, however, is that while the Christian consolation yields intellectual satisfaction, the memory of the joy he took in his "lov'd boy" and the guilt he feels for his inordinate (and therefore sinful) hopes of support and comfort from his son intensify his feeling of loss.

In the tenth line, Jonson alludes to the Greek term for poet, *maker*, calling his son "his best piece of *poetrie*." This bilingual pun is an enormous tribute. It can be appreciated only in light of Jonson's profound respect for poetry and a knowledge of the immortality he hoped to achieve through it. If his son is his best piece of poetry, then the significance of the child's death is very great indeed. This equation of Jonson's initially discrete roles as poet and as father reverberates with implications for the whole poem. In retrospect, the wish to "loose all father, now" becomes even more haunting than it was originally. More than that, it becomes sadly ironic, for the poem itself testifies to Jonson's continuing acceptance of his dual role despite the pain such a role exacts of him.

The relationship of father and son is also pertinent to the ambiguous conclusion. The distinction Jonson makes in line 12 between "loves" and "like" is in part a distinction which stems from his obligations as a father and as a Christian.[15] As a father he is obligated to love his children and to be attentive to their welfare. As a Christian, he knows that his son's best interest is served by death. But Jonson not only loves his son according to his obligations as a Christian father, he also genuinely likes the boy, and this latter affection makes the loss of his son difficult to bear even as he is able to place it within a Christian framework. Thus, the "sinne" of "too much hope of thee" of line 2 is also the liking too much of line 12. In the conclusion, the poet hopes henceforth to love only in a Christian context and never to reveal "of the resurrection little trust" (*E*. 34, l. 2) by mourning the death of "the just" (*E*. 34, l. 1). But the beauty of the poem, finally, is that Jonson never fully resolves this paradox of human love. The pain of loss exists alongside the Christian wisdom he has gleaned from the loss. It is this complexity of feeling, as well as its masterful expression, which makes "On My First Sonne" one of Jonson's most moving poems.

The "Epitaph on S[alomon] P[avy] a Child of Q[ueen] El[izabeth's] Chappel" (*E*. 120) is a beautiful *tour de force*. The subject of the poem, a boy actor who performed in some of Jonson's own plays and who died at the age of thirteen, is celebrated as so consummate a player of old men that, ironically, the fates "thought him one, / He plai'd so truely" (ll. 15–16). The fates have since repented of their error and have sought to revive the boy, "But, being so much too good for earth, / Heaven vowes to keepe him" (ll. 23–24). The poem lacks the repressed emotion of the epitaphs for Jonson's own children, but its graceful tenderness reflects genuine feeling. The form of the work is very intricate, with its varying masculine and feminine endings and line-lengths, but its artifice is wholly in keeping with its subject. The hyperbole of the central conceit and the large personifications also call attention to the frankly artificial nature of the poem but without in any sense qualifying its sincerity of tone. Indeed, one of the miracles of Jonson's art here is his ability to be at once playful and earnest, witty and sincere, ironic and tender. This lovely tribute ranks among Jonson's wittiest and most imaginative achievements.

The epistolary "Inviting a Friend to Supper" (*E*. 101) is also among Jonson's finest works. Based on three of Martial's poems and infused with a spirit of classical urbanity, it is thoroughly Jonsonian. It articulates a code of hospitality and grace which is central to Jonson's notion of civilized fellowship. The aesthetic and social values embodied in the poem are precisely those values the poet prizes in the commendatory epigrams when he hails his exemplary heroes and heroines as anachronistic emblems of earlier and better ages. "Inviting a Friend to Supper" is more than a charming invitation to a feast. It is also a declaration of social principle in which courtesy, moderation, and freedom are the preeminent virtues.

The poem breathes an air of self-confident control and shows

Jonson's mastery of the pentameter couplet. It is marked equally by
an air of courteous deference, as in the opening lines:

> To night, grave sir, both my poore house, and I
>   Doe equally desire your companie:
> Not that we thinke us worthy such a ghest,
>   But that your worth will dignifie our feast,
> With those that come; whose grace may make that seeme
>   Something, which, else, could hope for no esteeme.
> It is the faire acceptance, Sir, creates
>   The entertaynment perfect: not the cates. (ll. 1–8)

Part of the good humor of this courtesy comes from the marvelous
catalogue of "cates" which follows, and from the capping line, "Ile tell
you of more, and lye, so you will come" (l. 17). But Jonson's feast
includes more than merely food, as he incorporates the joys of
literature into the rites of friendship. He and his guests will discuss
Vergil, Tacitus, Livy, or "some better booke" (l. 22). Following
Martial's lead, the considerate host adds, "And Ile professe no verses
to repeate" (l. 24). The feast will be accompanied by "that, which
most doth take my *Muse*, and mee" (l. 28): "a pure cup of rich
Canary-wine, / Which is the *Mermaids*, now, but shall be mine" (ll.
29–30). Jonson's courtesy and urbanity in these opening lines are
endearing. He knows that interesting and discriminating guests are
what make a good party. Literary discussion is as natural a part of the
evening as the wine. The food he serves is good and carefully
selected, even though simple and inexpensive. He is sophisticated
but not pretentious.

The whole poem and the social code it embodies are perceptibly
deepened by the conclusion in which the poet declares "we will sup
free, but moderately" (l. 35). The last lines of the poem indicate more
fully and more concretely the meanings of freedom and moderation
Jonson intends:

> And we will have no *Pooly'*, or *Parrot* by;
> Nor shall our cups make any guiltie men:
>   But, at our parting, we will be, as when
> We innocently met. No simple word,
>   That shall be utter'd at our mirthfull boord,
> Shall make us sad next morning: or affright
>   The libertie, that wee'll enjoy to night. (ll. 36–42)

As so often in Jonson's poems, the concrete particulars of an immediate occasion unobtrusively come to symbolize large ethical issues which embrace far more than the particular or the immediate. The references to *Pooly* and *Parrot* are to government informers, the spies he attacks in *Epigram* 59. "Pooly" is probably Robert Poley who was present at the famous supper at which the young playwright and poet Christopher Marlowe was stabbed. The emphasis in the poem on trust, safety, innocence, moderation, mirth, and liberty reveals the ultimate seriousness beneath its veneer of lightness. What Jonson does in this delightful poem is nothing less than to present a vision of the integrated life, an ideal threatened by public danger and private failure. The integrated life is one in which the sacred rites of friendship mirror the private and public virtues of courtesy, moderation, trust, and liberty, all infused with a passionate love of good verses.

The variety and conscious artistry of *Epigrams* help explicate Jonson's claim for it as "the ripest of my studies." The volume concludes with the scatological mock-epic "On the Famous Voyage" (*E.* 133), a poem whose indecorous subject is partially redeemed by infectious wit and comic delight.[16] Perhaps intended as a broad satire of Jacobean England, the poem has certain obvious affinities with the satiric epigrams, although not even by Jonson's broad conception of the genre could one classify "On the Famous Voyage" as an epigram. Jonson's volume, then, is more diverse than its name might suggest. Its 133 poems include celebrations of the poet's king and tender farewells to his children, the harsh attacks on foolish and vicious courtiers and the commendations of contemporary heroes and heroines. But the unifying sensibility of Jonson emerges from this variety. His personality dominates all of these poems. Idealist and realist, moralist and parodist, in the *Epigrams* he is foremost a poet of his own times who brings to his responsibilities a sense of the past and a vision of the possible. He fulfills the obligations of the poet which he sketches in *Discoveries:* "Wee doe not require in him meere *Elocution;* or an excellent faculty in verse; but the exact knowledge of all vertues, and their Contraries; with ability to render the one lov'd, the other hated, by his proper embattaling them" (*Disc.*, ll. 1038–41).

II The Forest (*1616*)

The Forest first appeared in the 1616 folio *Works*, immediately following *Epigrams*. It consists of fifteen poems in various forms and concerning diverse subjects. Although a small book, it includes lyrics, epistles, odes, and topographical poems, and considers such subjects as love, hospitality, and religious devotion. In sum, it is very different from *Epigrams* in its size, the range of its content, and the variety of its verse forms, although the same moral and social preconceptions inform this collection as well.

The significance of Jonson's title and his high regard for this book can best be understood in light of the explanatory note "To the Reader" which he appended to the posthumous publication of *The Underwood* in the 1640–41 folio: "With the same leave, the Ancients call'd that kind of body *Sylva*, . . . in which there were workes of divers nature, and matter congested; as the multitude call Timber-trees, promiscuously growing, a *Wood*, or *Forrest:* so am I bold to entitle these lesser Poems, of later growth, by this of *Under-wood*, out of the Analogie they hold to the *Forrest*, in my former booke, and no otherwise." Thus, the title, on ancient authority, implies diversity of form and subject, and the sylvan analogy Jonson employs in naming his books indicates his higher regard for the poems of *The Forest* than for the later ones of *The Underwood*. Actually, the two collections are of such different scope as to make such comparisons impossible. Still, it is true that the fifteen poems of the earlier book are surprisingly various for their small number, and among them are some of Jonson's most famous and most admired poems.

Seven of the fifteen poems concern love, a subject in which Jonson is sometimes thought to lack interest. Admittedly, the poet himself helps foster this impression. In *The Forest*, for instance, he entitles a poem "Why I Write Not of Love" (*F*. 1) and, in another poem, he expels Cupid, declaring, "His absence in my verse, is all I aske" (*F*. 10, l. 21). And in several later poems, he presents himself as an unlikely lover: old, gray-haired, and with "so much wast, as she cannot imbrace / My mountaine belly, and my rockie face" (*U*. 9, ll. 16–17). But the surprising diversity and large number of love poems in Jonson's canon, as well as the high quality of the best of them, suggest that in his erotic verse he is doing something more insistently engaging than merely demonstrating "that a poet should be able to write exhaustively about almost anything."[17] That Thomas Dekker, in *Satiro-mastix*, pictures Jonson laboring over a love lyric may indicate begrudging recognition of the poet's aspiration in this genre.[18] Noteworthy, too, is that Jonson read or quoted several of his own love poems on his famous visit to William Drummond of

Hawthornden. Moreover, the very lyric which exiles Cupid serves as prelude to the "Epode" (*F.* 11), which sings of virtuous love. And the explanatory poem "Why I Write Not of Love" may itself be considered a love poem: it makes a subtle and touching statement about the human need for love. Further, in the poems which emphasize the speaker's unsuitability for love, Jonson cultivates a vital tradition of the *senex amans,* traceable at least to Horace, whose own complaint at having fallen in love with a beautiful boy at the unseemly age of fifty (*Odes,* IV. i) Jonson translates as *Underwood* 86. Finally, love is a dominant theme of the masques, those productions which "ought to be the mirrors of mans life" (*L. T.,* ll. 3–4). The love poetry, then, is not peripheral to Jonson's total achievement, but an integral part of it.

The love poems are, however, often quite unconventional. "Why I Write Not of Love" (*F.* 1), for instance, imaginatively plays with the reader's expectations in order to thwart them in an unpredictable manner. The poem pivots on the two different meanings of "Love"—as the personification Cupid and as human emotion—and on a contrast of the artificial and the real. It appears from its opening to be simply a witty fable about Cupid, but then deepens into a conclusion about human love which starkly contrasts with the playfulness and artificiality of the beginning. The opening couplet, "Some act of *Love's* bound to reherse, / I thought to binde him, in my verse," introduces the controlling imagery of bondage, used in many senses throughout the poem. It also suggests the idea, implied in the apologetic tone of the title as well, that poets are bound to write of love, and by "binding" Cupid in their verse the poets reduce the power of love to the graceful mythology recounted in the fable which follows. In the conclusion, however, Cupid flees the bonds of art, but—in another and more important meaning—love does not:

> With which he fled me: and againe,
> Into my ri'mes could ne're be got
> By any arte. Then wonder not,
> That since, my numbers are so cold,
> When *Love* is fled, and I grow old. (ll. 8–12)

The escape of Cupid is the poet's explanation of his refusal to write the artificial rehearsals of Love's acts, an example of which is the center of this very poem (ll. 3–7). But in the direct address to the reader of the last three lines, the poet abandons the artificial and the mythological. He speaks as a real person subject to age and death and in need of

love. Paradoxically, his explanation, "my numbers are so cold, /
When *Love* is fled, and I grow old," actually binds the human
emotion of love in art, and in an art more real and more affecting than
any fable of Cupid, Vulcan, and Venus could ever be. "Why I Write
Not of Love" is ultimately a love poem because it dramatizes in art an
important distinction between conventional poetic treatments of love
and the real human need for love in the face of time.[19]

The companion poems *Forest* 10 and 11 celebrate chaste neoplatonic love. *Forest* 10 serves as prologue to *Forest* 11 and establishes
the poet's credibility. He abandons the conventional mythological
subjects and inspirations and declares, "I bring / My owne true fire"
(ll. 28–29). The end of *Forest* 10 introduces *Forest* 11: "Now my
thought takes wing, / And now an *Epode* to deepe eares I sing" (ll.
29–30). An epode is a classical form which alternates long and short
lines and is usually serious in nature. Indeed, in an earlier version of
this poem, Jonson specifically contrasts an epode with an elegy, the
classical form most often used in love lyrics: "An elegie? no, muse;
that asks a straine / to loose, and Cap'ring, for thy stricter veyne."
The seriousness and strictness of *Forest* 11 is well conveyed by the
dignified meter of the epode.

Commending the virtuous love of the Phoenix and the Dove
(variously identified), *Forest* 11 disappoints in many ways. It is too
long, too didactic, and too predictable. Nonetheless, it is important
for the idealism of its attitude toward love and for its occasional
moments of lyrical beauty. The opening of the poem establishes the
moral tone of the whole: "Not to know vice at all, and keepe true
state, / Is vertue, and not *Fate*" (ll. 1–2). Jonson contrasts the passions
of love which "still invade the minde, / And strike our reason blinde"
(ll. 29–30) with "true Love" (l. 43) defined in neoplatonic terms. This
reasonable love is celebrated in the poem's finest and best sustained
passage:

> That is an essence, farre more gentle, fine,
>   Pure, perfect, nay divine;
> It is a golden chaine let downe from heaven,
>   Whose linkes are bright, and even,
> That falls like sleepe on lovers, and combines
>   The soft, and sweetest mindes
> In equall knots: This beares no brands, nor darts,
>   To murther different hearts,
> But, in a calme, and god-like unitie,
>   Preserves communitie. (ll. 45–54)

In the last four of these lines, Jonson brilliantly juxtaposes neoplatonic and Petrarchan machinery in order to emphasize the peace
and satisfaction of ideal love.[20] Jonson's neoplatonism is an important
aspect of his love poetry, particularly that in *The Underwood,* where
it is used more subtly and for greater effect than it is here.

Many of Jonson's love lyrics have a lightness of tone quite foreign to
the seriousness of the "Epode." This playfulness dominates *Forest* 7,
"That Women Are But Mens Shaddowes." A lovely trifle, the poem
dwells ingeniously on the paradoxical nature of courting rituals:

> Follow a shaddow, it still flies you;
> Seeme to flye it, it will pursue:
> So court a mistris, she denyes you;
> Let her alone, shee will court you. (ll. 1–4)

The lyric is not weighty enough to be included among Jonson's best
love poetry, but its sophisticated grace makes it far more than simply
an exercise in a popular anti-Petrarchan mode. Surely Jonson's
editors fail to apprehend the peculiar delicacy of tone here when they
remark that the song reflects "faithfully enough the cynical view of
women at large which no admiration for a few ever dislodged from his
mind."[21] Jonsonian courtesy robs the poem of the cynicism potential
to the tradition of paradoxical wit. This courtesy, in fact, helps
distinguish Jonson's love poetry from much of that written by Donne
and by the "Sons of Ben."

Jonson often individualizes his love poems by casting an aura of
secrecy over the attachments they depict. The need for concealment
in love is stressed by such different writers as Ovid and Baldassare
Castiglione. The secrecy in Jonson's love poetry probably owes more
to the latter, who in *The Courtier* emphasizes the importance of
concealing virtuous love, than to the former, who in *The Art of Love*
urges the practical necessity and amorous delights of concealing illicit
relationships. At any rate, Jonson's fondness for identifying his
subjects as existing in real time and locale outside of the poetic fiction
makes the secretiveness of many of his love lyrics especially striking.

The lovers of *Forest* 6 exclude the envious world to create a private
refuge of cleanly wantonness. Using a favorite Jonsonian technique of
contrast, the speaker assures Celia that he is a "warie lover" (l. 1) who
"Can your favours keepe, and cover" (l. 2) and not "the common
courting jay" (l. 3) who "All your bounties will betray" (l. 4). This
poem, partly an adaptation of Catullus VII, has been praised mainly

for Jonson's superb anglicizing of the classical details.[22] But the theme of secrecy is thoroughly Jonsonian, and Jonson's own. This motif helps convey a sense of the intimacy shared by the lovers, and it promotes a delicious feeling of mysterious sanctuary in the midst of an envious world. Despite the emphasis on "stolne delights" (l. 18), however, Jonson's poem avoids the libertinism of Catullus. A sweetness and a sincerity of tone in this and other Jonsonian persuasions to love differentiate them from the classical tradition of illicit pleasure. Nothing here, for instance, is equivalent to the furtiveness of Ovidian love. Jonson's individualized tone is achieved by the realistic details which place love's hyperbole in a recognizable setting, by the useful contrast of the "warie" speaker and the "common courting jay" eager to boast of amorous conquests, and by the essential innocence of the kisses.

The famous song "Come my Celia, let us prove" (F. 5) also employs the idea of secrecy, but the very lack of the speaker's innocence transforms what at first glance appears to be a persuasion to love into a cynical invitation to lust. The speaker's sinister *carpe diem* serves more to characterize him than to convince Celia. Heavily indebted to Catullus V, Jonson's poem undercuts the Catullan spirit by gradually introducing moral values which become more and more explicit until the poem concludes with the cynical statement, "To be taken, to be seene, / These have crimes accounted beene" (ll. 17–18). Even without knowledge of its original dramatic context in *Volpone*, readers cannot fail to grasp Jonson's satiric mode here.

One of Jonson's most nearly perfect lyrics depends for much of its tension on the premise of covert communication. "Drinke to me, onely, with thine eyes" (F. 9), based on several discrete passages from the letters of Philostratus, is finally much different from its classical sources, having a delicate tone completely foreign to them.[23] The inability of the speaker to communicate openly with Celia enables him to misinterpret her rejection of him. His need to believe that she returns his affection even in the face of contrary evidence reveals him as affectingly vulnerable and gives the poem considerable depth as well as grace. The lyric divides into two eight-line sections with corresponding and intricate rhyme schemes. The first section pleads for the lady to drink to the speaker or at least "leave a kisse but in the cup, / And Ile not looke for wine" (ll. 3–4). The speaker's love is elevated by his compliment in lines 5–8:

> The thirst, that from the soule doth rise,
>   Doth aske a drinke divine:

> But might I of JOVE'S *Nectar* sup,
> I would not change for thine.

Although the last two lines are sometimes interpreted to indicate that the speaker would prefer Jove's nectar to Celia's kisses, surely the more likely meaning is precisely opposite. The second section of the poem develops around the speaker's sending Celia a "rosie wreath" (l. 9) which she returns. What gives the poem its touching quality is the rebuffed speaker's determined self-deception, his need to imagine that his lady returns his love as well as the rosy wreath. The perfect diction, delicate tone, and subtle betrayal of the speaker's vulnerability all make this one of Jonson's most beautiful poems.

Several of the poems in *The Forest* are verse epistles, a classical form especially congenial to Jonson since it calls for a familiar style and reveals the poet in his own person. As D. J. Palmer observes, "The epistolary form answered well to a new desire for a more informal use of language and a more empirical sense of reality. . . ."[24] Introduced into England in the late sixteenth century, the English adaptation was perfected by Donne and Jonson. The two most important classical masters of the form are Horace and Seneca, writers whose moral concerns and stoic philosophy are particularly attractive to Jonson. The most important aim of the classical form is to define the good life, an attempt congruent with Jonson's own notion of the function of poetry. The verse epistle is, thus, attractive to Jonson because it is a form at once public and private. It demands an intimate communication between poet and an addressed reader, yet it is an excellent medium for the expression of moral and social points of view. Rooted in the actual experience of the poet who speaks without an obvious mask, the verse letter applies the writer's observations to issues which transcend the personal.

The *"Epistle* To Elizabeth Countesse of Rutland" (F. 12) disappoints because it sacrifices intimacy in an attempt to accomplish disparate goals. Sent to the Countess, a daughter of Sir Philip Sidney, as a New Year's Day gift in 1600, it makes much of the Countess's relationship with her illustrious father and becomes itself a defense of poetry. Opening with a harsh attack on misplaced values in a gilt age, the poem deepens into a celebration of poetry's immortalizing power. The epistle's finest moment comes when Jonson contrasts poetry with wealth, beauty, and nobility:

> It is the *Muse,* alone, can raise to heaven,
> And, at her strong armes end, hold up, and even,

The soules, shee loves. Those other glorious notes,
　Inscrib'd in touch or marble, or the cotes
Painted, or carv'd upon our great-mens tombs,
　Or in their windowes; doe but prove the wombs,
That bred them, graves: when they were borne, they di'd,
　That had no *Muse* to make their fame abide. (ll. 41–48)

The confident dignity and subdued passion of these lines make them
among the finest Jonson ever wrote. This faith in good verses is an
important aspect of his personal philosophy, and it is not surprising to
find it expressed in a verse epistle, which traditionally lends itself to
discussions of literature. But in this poem it so overpowers the
subject, who is defined only in terms of her devotion to a muse which
may make her shine in conjunction with "that other starre" (l. 65),
Lucy, Countess of Bedford, as to destroy any feeling of intimate
communication between poet and subject.

The "*Epistle*. To Katherine, Lady Aubigny" (*F.* 13) is altogether
more successful; it is more familiar and it more naturally integrates
the poet's public and private concerns. Addressed to the wife of one of
Jonson's closest friends, Esmé Stuart, Seigneur d'Aubigny, with
whom Jonson lodged for five years, and to whom he addresses
Epigram 127 and dedicates *Sejanus,* the epistle gains power by its
intimacy of detail, sincerity of tone, and reliance on the poet's
personal experience. In a characteristic Jonsonian manner, the poem
opens by portraying a debased age in which virtuous individuals are a
lonely few. The poet forcefully asserts his own integrity in the
opening lines, an integrity maintained at high personal cost in a
vicious world. Illustrating the Horatian observation that "The good
hate vice because they love virtue" (*Epistles,* I.1.52), he recounts his
own suffering and stoic resolution, culminating in line 21 with the
first mention of Lady Aubigny: "I, *Madame,* am become your
praiser." The purpose of this self-congratulation is not mere indulgence. The personal experience of the poet establishes his
credentials, and inasmuch as it is an exemplum of lonely virtue, it
reflects the very qualities Lady Aubigny comes to embody in the
course of the poem which mirrors the beauties of her mind.

Foremost of these qualities is her independence of thought and
stoic indifference to fashion:

　　　　　wisely you decline your life,
　　　Farre from the maze of custome, error, strife,
　　And keepe an even, and unalter'd gaite. (ll. 59–61)

Like the poet, the lady finds comfort in her conscience, her isolated virtue, even amidst the "turning world" (l. 64) and its vicissitudes. Beyond this, Lady Aubigny will triumph over the debased age, for she possesses virtue which alone "can time, and chance defeat" (l. 51). Jonson's praise for the beauty of the lady's mind is in contrast to the world's praise of superficial and cosmetic physical beauty, and it is reminiscent of the compliment extended to Lucy, Countess of Bedford in *Epigram* 76. Interestingly, Jonson also praises Lady Aubigny as an exemplary wife whose "chast love" (l. 96) for her husband yields a "noble stemme" (l. 97). The account of the love of Lord and Lady Aubigny, whose "soules conspire, as they were gone / Each into other, and had now made one" (ll. 119–20), is gently intimate and helps make concrete what might otherwise seem a portrait of abstract virtue.

The epistle's final lines return to the controlling metaphor of the mirror and to the theme of Lady Aubigny's consistent independence of thought:

> and as long yeeres doe passe,
> *Madame*, be bold to use this truest glasse:
> Wherein, your forme, you still the same shall finde;
> Because nor it can change, nor such a minde. (ll. 121–24)

This is an especially effective conclusion, resolving a number of issues touched upon earlier. It tactfully implies what is explicit in *Forest* 12, where the poet declares that—in contrast to poetry—beauty and wealth and blood are all subject to mutability and decay. At the end of this poem, Jonson looks ahead to the passing of time and recognizes that only in the frozen art of his "truest glasse" will Lady Aubigny's form remain untouched by time's passage. But whereas in *Forest* 12 poetry's immortalizing power is self-servingly, though movingly, asserted, here the promise of immortality stems from richer and more complex associations. It is the truth of the poem as a faithful mirror of Lady Aubigny's constant virtue which assures her immortality. Thus the conclusion is not self-congratulatory; it is a graceful extension of the compliment which the poem as a whole represents. It explicates the earlier assurance that virtue "can time, and chance defeat" (l. 51). By tactfully implying the physical changes inevitably to be wrought by time, and finding a parallel between unchanging poetry and unchanging virtue, the conclusion is a moving declaration of faith in true poetry and true virtue at a time when both are imperiled.

"To Penshurst" (*F*. 2), which inaugurated a significant English tradition of poems in praise of country houses, may be Jonson's supreme success in creating verse which is simultaneously public and private.[25] Formally an ode and directed to the estate of Sir Robert Sidney, Lord Lisle, rather than to him personally, it is nevertheless very similar to the verse epistle, since it addresses the country house as though it were a person. The poem's tone is one of dignified familiarity, thus creating an illusion of genuine communication between poet and patron; and Jonson bases his praise of the illustrious family on his own personal experience, casting himself as a recipient of Penshurst's hospitality. As J. C. A. Rathmell has demonstrated, the poem reveals the poet's knowledge of the estate's intimate domestic details and may be viewed as a discreet reminder to the financially troubled Lord Lisle of the true nature of his fortune.[26] But "To Penshurst" is clearly more than a poem of advice to an individual patron. It articulates an ideal of civilized life in a well-ordered society. It presents Penshurst as a positive ideal, a pattern to guide readers in search of the good life; and in doing so it employs a negative formula of praise, contrasting the Sidney estate with others which fall short of that ideal. By these contrasts, it communicates an urgent awareness of the forces which threaten to undermine the values which Penshurst represents.

The opening of the poem establishes the bases of Penshurst's claim to praise. Unlike ostentatious new estates built to prideful and expensive "show" (l. 1) and resented by their communities, Penshurst has grown from ancient traditions and is "reverenc'd" (l. 6). Whereas the beauty of the other estates lies in gaudy decoration, the beauty of Penshurst is natural. Its "better markes" (l. 7) are those of the four elements, and the estate comes to epitomize the harmonious coexistence of man and nature within God's great chain of being. In lines 45–47, another contrast between Penshurst and other country houses is implied. While the building of lavish estates often resulted from capitalistic exploitation and led to agrarian disruption, Penshurst's walls are "rear'd with no mans ruine, no mans grone, / There's none, that dwell about them, wish them downe" (ll. 46–47). The enlightened, traditional social attitudes of the Sidneys earn them the respect and esteem of their tenants and neighbors. Moreover, the hospitality at Penshurst is in marked contrast to that of other great houses:

And I not faine to sit (as some, this day,

> At great mens tables) and yet dine away.
> Here no man tells my cups; nor, standing by,
> A waiter, doth my gluttony envy. (ll. 65–68)

The complaint of a guest being served food inferior to that enjoyed by the host is a frequent one in classical literature, and Jonson undoubtedly intends his readers to recognize an allusion to Martial, *Epigrams* III.ix. But the contrast here between Penshurst and other great houses may be more localized and based on more than bookish knowledge, for Jonson apparently experienced in reality the same poor hospitality of which Martial complains. He told William Drummond that he protested to Robert Cecil, Earl of Salisbury, owner of the lavish country estate Theobalds, "My Lord . . . yow promised I should dine with yow, bot I doe not . . ." (*Conv.*, ll. 318–19). A further contrast made in "To Penshurst" concerns the chastity of Lady Lisle, whose children her husband can be certain are his, "A fortune, in this age, but rarely knowne" (l. 92). The domestic life at Penshurst thus incorporates a code of sexual morality which has become increasingly rare in the larger world. The poem concludes with a contrast paralleling that made in the opening lines:

> Now, PENSHURST, they that will proportion thee
>   With other edifices, when they see
> Those proud, ambitious heaps, and nothing else,
>   May say, their lords have built, but thy lord dwells. (ll. 99–102)

The precise diction here implies the true measure of Penshurst, not as a building but as a way of life transcending individual pride. The use of contrast is, of course, a characteristic technique of Jonson's praise throughout his works, but it functions particularly well in "To Penshurst" to establish a social context in which to view the ideal which the Sidney estate represents. This context gives the celebration an urgency it might otherwise lack.

Each of the two large divisions of the poem is organized to adhere to the hierarchical structure of the great chain of being and of the traditional social order, itself a reflection of that chain. It is important to stress that these hierarchies are not oppressive. Just as the fish and the game and the fruit are eager to serve man, so each group of people look with love and respect on those higher in the social order. The first large section of the poem, lines 1–47, concentrates on the external features of the estate, emphasizing its natural harmony and bounty. The mythological figures introduced in lines 10–17 serve to connect the estate with classical ideals, particularly with Julius Caesar's estate at Tartessus which was celebrated by Martial in *Epigrams* IX.lxi, and to establish poetry as a natural part of the estate which contains "That taller tree" (l. 13) planted in honor of the birth of Lord Lisle's deceased elder brother Sir Philip Sidney, in whom "all the *Muses* met" (l. 14). Jonson's conception of Penshurst may be significantly influenced by the description of Kalander's house in Sir Philip's prose romance *The Arcadia*, so this courteous allusion to Penshurst's poetic son is especially appropriate.

Since poetry is a valued part of the estate's ancient traditions, it is not surprising to find the poet himself comfortably ensconced in the poem's second half, which depicts life indoors. The poet is assigned a middle position in the order which reflects the good life, as necessary to the social fabric as the peasants or the royalty who are also depicted. He is an honored guest, "all is there; / As if thou, then, wert mine, or I raign'd here" (ll. 73–74), and the same hospitality extended to the poet is accorded King James and Prince Henry when they pay an unexpected visit. It is noteworthy that the entertainment extended to the King and his son is "sodayne" but not "great" (l. 82), fit but not lavish, perfectly in keeping with the ideal of moderation espoused in "Inviting a Friend to Supper" (*E*. 101). Lady Lisle's "high huswifery" (l. 85) earns praise on that occasion, but her greater merit lies in being "noble, fruitfull, chaste withall" (l. 90). Moreover, the Sidney children "are, and have beene taught religion" (l. 93) and may "Reade, in their vertuous parents noble parts, / The mysteries of manners, armes, and arts" (ll. 97–98). By introducing children into the poem, Jonson looks forward to the future, intimating the continuation of those values which the "ancient pile" (l. 5) has inherited from the past. The "mysteries of manners, armes, and arts" are the lessons of an integrated life within a harmonious order in which man and nature, lord and tenant, poet and patron, husband and wife, parents and children all function to form an organic unit.

The verse epistle "To Sir Robert Wroth" (*F*. 3) is informed by the same vision expressed in "To Penshurst," but it is directed more narrowly toward praise of the country life. Moreover, its intention is not to articulate a social ideal but, more pointedly, to convince Wroth that his life in the country is happier than it would be in the city. It idealizes country life and satirizes city vice, but its portrayal lacks the stately dignity and broad scope of "To Penshurst." Influenced by a rich classical tradition of poems in celebration of rural retirement, a tradition which includes Horace's *Epode* II and Vergil's *Georgics,* it sings the "securer rest" (l. 13) of the owner of the country estate Durrants and the husband of Sir Robert Sidney's daughter, Lady Mary. At Durrants, Wroth enjoys the pleasures of the Golden Age: rural sports, the variety of the seasons, mirth and cheer, poetry and dance, and the easy mingling of diverse social classes. The hospitality at Durrants is beautifully sketched in lines 53–60, the description of a winter festivity, which invokes the estate's connection with the illustrious Sidney family while simultaneously offering a vision of good fellowship that temporarily transcends class structure. Throughout the poem, Jonson contrasts the prideful acquisitiveness, competitiveness, and vice of the city and court with the natural bounty and innocence of the country. These contrasts have a far sharper satiric edge than those in "To Penshurst," as in lines 67–90. Within the poem, the vigor of such attacks gives force to Jonson's advice to Wroth to be content with his lot even if city life might superficially appear attractive and exciting.

The poem's argument for Wroth's acceptance of a country life is given religious justification in a conclusion indebted to Juvenal's tenth satire: God "alwayes gives what he knowes meet;/Which who can use is happy: Such be thou" (ll. 98–99). The nature of this advice and the terms in which it is given prompt speculation that perhaps Wroth's retirement was not altogether voluntary. Jonson, though he apparently did not like him, actually knew Sir Robert very well, addressing his wife in *Epigrams* 103 and 105 and in *Underwood* 28 as well as dedicating *The Alchemist* to her. Yet he appears uncertain whether Wroth lives in the country by "choice, or fate" (l. 2). Coupled with the poem's vociferous attack on city life, this studied uncertainty may suggest by reticence that Wroth's ambitions in the larger world have been frustrated. Jonson encourages him to adopt the Ciceronian viewpoint that it is blessed "for the soul, after having, as it were, finished its campaigns of lust and ambition, of strife and enmity and of all the passions, to return within itself, and, as the saying is, 'to live apart'!" (*De Senectute,* XIV.49). Jonson fulfills his self-imposed obligation to advise his patrons discreetly but forthrightly. Whatever its immediate motivations, "To Sir Robert Wroth" is a fine tribute to the joys of life apart from the city's vice.

The celebration of country life in "To Penshurst" and "To Sir Robert Wroth" and in other poems and masques makes clear the nature of Jonson's conservative ideal in a changing society. The contrast between town and country was particularly acute in the early seventeenth century when the London metropolitan area was rapidly growing into a capitalist center dominated by "new men" whose fortunes were based upon trade and finance rather than upon the land. The decline of the old order and the rise of capitalism were accompanied by inevitable social strain and by the rise of religious Puritanism. Jonson directs much of his satire against the vices he particularly associated with the city: corruption and affectation, usury and financial exploitation, hypocrisy and intolerance. Conversely, he praises the countryside as the home of established order, proven tradition, and innocent pleasures. But it may be a mistake to read Jonson's criticism of urban life too literally as an attack on contemporary social conditions. The dispraise of cities and the celebration of rural retirement are persistent themes in classical literature, and the vices which the poet attacks are conventional targets. In any case, Jonson, among the most urban-oriented of English poets, who lived almost his entire life in London, is also a poet with very deep affinities for the pastoral.

Like "To Sir Robert Wroth," another poem addressed to a member of the Sidney family also offers advice. The "Ode. To Sir William Sidney" (*F*. 14) celebrates its subject's twenty-first birthday in November 1611. A complexly organized, ceremonial poem usually designed for utterance on a public occasion, the ode is another form for which Jonson has a natural proclivity. The Sidney ode is written in the most complex stanzaic form of any of Jonson's poems. Despite the intricacy of rhyme and meter, however, the poem's diction is simple and its syntax natural. It frankly but gracefully advises the young man, the eldest son of Sir Robert Sidney, to "Strive all right wayes . . ./T'out-strip your peeres" (ll. 25–26). Jonson pointedly stresses that the Sidney heir apparent cannot rely on the achievements of his famous forebears: "For they, that swell/With dust of ancestors, in graves but dwell" (ll. 39–40). This advice may have been particularly welcomed by Sir William's parents, since the young man seems to have been a disappointment to his family. He sparked a scandal some years previous to the poem by seriously wounding his schoolmaster.[27] Throughout the ode, there is a fine tension between Jonson's desire to celebrate Sir William on his birthday and his need to admonish him to live up to his name and responsibilities. Jonson resolves this tension by creating a voice which is simultaneously— and naturally—celebratory and admonitory. The intricate song stanza contributes to the celebratory tone, thus helping make the admonition palatable. The advice itself stems naturally from the poem's ceremonial occasion: "This day sayes, then, the number of glad yeeres / Are justly summ'd, that make you man" (ll. 21–22). The poem is a tactful but firm reminder of human and social responsibilities.

The Forest includes two remarkable poems which reveal Jonson in a melancholy mood and help place in perspective the image of conviviality which he often cultivates. The first of these, "To the World" (F. 4), is subtitled "*A farewell for a Gentle-woman, vertuous and noble.*" Having been abused and betrayed in her youth, the mature lady is repulsed by the decayed and corrupted world. She accepts unhappiness as her inevitable lot in a postlapsarian era:

> I doe know, that I was borne
> To age, misfortune, sicknesse, griefe:
> But I will beare these, with that scorne,
> As shall not need thy false reliefe. (ll. 61–64)

She retreats from the contemptible world, finding peace in stoic resolution. She vows to "make my strengths, such as they are, / Here in my bosome, and at home" (ll. 67–68). This ideal of the "gather'd selfe," as it is termed in *Epigram* 98, is frequently voiced in Jonson's work. It reflects his philosophical adherence to Christian stoicism and reveals another facet of the idealism which animates so much of his poetry. His contempt for the world and his attacks on the misplaced values of a debased age give urgency to the personal and public ideals he celebrates and add poignancy to the individual and social possibilities he envisions.

The speaker of "To Heaven" (F. 15) lacks the mature self-confidence of the gentlewoman in *Forest* 4. Among Jonson's most enigmatic poems, "To Heaven" is an intensely personal self-inquisition.[28] Its tension stems from the speaker's doubt of his own motives. More specifically, he is uncertain whether his discontent with the world, his longing for "ease" (l. 4), his death wish, results from the dangerous despair of melancholy or from his soul's hunger to be with God. This is a crucial question, for the answer to it makes all the difference as to the speaker's salvation. Christian theologians almost unanimously condemn suicide, St. Augustine characterizing it as the one unforgivable sin, for the sinner has no opportunity to repent.[29] But not everyone who longs for death is guilty of suicidal

impulses. Even St. Paul prayed for release from this life, as Jonson
indicates in line 24, alluding to Romans 7:24. The test for deciding
whether a death wish is sinful or laudable is a test of the individual's
motivation. John Donne in his daring study of suicide, *Biathanatos*,
explains the acceptable motive for wanting to die and cites John
Calvin as his authority: "yet certainly S. *Paul* had some allowable
reasons, *to desire to be dissolved, and be with Christ.* And Calvin by
telling us upon what reason, and to what end he wished this, instructs
us how we may wish the same. He sayes, Paul desired not death,
for deaths sake, for that were against the sense of Nature, but he
wished it to be with Christ."[30] "To Heaven" reveals Jonson in a
troubled mood, "laden with my sinnes" (l. 4) and longing for release
from earthly life.

The most remarkable aspect of the poem is its speaker's acute
self-consciousness. In *Epigram* 119, Jonson extols Sir Ralph Shelton,
a wealthy Catholic, for knowing his own way, "Which is to live to
conscience, not to show" (l. 14). Here Jonson is not quite sure of his
own conscience and he wonders if he might not be living for show.
The only certainty he knows is the spiritual crisis he feels. Long
infatuated with worldly things, he unexpectedly feels God stoop to
touch his heart (l. 14). "Where have I beene this while exil'd from
thee?" (l. 13), he asks, and implores God, "Dwell, dwell here still" (l.
15). But his longing to be with God and to escape from the miseries of
the world may itself be sinful, reflecting his melancholy weariness of
life rather than his love of God. Throughout the poem, he alternates
between self-accusation and assertions of guiltlessness. He appeals to
God as final arbiter, tellingly echoing Psalm 26, David's song of
innocence:

> O, be thou witnesse, that the reynes dost know,
>   And hearts of all, if I be sad for show,
> And judge me after: if I dare pretend
>   To ought but grace, or ayme at other end. (ll. 5–8)

The very intensity of the protest betrays self-doubt.

Jonson's self-doubt is also apparent in his moving assertion of
self-knowledge. These lines, reminiscent of the gentlewoman's resignation from the world in *Forest* 4, acknowledge vulnerability:

> I know my state, both full of shame, and scorne,
>   Conceiv'd in sinne, and unto labour borne,

Standing with feare, and must with horror fall,
    And destin'd unto judgement, after all. (ll. 17–20)

But whereas the lady's acceptance of the human condition in a
corrupt world mirrors her secure self-reliance, this speaker's intellectual assessment of his state reflects a much more complex response.
This difference is related to a fundamental difference between the
two speakers: the gentlewoman's confident virtue insulates her from
doubt while the speaker in "To Heaven" undergoes a more immediate spiritual crisis in which he feels his guilt even as he protests
his innocence. His genuine sense of sinfulness coexists with what he
fears may be a prideful rejection of the world. The phrase "after all" in
line 20, following as it does a list of tribulations to which man is heir in
this world, conveys a distinct hint of petulance: after all these earthly
miseries, there is still the ordeal of judgment. The speaker adds, "I
feele my griefes too, and there scarce is ground, / Upon my flesh
to'inflict another wound" (ll. 21–22). These telling lines, recalling
Ovid's complaint that the gods are conspiring against him (*Epistulae
Ex Ponto* II.vii.41–42), sound a note of despair, make explicit the
threat of self-destruction which haunts the poem, and indicate the
depth of Jonson's spiritual crisis.
    The conclusion resolves the issue of suicide. The speaker dares not

complaine, or wish for death
    With holy PAUL, lest it be thought the breath
Of discontent; or that these prayers bee
    For wearinesse of life, not love of thee. (ll. 23–26)

This conclusion is unconvincing in the terms in which it is
presented. The whole poem has been a complaint. The concern "lest
it be thought" (l. 24) parallels other statements in which Jonson fears
his religious motivations might be misunderstood. But the earlier
statements might be interpreted as reasonable fear that other people
might think him a hypocrite (cf. Matthew 6:16–18), while the
conclusion indicates apprehension that God might somehow err in
judgment. This suggestion is ludicrous, even blasphemous, and
incongruent with the earlier assertions of trust in God, if the poem is
taken to be a prayer as that term is popularly understood. Actually,
despite its title and its direct address to God, the poem is not so much
a prayer as a self-inquisition into the speaker's longing for death. This
self-examination is what in the seventeenth century might be de-

scribed as meditation: "a diligent and forcible application of the understanding, to seeke, and knowe, and as it were to tast some divine matter; from whence doth arise in our affectionate powers good motions, inclinations, and purposes which stirre us up to the love and exercise of vertue, and the hatred and avoiding of sinne."[31] By meditating on his longings for death, the speaker attempts to avoid the sin to which the longings might lead. "To Heaven" is a fascinating exploration of religious consciousness and the one poem in which Jonson approaches the spiritual passion and introspection of Donne.

The Forest is a small, but rewarding selection which reveals Jonson in a variety of moods and forms. In the brief span of this gathering, he is love poet, devotional poet, and public poet. He displays intensely private emotion as well as genuine engagement with social issues. He is both "morose Ben Jonson" and the convivial singer of hospitality. *The Forest* gives a good indication of Jonson's versatility and of his mastery of diverse forms from the love lyric and the familiar epistle to the formal ode. It is Jonson's most carefully pruned collection. His criteria for inclusion were the simple ones of poetic excellence.

III   The Underwood *(1640–41)*

The Underwood was first published in the posthumous folio *Works* of 1640–41, seen through the press by Jonson's friend Sir Kenelm Digby, who gained access to the manuscripts upon the poet's death in 1637. Jonson apparently planned to publish the collection in 1631, when he wrote the brief, apologetic preface referring to its contents as "these lesser Poems, of later growth." It is impossible to determine exactly how much effort Jonson himself spent in the arrangement of the poems within the collection. There is, in fact, no obvious thematic organization, but there may be a rough chronological order: most of the first forty-two poems were probably written before Jonson's famous visit to Scotland in 1619, while the latter forty-six probably were composed after the visit.

Dating from as early as 1600 and including some poems which were deliberately excluded from *The Forest*, the individual pieces of *The Underwood* vary widely in quality. But the collection itself is not much inferior to the *Epigrams* or *The Forest*. It contains far more successes than failures. Indeed, the later poems eloquently give evidence to Jonson's continuing power as a nondramatic poet throughout his life. Among the poems of *The Underwood* are some of

Jonson's finest and most ambitious efforts. In this final gathering he continues to fulfill the social functions he accepted as his responsibility, but more frequently than in the earlier books he focuses upon himself as an idiosyncratic and vulnerable individual. Thus the book as a whole seems somewhat more personal than the two earlier ones.

The Underwood opens with a nonidiosyncratic though nevertheless personal work, the *"Poems* of Devotion" (*U*. 1), fittingly divided into three parts to form a contemplative trio of religious lyrics. Each of the three pieces is self-contained and may rightly be regarded as a separate poem, yet the series as a whole is greater than the sum of its parts. Each lyric progresses from a conviction of personal unworthiness to a meditation on God's love and culminates in an assurance of salvation, mirroring in effect the movement of the whole toward a celebration of Christ's nativity, the event which makes us all "heires of glory!" (iii, l. 21). In addition, each succeeding lyric builds upon the preceding one. The first piece ends with a vision of mystical union, thus imparting great confidence to the second, an assurance which expands into restrained but joyous celebration in the third. The series is personal but not eccentric. Throughout one is aware of an individual speaker's relationship with God; the thoughtful articulation of faith has very much a personal tone. But the details of sin, contrition, and manifestations of mercy are generalized. God's love is embraced as an offer of salvation to all men, and not alone to the speaker. The Christmas hymn ends with the universal question "Can man forget this Storie?" (iii, l. 24). There are moments of anguish and rapture, but in general the emotion is understated. This understatement may betray the influence of the medieval religious lyric, an influence which may also explain the intricate metrical patterns of the poems alongside the apparent simplicity of their religious feeling.[32]

The first of the lyrics, "The Sinners Sacrifice" (*U*. 1, i), is subtitled *"To the Holy Trinitie."* It is structured according to the meditative pattern of St. Bernard of Clairvaux.[33] The initial step in meditation is what Bernard describes as the *humilitas,* a process of purgation and self-knowledge. In this section, Jonson depicts himself as "harrow'd, torne, and bruis'd/By sinne, and Sathan; and my flesh misus'd" (ll. 5–6). Presenting to "All-gracious God" (l. 9) his broken heart, he begs forgiveness. In the second section, the *compassio,* Jonson moves from a narrow self-absorption to a comprehension of the plight of all human beings. Lovingly addressing each part of the Trinity, he makes a universal plea for "The gladdest light, darke man can thinke upon" (l. 35). The final division of the lyric, the *contemplatio*, is an exalted adoration of God's tripartite mystery and an intensely felt vision of ultimate acceptance:

> My Maker, Saviour, and my Sanctifier:
> To heare, to mediate, sweeten my desire,
> With grace, with love, with cherishing intire. (ll. 41–43)

The lyric moves from personal anguish to an apprehension of the speaker as a member of the human community, and, finally, to a mystical vision of unity with the three-personed God.

Jonson's treatment of the Trinity in this first lyric is an orthodox reflection of Anglican attitudes. The first of the articles of religion in the Anglican Church (as reestablished by the Convocation of 1563) is "Of Faith in the Holy Trinity." It declares that "in unity of this Godhead there be three Persons, of one substance, power, and eternity; the Father, the Son, and the Holy Ghost," a position restated by Jonson in his tenth stanza. Similarly, the poem is informed by the second article, "Of the Word or Son of God, which was made very Man." This article stresses Christ's duality: he "took Man's nature . . . so that two whole and perfect Natures, that is to say, the Godhead and Manhood, were joined together in one Person, never to be divided, whereof is one Christ, very God, and very Man; who truly suffered, was crucified, dead, and buried, to reconcile his Father to us, and to be a sacrifice, not only for original guilt, but also for actual sins of men." Jonson's second stanza reflects this theology, occasionally echoing the wording of the article itself. Jonson contemplates the Holy Ghost as "*Eternall Spirit,* God from both proceeding, / Father and Sonne" (ll. 25–26), thus recalling the fifth article which states, "The Holy Ghost, proceeding from the Father and the Son, is of one substance, majesty, and glory, with the Father and the Son, very and eternal God." Rooted as it is in the Anglican articles of religion, the poem testifies to the poet's reconciliation with the Established Church, a reconciliation which, he told Drummond, he celebrated by drinking up the whole cup of communion wine (*Conv.*, ll. 314–16). Jonson's editors are correct when they remark of "The Sinners Sacrifice" that "he produces the current theology in the current phrases,"[34] but they are wrong to see this as pedanticism or lack of personal commitment. The poems of devotion deliberately submerge individual eccentricity into a larger, more universal vision of the human community united by God's love. The echoes of communal religious belief are thus appropriate and meaningful.

The second lyric, although it admits the speaker's sin and asks God to "Use still thy rod" (l. 4), lacks a sense of spiritual doubt. Any potential anguish has been dissipated by the first lyric and by the theological bias of the whole. In "A Hymne to God the Father" (*U*. 1, ii), Jonson accepts his sinfulness as original sin, "the fault and corruption of the Nature of every man, that naturally is engendered of the offspring of Adam; whereby man is very far gone from original righteousness, and is of his own nature inclined to evil, so that the flesh lusteth always contrary to the Spirit," as it is described in the articles of religion. He gladly embraces God's sacrifice of his Son "To free a slave" (l. 20).

In the final piece, "A Hymne On the Nativitie of my Saviour" (*U*. 1, iii), Jonson focuses on that sacrifice, the issue of God's love.[35] He echoes the "gladdest light" of the first lyric in the opening couplet of the third: "I sing the birth, was borne to night, / The Author both of Life, and light." In lines packed with theological significance, but presented with studied disingenuousness, he celebrates Christ's nativity, the birth of "the Babe, all innocence; / A Martyr borne in our defence" (ll. 22–23). Jonson concentrates on Christ as Theantropos, the Word of God become man:

> Both wills were in one stature;
> And as that wisedome had decreed,
> The Word was now made Flesh indeed,
> And tooke on him our Nature. (ll. 15–18)

By emphasizing Christ's duality, the final lyric partakes of that unity of man with God which concluded "The Sinners Sacrifice." The simple statement and conversational ring of these lyrics, achieved within varied and intricate patterns, are reminiscent of the poetry of George Herbert. As with Herbert, Jonson's apparent simplicity, a simplicity born of tone and diction rather than of any poverty of ideas, gives his religious expression a feeling of humility in the presence of sacred mystery. In his works Jonson only occasionally appears truly humble, thus the humility of these religious lyrics is all the more affecting.

A surprisingly large number of poems in *The Underwood* concern love. Although Jonson is seldom recognized as an important love poet, he merits such consideration, as the poems of *The Forest* suggest and those of *The Underwood* verify. He is often labeled cynical in his attitudes toward love and women, but apart from a few exercises in a tradition of wit in which he is both uncomfortable and ill-equipped, this charge cannot be supported by the poetry itself. Even in poems in which he adopts the popular anti-Petrarchan stance, he characteristically tempers the cynicism common to such works. For instance, in the two *Underwood* poems in which he assumes a female persona to defend the promiscuity of women (*U.* 5 and 6), the poet prevents them from being read as serious indictments. Self-reflexive humor and a lightness of tone—a true Anacreontic gaiety—rescue them from that undercurrent of gravity which disturbs the superficial playfulness of Donne's poems on the same subject. Ringing changes on a familiar theme, the woman speaker of *Underwood* 6 defends inconstancy with great verve and wit. In closing, the poem neatly reverses itself to declare, "were the worthiest woman curst / To love one man, hee'd leave her first" (ll. 23–24).

Rather than being cynical, Jonson is most often idealistic in his approach to love. His most important statement of ideal love is *Underwood* 88, his beautiful translation of a supposed fragment of Petronius Arbiter:

> Doing, a filthy pleasure is, and short;
> And done, we straight repent us of the sport:
> Let us not then rush blindly on unto it,
> Like lustfull beasts, that onely know to doe it:
> For lust will languish, and that heat decay.
> But thus, thus, keeping endlesse Holy-day,
> Let us together closely lie, and kisse,
> There is no labour, nor no shame in this;
> This hath pleas'd, doth please, and long will please; never
> Can this decay, but is beginning ever.[36]

The contrast between bestial lust and human love is a crucial one for Jonson. He opposes the guilt of the former to the innocence of the latter, the brief impermanence of lust to the enduring pleasure of love. Like Shakespeare's Sonnet 129, "Th' expense of spirit in a waste of shame," and Donne's "Farewell to Love," *Underwood* 88 realistically acknowledges conflicting impulses in the instinct to love. It avoids overt moralizing to concentrate on the fullness of emotional satisfaction. It thereby convinces by means of psychological insight, rather than through conventional interdiction. For Jonson, the keeping of endless holiday is the liberating ideal of a love which continually renews itself. This ideal is never far from the poet's apprehension of love, even when he depicts relationships which question the possibility of the ideal.

Of immense significance to an understanding of Jonson's attitude toward love is the submerged neoplatonism of *Underwood* 88, a philosophy of love which subtly informs much of Jonson's serious amorous verse. Perhaps the most revealing gloss of *Underwood* 88 is the impassioned oration of Bembo in the fourth book of Castiglione's *Book of the Courtier*, a work which exerted great influence on Jonson. Bembo condemns physical love in terms similar to those of Jonson's translation, observing that sensual lovers, "as soone as they be come to the coveted ende . . . feele a fulnesse and lothsomnesse."[37] He also remarks that "Too unluckie were the nature of man, if oure soule (in the which this so fervent covetinge [of beauty] may lightlie arise) should be driven to nourish it with that onelye, which is commune to her with beastes, and could not tourn it to the other noble parte, which is propre to her" (p. 352). Although beauty completely severed from the physical body which originally inspires it may be the most perfect, Bembo does allow Platonic lovers "lawfullye and without blame [to] come to kissinge" which is "a knitting together both of body and soule":

the reasonable lover woteth well, that although the mouthe be a percell of the bodye, yet is it an issue for the wordes, that be the enterpreters of the soule: and therfore hath a delite to joigne hys mouth with the womans beloved with a kysse: not to stirre him to anye unhonest desire, but because he feeleth that, that bonde is the openynge of an entry to the soules. . . . Whereupon a kisse may be said to be rather a cooplinge together of the soule, then of the bodye, bicause it hath such force in her, that it draweth her unto it, and (as it were) separateth her from the bodye. For this do all chaste lovers covett a kisse, as a cooplinge of soules together. And therfore Plato the divine lover saith, that in kissing, his soule came as far as his lippes to depart out of the body. (pp. 355–56)

Thus physical love can serve as a means to higher union. The ending of *Underwood* 88, which emphasizes the circular perfection of "endlesse Holy-day" and its "beginning ever," echoes the neo-platonic commonplace that "love is a circle, which turnes from good to

good by an everlasting revolution,"[38] an idea further illuminated by
Bembo's explanation that "beawtie commeth of God, and is like a
circle, the goodnesse wherof is the Centre" (p. 348).

Jonson often submerges the philosophical underpinning of his
poetry. As a consequence, the idealistic cast to the love poetry has
been mostly overlooked. Yet the importance of neoplatonism to
Jonson's love poetry can hardly be overestimated. It may be that full
appreciation of even a non-platonic poem hinges on familiarity with
neoplatonic documents. For instance, in "The Houre-glasse" (U. 8),
Jonson questions his readers about the dust "running in the Glasse"
(l. 2):

> Could you beleeve, that this,
>   The body ever was
>   Of one that lov'd?
> And in his M^rs. flame, playing like a flye,
>   Turn'd to cinders by her eye?
> Yes; and in death, as life, unblest,
>   To have't exprest,
> Even ashes of lovers find no rest. (ll. 4–11)

Usually traced to Girolamo Amaltei's *Horologium Pulverum* (1603),
this wry poem may be at least partially informed by the characterization in *The Courtier* of foolish women who attempt "to gete them a
great number of lovers, and (if it were possible) they would have them
al to burne and make asshes, and after death to retourn to lief, to die
again" (p. 285). Neoplatonism, then, is an essential ingredient in
Jonson's poetry, adding depth and meaning to the realistic depictions
of sexual attachments. Characteristically, Jonson's neoplatonism is a
moderate philosophy which permits sensuality but not excess; he
adopts a sensible, middle position which avoids both the unrequited
worship of the Petrarchan lover and the otherworldly spiritual ecstasy
of extreme neoplatonists like Marsilio Ficino, but preserves the
idealism of both. As Hugh Richmond observes of other poets who
employ neoplatonic ideas, Jonson uses "the theories not for their own
sakes but to illuminate essential features of the dramatic situations
. . . in his lyrics."[39]

Apart from a few lyrics in a pastoral vein which celebrate idealized
love in a mood of timeless holiday, most of Jonson's love poems are
highly concretized inventions, set in real worlds of particularized
locales and involving individualized characters. The realism of such
poems is calculated to be measured against the ideals of the transcen-

dent love described in *Underwood* 88 and implied within the particular poems themselves. The concreteness of experience tempers the philosophical and religious preconceptions of neoplatonism and concentrates them into private worlds of individual sensation, thereby rescuing the poetry from any tendencies toward the remote or the overtly didactic. On the other hand, the awareness of the transcendent deepens the experience of the actual, and the contrast of the real and the ideal sometimes leads to complex questioning of the experienced world and creates poetry of unusual power and implication.

"An Elegie" (*U.* 22), one of Jonson's finest poems, gains great emotional power when experience intrudes upon idealism. Singing a lady's perfect combination of beauty and virtue, the speaker reflects conventional neoplatonic attitudes. His hymn culminates in the lady's apotheosis into Love himself in lines 25–28. This graceful, conventionally exaggerated praise is suddenly deepened. In a startling merger of the realistic with the ideal, the speaker asks for "One sparke of your Diviner heat / To light upon a Love of mine" (ll. 31–32):

> Which if it kindle not, but scant
>   Appeare, and that to shortest view,
>   Yet give me leave to 'adore in you
> What I, in her, am griev'd to want. (ll. 33–36)

This turn is no less disquieting for the casualness of its accomplishment. The conclusion throws the whole poem into new perspective.[40] The intrusion of the real upon an idealized landscape forces a contrast between the experienced real and the celebrated ideal. The contrast may expose the artificiality of the ideal. But, by revealing the speaker's private attachment to a love at odds with the ideal he praises, the contrast also adds deep and surprising poignancy to his public adoration of the lady's neoplatonic virtue. The poem may be seen as a nostalgic tribute to idealized values almost extinct in the real world of the speaker's experience.

"My Picture left in *Scotland*" (*U.* 9) also demonstrates the failure of neoplatonic ideals in an imperfect world. Brilliantly manipulating traditions such as Cupid's blindness and the *senex amans* convention, Jonson achieves great pathos by portraying a vulnerable persona in realistic and self-mocking detail. The poem is at once genuinely humorous and deeply moving. It has an exactness of detail and title which convinces us of the speaker's sincerity and of his pain, making the poem seem far more personal than conventional. It is a poem in which experience challenges idealistic hopes. The defeat of those hopes is at the core of its precarious balance of wit and pathos. The speaker's attempts to woo through poetry have failed, not for any fault of his verse, but because the poetry cannot obscure his unattractive physical appearance. Indeed, the realistically depicted lover—like Jonson, forty-seven years old, gray haired, mountain bellied, and rocky faced—appears particularly incongruous in an idealized landscape of the "shadow of *Apollo's* tree" (l. 10). As noted earlier, the *senex amans* convention is one Jonson knew firsthand from Horace, and the question of whether an older man could be a lover is a familiar one in both classical and Renaissance discussions of love. But if Ovid thought that " 'Tis unseemly for the old man to soldier, unseemly for the old man to love,"[41] the immediate impetus for Bembo's neoplatonic theorizing in *The Courtier* is to defend the proposition that "olde menne maye love . . . more happilye then yonge" (p. 342). Significantly, Bembo urges lovers to "laye aside . . . the blinde judgemente of the sense" and love with the eyes and ears, those "ministers of reason" (p. 353). But the speaker of Jonson's poem learns from his experience that the ministers of reason are impaired, "I now thinke, Love is rather deafe, then blind" (l. 1). Even as Jonson exploits the inherent humor of the speaker's self-mockery, a sense of failed idealism contributes to the pathos of the poem.

"My Picture left in *Scotland*" in effect questions the power of poetry. But with characteristic Jonsonian irony, the very questioning is tempered by the high quality of the poetry itself. If the speaker is an incongruous lover, he nevertheless is moving in his candor and convincing in his command of language. The metrical *tour de force* of the first stanza confirms his baroque virtuosity, while the self-deprecation of the second persuades of the honesty of his "conscious feares" (l. 11). The authenticity of feeling in "My Picture left in *Scotland*" is especially noteworthy since the poem is frankly artificial, particularly in the first stanza where the speaker duplicates the love poetry he describes. This authenticity results from the poem's solid rooting in experience, and from Jonson's too little appreciated ability to convey fine shades of feeling. The wit balances, then finally intensifies, the pathos. The speaker's self-knowledge qualifies the brittle artificiality of the first stanza, and his honesty precludes the maudlin self-pity potential in a poem of complaint.

As is apparent in "My Picture left in *Scotland*" and "An Elegie" (*U.*

22), Jonson makes his treatment of love concrete by imagining realistic personae and by presenting carefully delineated dramatic situations. Patrick Cruttwell comments of Shakespeare and Donne as love poets, "these two had a great deal in common, and what they had in common was that the basic stance of both was a *dramatic* stance."[42] The same could be said of Jonson. The drama of his poetry is expressed in a number of ways: through the personal tone, through the adaptation of conventional poses and exhausted conceits for new and unexpected effects, and through the distinctive aura of secrecy—noticed earlier in the love lyrics of *The Forest*—which gives a surprising number of poems the illusion of private engagement.[43] Jonson's quiet but vivid articulation of dramatic context is at the center of his illumination of human experience.

Essential to the drama of one of Jonson's most nearly perfect lyrics is the secrecy motif. Beautiful and deceptively simple, the song "Oh doe not wanton with those eyes" (*U.* 4) conceals fullness of emotion beneath a veneer of elegant polish. The suggestiveness and grace of this song earn it a place among the most intriguing and delightful of seventeenth-century minor lyrics. Reminiscent of a host of Petrarchan and neoplatonic lyrics which sing the importance of eyes in love, the poem recalls Spenser's *Amoretti* VII in some specific details, but the compelling drama and powerful immediacy of Jonson's song make it unique.

The qualities central to "Oh doe not wanton with those eyes" stem from a dramatic situation in which secrecy is required. The speaker is hopelessly in love with the lady, so much so that he finds himself almost unbearably uncomfortable in her presence. However she conducts herself, she torments him. This discomfort arises from the fact that the two are unable to communicate openly. The sensitive, silent communication between the two may suggest an enviable intimacy, but such communication is rife with terror, particularly so if, like the dramatic situation of *Forest* 9, the lady is uncooperative, perhaps even unaware of her effect on the speaker. If she "wantons" with her eyes, the speaker sickens because of the impossibility of fulfillment; if she casts them down, he fears they may be consumed by guilt. The lady's anger can kill him, and even her kindness can excite unrealistic hopes which may (with a sexual quibble) "spill" him. If the lady weeps, the lover will be slain with sorrow; if she becomes distracted with fear, which his own eyes "enough betray" (l. 12), then their love may be exposed with presumably disastrous consequences. The suggestiveness of the poem, its consummate and economical exploitation of an implied dramatic situation, is remarkable. With shrewd psychological insight, Jonson reinvigorates a tired conceit to explore the painful isolation which a necessity for concealment exacts of the lovesick persona.

The peculiar circumstances which require secrecy in Jonson's sequence of love elegies, *Underwood* 38, 40 and 41, are not made explicit, but it may be that the lady is of a much higher social rank than her "servant" who vows never to reveal her "blazon" (*U.* 40, l. 13).[44] The sequence rivals "A Celebration of Charis" (*U.* 2) as Jonson's most ambitious exploration of love, and it is distinguished by a highly particularized dramatic situation. The first poem in the series is too long and repetitious; but it establishes the dramatic context, characterizes the narrator, and pleases with a fine urgency. The speaker has offended his mistress, perhaps by revealing her identity in a moment of drunkenness, and he addresses her in a mood of excited contrition. Throughout the poem, Jonson returns to the imagery of light and darkness which dominates the opening lines and continues the characterization of the speaker as resourceful and contrite. The narrator's nimbleness of thought prevents him from ever appearing exactly abject, but his adoration of the lady and his frank admission of error make him seem distinctly human. "Thinke it was frailtie, Mistris, thinke me man" (l. 31), he pleads. The flaws of the narrator humanize the dramatic situation. His confession of weakness balances the exaggerated and unrealistic praise of the mistress. This balance particularizes the relationship of the two, making it seem distinctive and unconventional.

The narrator describes the lady in spiritual terms, often using analogies which equate her with divinity. For example, he tells her, "I am regenerate now, become the child / Of your compassion" (ll. 39–40). Similarly, he asks her to "imitate that sweet Serenitie" (l. 77) of God, and to "view the mildnesse of your Makers state, / As I the penitents here emulate" (ll. 85–86). But such witty idealism is tempered by the easy integration of realistic detail within the analogies, as in lines 87–98. The realism of such details serves further to particularize the dramatic context. It also places the celebrated love within a recognizable social setting, and it incorporates within that public milieu a space for the personal and the private.

Underwood 38 ends by establishing the dramatic context of leave-taking, the event with which the other poems in the series are more narrowly concerned:

> O, that you could but by dissection see
>   How much you are the better part of me;
> How all my Fibres by your Spirit doe move,
>   And that there is no life in me, but love.
> You would be then most confident, that tho
>   Publike affaires command me now to goe
> Out of your eyes, and be awhile away;
>   Absence, or Distance, shall not breed decay. (ll. 109–16)

There is exquisite feeling in this beautiful passage. These lines are a culmination of all that has preceded, and the narrator draws confidence from the success of his earlier arguments. He thus speaks with greater assurance and with a sincerity which has already been tested. The conventional tropes are freshened by the graceful but strong lines and by the very particularized dramatic situation in which they are placed. The dramatic context of situation, character, and event established here are assumed in the two other poems which follow in the sequence.

This dramatic situation compels the speaker in *Underwood* 40 to address a number of specific issues. Foremost, he assures his mistress that he will keep "The Jewell of your name, as close as sleepe / Can lock the Sense up" (ll. 42–43). Separated from the lady, the lover may assuage his sorrow in drink, but—in lines 9–14, a fine passage which deepens the poet's cultivated image of sociability and beautifully attests to the essential privacy of individual emotion even on public occasions—he promises that he will not expose their secret. Moreover, in order to conceal the identity of his real love, he will even mislead others into thinking he loves elsewhere.

What makes this poem so interesting is that in it Jonson manages to do a number of things at once. The valediction explains how the lover copes with absence; it characterizes the speaker as a highly individual lover who can be distinguished from various kinds of lovers; and it reassures the mistress of the lover's trustworthiness. Poems about such subjects are at least potentially quite emotional, but Jonson restrains emotion here, allowing the various feelings evoked by the subjects to balance each other in a mood of assured tranquility, a mood more like the ending of *Underwood* 38 than its abrupt and agitated beginning. This restraint, coupled with an aura of secrecy, creates controlled tension. The secrecy motif contributes to the dramatic tension by prompting speculation on the reasons for secrecy, both helping make concrete an individualized relationship and providing an excuse for withholding specific details by which the characters within the poem could be identified in the world outside it.

The final lyric in the three-poem series of love elegies, *Underwood* 41 focuses more narrowly on the issue of leave-taking. In this poem, the tone modulates into a deeper strain, reflecting both the success of the other two poems in recovering the lady's trust and the imminence of the actual separation. The most concentrated and most moving of the three poems, it develops wholly conventional conceits into a fresh and unified statement of the pain of parting. The first third of the poem self-consciously skirts hyperbole to describe the effects of the mistress's absence:

> It is as if a night should shade noone-day,
>   Or that the Sun was here, but forc't away;
> And we were left under that Hemisphere,
>   Where we must feele it Darke for halfe a yeare. (ll. 5–8)

These lines may deliberately echo Sir Philip Sidney's *Astrophil and Stella* 89; certainly they develop the conceit which concludes *Underwood* 38, a passage which itself probably intends a slighting reference to Sidney's Stella in the phrase "common Stars":

> Others by common Stars their courses run,
>   When I see you, then I doe see my Sun,
> Till then 'tis all but darknesse, that I have;
>   Rather then want your light, I wish a grave. (ll. 119–22)

Along with this conventional trope, *Underwood* 41 also plays upon the familiar exchange of lovers' hearts, an idea intimated near the end of *Underwood* 38 when the narrator tells the lady, "Your forme shines here, here fixed in my heart" (l. 117). *Underwood* 41 interestingly yokes together the two conceits:

> Alas I ha' lost my heat, my blood, my prime,
>   Winter is come a Quarter e're his Time,
> My health will leave me; and when you depart,
>   How shall I doe, sweet Mistris, for my heart? (ll. 11–14)

He refuses her offer to restore his heart, for such an offer is "worth a feare, / As if it were not worthy to be there" (ll. 15–16). The conclusion is moving in its tender resignation to the necessary separation of the lovers, again echoing the close of *Underwood* 38:

> Come what can become
> Of me, I'le softly tread unto my Tombe;
> Or like a Ghost walke silent amongst men,
>   Till I may see both it [i.e., his heart] and you agen. (ll. 19–22)

The poem is a good example of Jonson's ability to infuse freshness and new grace into old conceits.

Underwood 41 succeeds in combining in a natural way several distinct love conventions which support rather than fracture the movement of the whole. The echoes which link *Underwood* 41 to *Underwood* 38 are important, for while *Underwood* 41 can stand alone without reference to *Underwood* 38 and 40, it gains greatly by being viewed as the culmination of a sequence. The other poems establish a dramatic situation which illuminates the nature of the relationship assumed here. And central to that relationship is a necessity for secrecy. This secrecy serves to isolate the lovers and to increase the poignancy of the speaker's duress. In addition, the motif helps illustrate how the dramatic situations reveal a great deal, but suggest more than they specify. Moreover, the sensitive reticence of the persona is an essential part of his individualized character and helps to create the distinctive tone of this series.

Jonson's most delightful love poem is the witty *tour de force* "A Celebration of Charis in ten Lyrick Peeces" (*U.* 2). Although the fourth lyric, *"Her Triumph,"* is frequently anthologized and is widely admired as one of Jonson's most beautiful songs, the sequence as a whole has only recently gained much attention.[45] It is sometimes misconstrued as a satirical attack on Charis and on the Jacobean court society which she is said to represent. But the tone of the celebration is too playful, and its execution too graceful, to be truly satiric. There are, of course, satiric and, especially, parodic moments within the sequence, but "A Celebration of Charis" is written primarily in a comic mode. Foremost, it is an amused and bemused narrative of an unlikely love affair between an aging lover and a fashionable lady of great beauty. In many ways, the poem is reminiscent of "My Picture left in *Scotland*" (*U.* 9). Both present Jonson as a realistically depicted lover in competition with conventionally idealized younger suitors, both contrast idealistic and realistic attitudes toward love, and both question the power of poetry in love.

More specifically, "A Celebration of Charis" tests the premise that

> it is not alwayes face,
> Clothes, or Fortune gives the grace;
> Or the feature, or the youth:
> But the Language, and the Truth,
> With the Ardor, and the Passion,
> Gives the Lover weight, and fashion. (i, ll. 7–12)

Much of the humor in the sequence results from Jonson's self-conscious depiction of himself as an old and possibly ridiculous lover, completely barren of the conventional attributes of the successful wooer. "Let it not your wonder move, / Lesse your laughter; that I love" (i, ll. 1–2), he pleads. In the second lyric, he describes his appearance after having been struck by his lady's "Lightning" (ii, l. 23):

> I stood a stone,
> Mock'd of all: and call'd of one
> (Which with griefe and wrath I heard)
> *Cupids* Statue with a Beard,
> Or else one that plaid his Ape,
> In a *Hercules*-his shape. (ii, ll. 27–32)

But if Jonson lacks the face, clothes, fortune, feature, and youth of the conventional lover, he is a poet, and—to reverse line 5 of the first lyric—poets, though human, are divine. The language and the truth, the ardor and the passion of a poet are tools he commands in this war of love. Indeed, in the individual lyrics of the sequence, he demonstrates a marvelous ability to ape various styles of love poetry.

The purpose of these imitations is not to satirize conventional love poetry, but to illustrate the aging poet's baroque artistry, his ability to have fun with issues which are quite serious to him. The variety of form and style in these lyrics—which include the gorgeously elegant *"Her Triumph"* (iv); the Donne-like, dramatically abrupt persuasion to love beginning "For *Loves*-sake, kisse me once againe" (vii, l. 1); and the Petrarchan parody of Cupid's voice in *"His discourse with Cupid"* (v)—demonstrates the poet-lover's facility and the range of his weapons in the contest for Charis. In the third lyric, he narrates his hopeless predicament as a victim of Cupid's arrow, but points to his poetry as a means of revenge:

> all my wreake
> Is, that I have leave to speake,
> And in either Prose, or Song,
> To revenge me with my Tongue. (iii, ll. 21–24)

This revenge with his tongue consists of his virtuoso poetic performances such as *"Her Triumph."* Appropriately, and wittily, these
performances are rewarded by Charis's kisses, a *quid pro quo*
explicitly enunciated in lyric vi, where he asks "if such a verse as this,
/ May not claime another kisse" (vi, ll. 35–36). For all his indulgence
in lover's complaints, Jonson actually is confident enough in the
power of his poetry to tease his lady about it. For example, he slyly
intimates that she is but one of his muses (v, ll. 7–9); he places his
praise of her in a long tradition of love poetry in celebration of Venus,
a traditional ploy which the lady might not find altogether pleasing
since it qualifies her uniqueness and since one of Vulcan's wives was
named Charis; and he playfully takes credit ("What my Muse and I
have done" [vi, l. 5]) for Charis's triumph at the Whitehall wedding
described in lyric vi, thus claiming another kiss by desert.

Whether the poet is finally successful in winning his lady is a matter
of debate and hinges on interpretation of lyric ix, where Charis
describes an ideal lover. Her description apparently undercuts the
major premise of the sequence as a whole, for she seems to prize
precisely those attributes of face, clothes, fortune, feature, and youth
which Jonson hopes do not invariably insure success in love. But
Charis's description is so idealized as to stretch credibility, and thus
invites suspicion that the final quatrain of her *"Dictamen"* may in fact
amount to a subtle declaration of love for Jonson with whom she
intends to continue a secret relationship:

> Such a man, with every part,
> I could give my very heart;
> But of one, if short he came,
> I can rest me where I am. (ix, ll. 53–56)

In effect, she declares herself content with her poet-lover unless she
should find the idealized young man she has described, an event so
unlikely as to be scarcely possible. The lady thus indicates her
willingness to accept the realistically flawed poet in the absence of an
impossibly idealized suitor.

The phrase "if short he came" is almost certainly intended innocently by Charis, but it is given bawdy implications in the final lyric, spoken by a coarse lady who has overheard Charis's pronouncement. Insofar as the phrase can be construed to indicate Charis's need for a flesh-and-blood lover rather than an idealized imaginary one, Jonson intends it to be suggestive and witty. But, unlike the lady of the final lyric, Charis herself is not vulgar. In lyric v, she is identified with Venus in every respect except one, "All is *Venus:* save unchaste" (v, l. 42), an epithet further clarified by the graceful tribute which closes the lyric, when Jonson tells Cupid:

> this Beauty yet doth hide
> Something more than thou hast spi'd.
> Outward Grace weake love beguiles:
> Shee is *Venus,* when she smiles,
> But shee's *Juno,* when she walkes,
> And *Minerva,* when she talkes. (v, ll. 49–54)

The qualities of Juno's dignity and Minerva's wisdom, which Charis possesses in addition to Venus's beauty, are utterly lacking in the lady of the final lyric, whose concerns are frankly and exclusively sexual. "What you please, you parts may call, / 'Tis one good part I'ld lie withall" (x, ll. 7–8), she declares. Her coarseness serves to characterize her own values rather than to implicate Charis in the courtly corruption. Indeed, the contrast between the two ladies may explain why Charis is determined to keep secret her alliance with a poet-lover who may appear ridiculous to those who value only titles, clothes, youth, beauty, and sexual endowment.

"A Celebration of Charis" is especially interesting for the easy integration of realism and idealism in its depiction of the lovers' attachment. While Jonson affectionately parodies the extreme forms of Petrarchan worship and is clearly interested in a sensual relationship with Charis, the poem is nevertheless infused with idealistic but commonsensical neoplatonic feeling. Part of the difficulty in interpreting the poem arises from the fact that so much of it is parodic, as Jonson demonstrates his ability to celebrate his love in various styles. But the gentle parody of Petrarchan conventions does not amount to a rejection of idealism in love. The sensual motives of the aging lover are not inconsistent with the moderate neoplatonism of Jonson's philosophy of love. The essential innocence of the relationship between Charis and the poet can best be measured in comparison with the blatant and exploitative sexuality of the final lyric. Even lyric vii, which parodies the sexual urgency of Donne's anti-Petrarchanism, is—it must be recalled—an invitation to a kiss. The lover's plea, "What w'are but once to doe, we should doe long" (vii, l. 12), distinguishes his desire from the purely sexual impulse, the fulfillment of which results in guilt and revulsion if it is unaccompanied by love, as explained in the apt opening lines of *Underwood* 88. Though it is neither the unrequited worship of the Petrarchan lover nor the antisexual otherworldliness of the neoplatonic theorist, Jonson's love of Charis is idealistic.

Jonson's idealism is also revealed in several poems which focus on friendship. These poems make clear that the poet valued friendship highly and that he recognized the difficulties in achieving intimate relationships with others. He characteristically contrasts false or casual friendship—the "issue of the Taverne, or the Spit" (*U.* 45, l. 8)—with a more sublime notion, sometimes using his own failures in friendship as a means of defining the ideal he seeks. Conceding that his idiosyncratic bluntness "is a Drug austere / In friendship" (*U.* 37, ll. 17–18), he strives for freedom, honesty, and self-knowledge, elevating friendship into a union of hearts and souls. If Jonson's exaltation of friendship sometimes echoes classical models, it nearly always is rooted in concretely personal situations.

The poet's awareness of his own failure to live up to the ideal of a friend colors several of the poems, investing them with a sincerity which makes them convincing and quietly moving. "An Epistle to Master *Arthur Squib*" (*U.* 45), for instance, opens with a statement of disarming honesty: "What I am not, and what I faine would be, / Whilst I informe my selfe, I would teach thee" (ll. 1–2). The speaker discovers that, true to classical friendship theory, real friendship is based on virtue alone and that he must be "Friend to himselfe, that would be friend to thee" (l. 22). The implied defensiveness of this poem is even more noticeable in the eminently tactful "An Epistle to a friend" (*U.* 37), where Jonson argues for the "comelie libertie" (l. 20) of intimacy, the right of friends honestly to "mixe spirits" (l. 12). This "comelie libertie" is equivalent to the "Freedome, and Truth" which "Epigram. To a Friend, and Sonne" (*U.* 69, l. 5) insists friends owe one another. As a friend, Jonson prized integrity and independence. In "An Epistle answering to one that asked to be Sealed of the Tribe of *Ben*" (*U.* 47), the speaker, who dwells "as in my Center, as I can" (l. 60), discovers self-knowledge and trust as essential ingredients in true friendship: "First give me faith, who know / My selfe a little. I will take you so" (ll. 75–76). Although most of the poem is a satirical attack on the false friend, probably the poet's collaborator and antagonist Inigo Jones, it also gives ethical and, with the witty biblical allusion of the title (Revelation 7:1–8), even religious significance to the circle of friends and "sons" Jonson gathered about him for evenings of wine and wit at the Mermaid and the Apollo Taverns.

In "An Epistle to Master *John Selden*" (*U.* 14), Jonson pays a warm tribute to an accomplished friend and also celebrates the learned Selden's friendship with his chamber-fellow Edward Hayward. The center of the poem is a beautiful passage which echoes several earlier poems, most notably "To William Camden" (*E.* 14) and "To William Roe" (*E.* 128). The poet portrays Selden, an eminent historian and legal scholar, as the consummate humanist. Lines 29–38 brilliantly convey the excitement of scholarship. Jonson sees Selden as a vicarious type of the epic hero. Secure in his own gathered self, the scholar adventurer explores the world about him and observes the past and present, informing his knowledge with commitment and trust, with "faith in things" (l. 36).

After rehearsing Selden's wide learning and good instruction, the tribute culminates in the praise of Hayward, to whom Selden had dedicated his work *Titles of Honor* (1614). Hayward will not only love and cherish Selden, but—as a scholar himself—he can appreciate the pains of scholarship. From his work in the "Mines of knowledge" (l. 76), Hayward has brought "Humanitie enough to be a friend, / And strength to be a Champion" (ll. 77–78). Jonson depicts the friendship of Hayward and Selden as a natural fruit of their humanistic learning. Their friendship in turn provides concrete evidence that Selden, like Hayward, has translated his knowledge and "faith in things" into humanity and strength.

Perhaps Jonson's greatest poem on the theme of friendship is his dazzling "To the immortall memorie, and friendship of that noble paire, Sir *Lucius Cary*, and Sir *H. Morison*" (*U.* 70). Among the earliest Pindaric odes in English, the poem is immensely complex.[46] Occasioned by the early death in 1629 of Sir Henry Morison, whose "life was of Humanitie the Spheare" (l. 52), it balances classical and Christian responses to life and death in a carefully modulated and superbly orchestrated elegy. Moving from classical stoicism in its opening stanzas to a Christian consolation, the poem envisions a "bright eternall Day" (l. 81) in which the poet himself will finally rest with Morison and his friend Cary. Jonson apparently was much more closely associated with Sir Lucius Cary than with the deceased, and the poem uses the friendship of Morison and Cary as a means of making intimate and poignant its consideration of issues raised by the premature death of a promising young man. Jonson intrudes himself into the poem in order to make clear his personal involvement in the mourning of a young man whom he may not have known very well. The poem is an elegy for Morison, a consolatory tribute to Cary, a celebration of friendship, and a deeply felt response to premature death. If a poem as complex as this can be said to have a single theme, it is that the quality of a person's life is more significant than its length.

Interestingly, the quality of Morison's life is judged by aesthetic standards, criteria which might well be applied to a poem or a musical composition:

> Life doth her great actions spell,
> By what was done and wrought
> In season, and so brought
> To light: her measures are, how well
> Each syllab'e answer'd, and was form'd, how faire;
> These make the lines of life, and that's her ayre. (ll. 59–64)

Although Morison's life was brief, it was as graceful as a lyric:

> All Offices were done
> By him, so ample, full, and round,
> In weight, in measure, number, sound. (ll. 48–50)

The loveliest stanza in the poem, lines 65–74, makes the theme explicit, and it illustrates the qualities of grace, ease, and proportion which Morison's own life is said to have embodied. The lyrical perfection of Morison's brief life prepares us for the graceful deference of the conclusion where Jonson ascribes the immortality of the Cary-Morison friendship not to his poem but to their deeds and their love, presenting the surviving friend with wine and laurel.

The end of the poem focuses on the friendship itself. The exaltation of the Cary-Morison friendship draws on tropes derived from classical theory and familiar in the large body of seventeenth-century friendship literature. It also reflects the very qualities Jonson stresses in his other poems on friendship. Not formed by chance or "leased out to'advance / The profits for a time" (ll. 100–101), nor the issue of the tavern or the spit, the friendship of Cary and Morison stems from "simple love of greatnesse, and of good" (l. 105). Characterized by honesty and self-knowledge, Cary and Morison's ideal friendship

makes them examples to future generations. The Cary-Morison ode
may rightly be regarded as the triumphant culmination of Jonson's
treatment of friendship.

The Underwood contains a number of tributes to worthy persons
whom Jonson casts as virtuous exemplars for their own and future
ages. Many of these seem formulary, and the ambitious enshrine-
ment of Lady Venetia Digby as "Eupheme" (*U.* 84) is incomplete and
uneven. Others, the best example of which may be the epistle to Sir
Edward Sackville (*U.* 13), confront the perpetual but not immediately
engaging question of the proper relationship of poet and patron. Still,
some of the tributes are distinguished by the intimacy of Jonson's
address and the subtlety of his didacticism. For instance, a gentleness
and a specificity of detail give "An Epitaph on Master *Vincent
Corbet*" (*U.* 12) surprising and understated power. The tributes to
gifted women such as Lady Mary Wroth (*U.* 28) and the Countess of
Rutland (*U.* 50), are similarly marked by tactful familiarity and
detailed knowledge, and frequently enlivened by wit. Wit, indeed, is
the most striking feature of the "Epistle. To my Lady *Covell*" (*U.* 56)
and "An Elegie On the Lady *Jane Pawlet*" (*U.* 83). But whereas the
self-deprecatory play of the poem to Lady Covell yields unsurpris-
ingly to a graceful compliment, the wit of the elegy is far more
complex.

The elegy for Jane Pawlet is a virtuoso piece, brilliantly inventive,
daring in its conceits, and self-assured in stretching the boundaries of
decorum. The speaker's self-dramatization gives the work a theatrical
quality reminiscent of poems by Donne. Its frequent changes of tone
are similar to those in the Cary-Morison ode, although here the
changes are abrupt and call attention to themselves, dramatically
juxtaposing one mood with another. The elegy is almost as long as the
ode, but it has more energy and less delicacy, and consequently the
experience of reading it is more compressed and more immediately
pronounced. The poem begins with a private drama in which the
poet himself is a participant, but concludes with a triumphant
celebration of faith accessible to all Christians.

The initial encounter of the speaker and the "gentle Ghost,
besprent with *April* deaw" (l. 1) self-consciously emphasizes the
grotesqueness of the graveyard setting. "Stiffe! starke! my joynts
'gainst one another knock!" (l. 9), the agitated narrator exclaims. The
poem then modulates into an apparently conventional recitation of
Lady Jane's genealogy and her individual virtues. But even these
familiar topics of praise are heightened by the histrionic response of

the poet. "Had I a thousand Mouthes, as many Tongues, / And voyce to raise them from my brazen Lungs" (ll. 23–24), he could not adequately sound the lady's virtue. The drama of Jane Pawlet's deathbed is exaggerated in a famous passage which approaches the comic, lines 49–56. She meets death with such confidence and faith that she "taught the Standers-by, / With admiration, and applause to die!" (ll. 61–62). In heaven, Lady Jane "through circumfused light . . . lookes / On Natures secrets" (ll. 69–70) and "Beholds her Maker! and, in him, doth see / What the beginnings of all beauties be" (ll. 73–74). The poem then addresses the lady's parents, enjoining them to be sad only "If you not understand, what Child you had" (l. 78), using enjambment for surprise. The conclusion affirms Christian faith, echoing but not testing the conventional sentiments of "On My First Sonne" (*E.* 45), and culminates in a sober and victorious coda:

> When we were all borne, we began to die;
> And, but for that Contention, and brave strife
> The Christian hath to'enjoy the future life,
> Hee were the wretched'st of the race of men:
> But as he soares at that, he bruiseth then
> The Serpents head: Gets above Death, and Sinne,
> And, sure of Heaven, rides triumphing in. (ll. 94–100)

The elegy for Lady Jane Pawlet is a *tour de force* in which Jonson skirts an excess of metaphysical wit in order to embrace a common religious consolation. Pleasing with its energy and its frenetic combination of the conventional and the startling, the poem demonstrates Jonson's ability in a mode of poetry he used only infrequently.

As the Cary-Morison ode and the Jane Pawlet elegy brilliantly demonstrate, Jonson's poetic powers did not wane in his later years. But many of Jonson's late poems concern specific personal problems, some of them occasioned by age and illness. His house burned in 1623, and in the fire he lost his library and several manuscripts. During the reign of Charles I, his prestige at court declined; with the ascendancy of Inigo Jones, he was employed less frequently in writing masques and other courtly entertainments, and consequently he was often in financial straits. A stroke paralyzed him in 1628 and confined him to bed for a long period. In 1629, his return to the popular stage met with disaster. Jonson experienced enough misfortune in his last years to have become an enfeebled and embittered old man. That he did not may be testimony to his own "faith in things," that favorite tribute of his to friends he admired.

Few of the late poems are self-pitying and many are imbued with a comic spirit surprising in light of the circumstances of their composition. "An Execration upon *Vulcan*" (*U*. 43), prompted by the fire of 1623, while it contains much satire in passing, is remarkably good-humored in its burlesque attack on the god of fire who is such a fool he "would his owne harvest spoile, or burne!" (l. 150). Even in "An Ode. To himselfe" (*U*. 23), Jonson avoids the bitterness and self-pity of his immediate reaction to the failure of *The New Inn*. In *Underwood* 23, he castigates himself for "ease and sloth" (l. 2) and resolves to "sing high and aloofe, / Safe from the wolves black jaw, and the dull Asses hoofe" (ll. 35–36). His contempt for his age and for "that strumpet the Stage" (l. 34) remains, but it is subordinated to his positive and healthy regard for his own poetic power, a gift for which he assumes full responsibility. In the "Epistle To M^r. *Arthur Squib*" (*U*. 54), he jokingly uses his own large girth as an opportune pretext to borrow money from his friend.

As a partial solution to his monetary problems, Jonson petitioned in 1630 "th'best of Monarchs, Masters, Men, King *Charles*" (*U*. 76, title) for an increase in the "free Poetique Pension" (l. 10) which King James had granted him in 1616. The request was honored, but the payment was sometimes late. In an epigram to a clerk in the Exchequer (*U*. 57) and in "An Epigram, To the House-hold" (*U*. 68), the poet complains, "If the'Chequer be emptie, so will be his Head" (*U*. 57, l. 28). The best of these begging verses is "To the Right Honourable, the Lord high Treasurer of *England*. An Epistle Mendicant" (*U*. 71), where the poet, using siege imagery, admits that

> *Disease*, the Enemie, and his Ingineeres,
> *Want*, with the rest of his conceal'd compeeres,
> Have cast a trench about mee, now, five yeares. (ll. 4–6)

As a consequence, "The *Muse* not peepes out, one of hundred dayes" (l. 9). The poet asks for "some saving-*Honour* of the *Crowne*" (l. 13) to relieve his "*Bed-rid* Wit" (l. 15). But for all the pathos inherent in the situation of a proud man wracked by illness and poverty, there is nothing maudlin in the poem. It maintains dignity in part by the martial imagery and the comparison of the poet with a distressed city, but more because of its note of honest and unsentimentalized need.

In his later years, Jonson regularly fulfilled the obligations of poet laureate, producing poems on the loss of the royal couple's first child (*U*. 63), the birth of the future Charles II (*U*. 65), and royal

anniversaries (*U.* 67, 72). These poems are filled with the royalist
fervor which mark the praise of King James in the *Epigrams.*
Occasionally, Jonson also reveals an awareness of the growing
political problems facing his monarch. In "An Epigram. To K.
Charles for a *100.* pounds he sent me in my sicknesse" (*U.* 62), the
poet alludes to the old belief that the king's touch could cure scrofula
(popularly known as the King's Evil). The ceremony itself asserts that
the king's authority derives from God and not from the will of his
unruly subjects.[47] Jonson uses the king's personal kindness to him as
the occasion for a political statement, one especially appropriate in
1629 when the king dissolved his increasingly rebellious parliament:
"What can the *Poet* wish his *King* may doe, / But, that he cure the
Peoples Evill too?" (ll. 13–14). The growing discontent which would
later fester into civil war is also at the core of "An Epigram. To our
great and good K. *Charles* On his Anniversary Day" (*U.* 64).
Beginning "How happy were the Subject, if he knew, / Most pious
King, but his owne good in you!" (ll. 1–2), Jonson attacks his
countrymen—particularly the Puritans among them—for failing to
appreciate their sovereign. "How is she barren growne of love! or
broke! / That nothing can her gratitude provoke!" (ll. 15–16), the poet
asks of his unhappy country, and attributes the discontent to "Surfet
bred of ease, / The truly Epidemicall disease!" (ll. 17–18). The poem
celebrates the beleaguered king by portraying him as a prophet
without honor in his own country. Jonson was a keen observer of his
age. His poems reflect his awareness of unhappiness in the land, and
he correctly perceives in this discontent danger to his monarch.

A large and uneven collection which the poet himself did not live to
see through the press, *The Underwood* is nevertheless a work of
Jonson's mature genius. The poems of *The Underwood* exhibit the
poet in a variety of moods and predicaments and, like the earlier
collections, attest to the large range of his interests. The book in
general reveals Jonson's personality more intimately and with greater
warmth than do the previous gatherings. It contains poems which are
both playful and serious, often simultaneously witty and moving. It
features a number of fine love lyrics and an almost equally distinguished group of poems focusing on friendship. In addition, a
number of poems unhesitatingly treat personal events and problems
in the aging poet's life. Throughout the work, Jonson appears more
idiosyncratic and more vulnerable than in the earlier collections, and
more frequently than before he casts himself as a character in the
poems, writing about his personal life in a way which is affecting but

not sentimental. He remains an idealist and a moralist in these poems and more of a public than a private poet. But his idealism often functions to unveil realistic human imperfections which are not despised, and his didacticism translates into a large and humane vision of individual and social possibilities. For all its unevenness and occasional failures, *The Underwood* is a fitting capstone to the career of a man who dedicated his life to the arduous and sometimes unrewarding art of poetry.

IV *Ungathered Verse*

Jonson's ungathered verse is a motley group of poems which he did not see fit to publish in his three collections. Most of these poems were written as prefatory or complimentary verses for works by friends or acquaintances or as contributions to miscellaneous anthologies, and some are poems which Jonson deliberately chose to suppress, as, for example, the wedding poem for the ill-fated Robert Carr, Earl of Somerset (U. V. 18). The uncollected poetry includes an intricate religious poem, *"The Ghyrlond* of the blessed Virgin *Marie"* (U. V. 41), assorted epitaphs and literary compliments, attacks on Inigo Jones (U. V. 34, 35, 36), and several royalist encomia.

The most famous and the finest of the ungathered verse is a literary compliment addressed to William Shakespeare. "To the memory of my beloved, The Author *Mr. William Shakespeare:* And what he hath left us" (U. V. 26) was first published in the 1623 folio of Shakespeare's *Works,* collected by John Heminges and Henry Condell, actors in Shakespeare's company and friends of Jonson. The poem should long ago have put to rest the recurrent suspicion that Jonson disliked, envied, or misunderstood his great contemporary.

It is true that Jonson disapproved of what he considered Shakespeare's occasional lapses of decorum and of verisimilitude and that he thought Shakespeare should have revised more often than he was rumored to do. *"I remember,* the Players have often mentioned it as an honour to *Shakespeare,* that in his writing, (whatsoever he penn'd) hee never blotted out line. My answer hath beene, Would he had blotted a thousand" *(Disc.,* ll. 647–50). Drummond reports, perhaps not entirely accurately, that his visitor declared, "Shaksperr wanted Arte" *(Conv.,* l. 50), a blunt statement explicitly contradicted in the poem which gives nature and art equal credit in fashioning the poet. Jonson took great pains to clarify his position regarding Shakespeare, and in doing so he praised both the man and his genius: "I lov'd the man, and doe honour his memory (on this side Idolatry). . . . He was (indeed) honest, and of an open, and free nature: had an excellent *Phantsie;* brave notions, and gentle expressions. . . . hee redeemed his vices, with his vertues. There was ever more in him to be praysed, then to be pardoned" (*Disc.,* ll. 654–68). In the poem to his fellow poet, Jonson honors the dead man's memory and demonstrates that he in fact both understood and sympathized with Shakespeare's greatness.

The poem opens with a long introduction in which Jonson details in what traditional ways he will not praise Shakespeare. He will not be motivated by ignorance, blind affection, or crafty malice. Having established his judiciousness, independence, and sincerity, he strikes a triumphant note: "Soule of the Age! / The applause! delight! the wonder of our Stage!" (ll. 17–18). This expansive new beginning releases the energy restrained in the cautionary introduction and intimates the two interconnected concerns developed more fully in the tribute which follows. Shakespeare is celebrated as a national hero and as an embodiment of *Zeitgeist.* But as the poem proceeds, he comes to be seen as one whose art conquers any limitations of time and space. To render Shakespeare justly, he cannot be compared with his English contemporaries John Lyly, Thomas Kyd, and Christopher Marlowe, but with Jonson's hallowed humanist heroes, the classical masters of tragedy and comedy "that insolent *Greece,* or haughtie *Rome* / Sent forth, or since did from their ashes come" (ll. 39–40). Shakespeare is a national hero, but he merits international acclaim: "Triumph, my *Britaine,* thou hast one to showe, / To whom all Scenes of *Europe* homage owe" (ll. 41–42). And if he is the "Soule of the Age!" (l. 17), he is also "not of an age, but for all time!" (l. 43).

The two external factors which bear upon the poem— Shakespeare's death in 1616 and the publication of the folio in 1623—are naturally integrated. The poem is an elegy, but it is also a commendatory verse for a book. The central theme of the poem is Shakespeare's immortality, but that state results more insistently from "what he hath left us" than from the conventional consolation in which the dead poet is stellified. Thus, Shakespeare is "alive still, while thy Booke doth live, / And we have wits to read, and praise to give" (ll. 23–24). His mind and manners shine "In his well torned, and true-filed lines" (l. 68). Even when the "Sweet Swan of *Avon*" (l. 71) is transfigured into the constellation Cygnus, the stellar poet influences the "drooping Stage" (l. 78) through his "Volumes light" (l. 80). As the poem easily integrates the two parts of its double function, it also exploits the tension inherent in them. Shakespeare is dead; his art lives. Although the man can no more return than can *"Eliza,* and our *James"* (l. 74), who so enjoyed his work, the "Starre of *Poets"* (l. 77) triumphs over his own death through the continuing vitality of his book.

Jonson's tribute to Shakespeare is a dignified but seriously witty celebration of a great artist. Like "On My First Sonne" (*E.* 45), the poem is filled with semantic play which never violates decorum. The puns on Shakespeare (ll. 37, 69), on Kyd and Lyly (ll. 29–30), on issue and race (l. 66), and on influence (l. 78) give the poem a liveliness which contributes to the triumphant tone of the whole. Elegiac verse demands extravagant praise, but even within the conventions of compliment, Jonson's tribute is extraordinarily generous. Yet for all its generosity and conventional exaggeration, it is finally a just, critical estimate by a scrupulously honest judge. Jonson's acuity here does both him and Shakespeare credit. The poem convinces and touches because of the sincerity and aptness of its sentiment. The great lines and epithets of the poem have by constant repetition become clichés, but they have been repeated precisely because in them Jonson conveys an accurate appreciation of Shakespeare's genius.

Ben Jonson is one of the two greatest poets of the earlier seventeenth century. In his various art, he mingles public and private concerns, Christian and classical points of view, idealistic and realistic attitudes, celebratory and satirical modes. He captures the fullness of Jacobean society, depicting it as it actually was, alternately sordid and magnificent, debased and robust, corrupt and just, but always measuring it against an exalted vision of human possibilities. Upon everything he wrote, he stamped the impress of his own vivid personality. His notion of the good life is a personal as well as a social ideal, and within his poetic commonwealth he insists upon room for the private emotions. Expressed in a style of passionate plainness admitting of wide tonal range, his individual sensibility is many faceted. Jonson may be the greatest occasional poet in English literature, but the occasions which prompted his poetry were not only public ones, but also personal occasions of love, friendship, and grief.

As a serious writer singlemindedly dedicated to his talent, Jonson thought himself neglected in his own time. *"Poetry,* in this latter Age, hath prov'd but a meane *Mistresse,* to such as have wholly addicted themselves to her . . ." (*Disc.*, ll. 622–24). He offered his work to posterity, confident of its verdict: "An other Age, or juster men, will acknowledge the vertues of his studies: his wisdome, in dividing: his subtilty, in arguing: with what strength hee doth inspire his Readers; with what sweetnesse hee strokes them: in inveighing, what sharpnesse; in Jest, what urbanity hee uses. How he doth raigne in mens affections; how invade, and breake in upon them; and makes their minds like the thing he writes. Then in his Elocution to behold, what word is proper: which hath ornament: which height: what is beautifully translated: where figures are fit: which gentle, which strong to shew the composition *Manly*. And how hee hath avoyded faint, obscure, obscene, sordid, humble, improper, or effeminate *Phrase* . . ." (*Disc.*, ll. 786–99). The very qualities Jonson enunciates here are those which distinguish his own carefully wrought poetry. They can be seen most clearly in the brilliant and affecting epigrams, the dignified yet familiar odes and epistles, the graceful and elegant songs, the touching and dramatic explorations of the need to love. These varied poems honestly earn Ben Jonson the immortality he honestly sought.

CHAPTER 6

Jonson's Reputation

WHEN Ben Jonson died in 1637, he was recognized as the greatest man of letters his age had produced. His death was greeted by an outpouring of elegies and commemorative tributes which mourned him, in English, Latin, and Greek, as "the most Excellent of English *Poets*," the "Mirror of our *Age!*" and the law-giver to the stage.[1] Even in a period of extravagant commemorative verse, this praise from fellow poets is extraordinary. More significantly, it is a measure of the position Jonson enjoyed late in his life as "rare Ben Jonson," a unique literary personality who had influenced a host of lyric and dramatic disciples. Indeed, apart from his own work, Jonson's greatest legacy is the pervasive influence he exerted on his contemporaries and "Sons."[2] The "Tribe of Ben" included poets as individual and accomplished as Robert Herrick, Thomas Carew, Sir John Suckling, and Richard Lovelace, as well as such fine lesser voices as Thomas Randolph, Richard Corbett, James Shirley, and William Habington. But Jonson's influence reached further than those who, like Herrick, recall with such vividness "those *Lyrick* Feasts" at London taverns "Where we such clusters had, / As made us nobly wild, not mad."[3] Almost no poet of the earlier seventeenth century escaped the impact of Jonson's humanist vision. It affected the whole age, even exerting influence on John Donne and touching the still greater genius of John Milton.

I *From Dryden to Eliot*

Jonson's best early critic is John Dryden, whose generous estimate concludes with what had already become almost obligatory, a comparison of Jonson and Shakespeare: "If I would compare him with Shakespeare, I must acknowledge him the more correct poet, but Shakespeare the greater wit. Shakespeare was the Homer, or father of our dramatic poets; Jonson was the Virgil, the pattern of elaborate

writing; I admire him, but I love Shakespeare."[4] Although Jonson
might well have appreciated being likened to Vergil, the ideal poet of
Poetaster, Dryden's comparison established the terms by which
Jonson's reputation precipitously declined in the eighteenth century,
a decline which has been reversed only recently. The most popular
comedies continued to be produced throughout much of the
eighteenth century, but Jonson—both the man and the artist—was
sacrificed upon the altar of Shakespearean bardolatry. The bar-
dolators attacked Jonson as a means of praising Shakespeare. As Jonas
Barish has observed, they came "to see in Shakespeare a Christ
figure, and in Jonson both the Judas and the mob demanding blood."[5]

The polemicist William Gifford, who in 1816 issued the first
scholarly edition of Jonson's works, largely silenced the attacks on the
poet's character.[6] But with the rise of Romanticism, the decline of
Jonson's artistic reputation accelerated in the nineteenth century.
The plays were produced less often than in the previous century, and
the poetry utterly failed to satisfy the Romantic appreciation of the
exquisite sensibility belonging to a more aureate tradition. To
nineteenth-century readers, Jonson seemed to lack those qualities
they valued most highly: a soaring imagination, a delicate tone, a
unique soul. His realism was seen as a failure of inspiration and an
inability to convey psychological subtleties. Although praised as a
dramatist and poet of learning and self-conscious classicism, he was
dismissed as a plodding pedant, devoid of the "natural" gift of lyric so
abundant in Shakespeare; and even his learning sometimes became
evidence of his lack of originality.

The nineteenth century did, however, produce some defenses of
the poet other than those of Gifford and his scholar friend Octavius
Gilchrist. Critics as diverse as Coleridge and J. A. Symonds offered
incidental appreciations.[7] Colonel Francis Cunningham revised and
reissued Gifford's edition in 1875,[8] and in 1889, Algernon Charles
Swinburne published *A Study of Ben Jonson*. Although an eccentric
critic too limited by his own impressionistic ardor, itself the product
of late Victorian sentimentality, Swinburne deeply appreciated
Jonson. Much of his book recapitulates standard critical prejudices,
as does his opening sentence, which draws the inevitable contrast
between Shakespeare and Jonson in terms of a distinction between
"gods of harmony and creation" and "giants of energy and invention":
"the supremacy of Shakespeare among the gods of English verse is
not more unquestionable than the supremacy of Jonson among its
giants."[9] But if Swinburne felt that Jonson was deficient in imagina-

tion and passion, he fully credited his "weight of matter, the solidity of meaning, the significance and purpose of the thing suggested or presented." And he affirmed that the author of *Discoveries* "was in every way worthy to have been the friend of Bacon and of Shakespeare."[10] Despite Swinburne's efforts, however, Jonson in the nineteenth century became a figure to be consigned to literary history, a footnote rather than a living author to be reinterpreted by each new generation. Thus T. S. Eliot began his 1919 essay on Jonson by remarking that his reputation "has been of the most deadly kind that can be compelled upon the memory of a great poet. To be universally accepted; to be damned by the praise that quenches all desire to read the book; to be afflicted by the imputation of the virtues which excite the least pleasure; and to be read only by historians and antiquaries—this is the most perfect conspiracy of approval."[11]

II   *The Current View*

In the twentieth century, Jonson's reputation has undergone a remarkable recovery, due largely to a number of academic critics who have appreciated the artist on his own terms.[12] The modernist reaction against the late Romantic sensibility and Eliot's critical belief that poetry should transform individual feeling into generalized truth set the stage for a sympathetic revaluation of Jonson's achievement as playwright and poet. Eliot called for "intelligent saturation in Jonson's work as a whole" as the necessary prerequisite for a new appreciation of him.[13] This task was made immeasurably easier by the massive scholarly edition of C. H. Herford and Percy and Evelyn Simpson, issued in eleven volumes between 1925 and 1952. Twentieth-century studies of Jonson have revealed the accuracy of the plays' depiction of the men and women of seventeenth-century England, their mastery of form and seriousness of purpose. The masques have come to be seen as more than ephemeral spectacles and to be appreciated for their combination of the topical and the transcendent. More recently, the nondramatic poetry, which had been eclipsed by Donne's, has been recognized as remarkable in its "range and strength and art," its dignity and scope.[14]

Jonson is among the greatest writers in English literature. Of the poets and playwrights of his own time, he yields place only to Shakespeare and Milton. A professional man of letters, whose livelihood derived directly or indirectly from his pen, he always looked beyond his own age, self-consciously writing for posterity. He took seriously the moral obligations of art, yet he is serious without being sober, moral without being grim. A literary critic and theorist, he imposed discipline on his work but did not sacrifice either spontaneity or vigor. More vividly than anyone else, he sketched the manners of his age, yet he probed beneath the superficial and the transient to reveal universal longings and common failings. A satirist who excoriated vice and folly, he is also supremely a poet of human possibilities. He never lost his "faith in things" (*U.* 14, 1. 36), and his humanist vision expressed "the life of man in fit measure, numbers, and harmony" (*Disc.*, ll. 2349–50). The variety and quality of his achievement merit the respect of all who love literature. More pointedly, the greatness of his art entitles Jonson to the "legitimate fame" (*E.* 17, 1. 3) he sought from intelligent readers.

Notes and References

Chapter One

1. For detailed accounts of the times during which Jonson lived, see the relevant volumes of The Oxford History of England: J. B. Black, *The Reign of Elizabeth, 1558–1603*, 2d ed. (Oxford, 1959); and Godfrey Davies, *The Early Stuarts, 1603–1660*, 2d ed. (Oxford, 1959). Also of value are the briefer studies in The Pelican History of England: S. T. Bindoff, *Tudor England* (Baltimore, Md., 1950); and Maurice Ashley, *England in the Seventeenth Century*, 2d ed. (Baltimore, Md., 1954). On Jonson's detailed knowledge of the social, political, economic, and religious currents of his day, see L. C. Knights, *Drama and Society in the Age of Jonson* (London, 1937; reprinted New York, 1968).

2. Of the rich scholarship on the theaters, the acting companies, and the audiences of Jonson's day, see, e.g., John Tucker Murray, *English Dramatic Companies, 1558–1642*, 2 vols. (Boston, 1910; reprinted New York, 1963); J. Q. Adams, *Shakespearean Playhouses* (Boston, 1917); Alfred Harbage, *Shakespeare's Audience* (New York, 1941); M. C. Bradbrook, *The Rise of the Common Player: A Study of Actor and Society in Shakespeare's England* (London, 1962); and G. E. Bentley, *The Jacobean and Caroline Stage*, 7 vols. (Oxford, 1941–68).

3. Letter of the papal secretary of state Cardinal Como to the papal nuncio in Madrid, written in December of 1580; quoted in Black, *The Reign of Elizabeth*, p. 178.

4. William Camden, *The Historie of the Most Renowned and Victorious Princesse Elizabeth, Late Queen of England* (i.e., *Annales rerum Anglicarum . . . regnante Elizabetha*), trans. Robert Norton (London, 1630), Book 2, pp. 68–69.

5. Volume I of H. & S. has a detailed life of Jonson; and it prints *Conversations with Drummond*, John Aubrey's notes on Jonson, and legal and official documents relating to the poet. Volume XI contains supplemental notes to Jonson's life and a reprint of Thomas Fuller's charming but brief and unreliable biography (1662). Marchette Chute's *Ben Jonson of Westminster* (New York, 1953) is a very readable lengthy account.

6. J. B. Leishman, ed., *The Three Parnassus Plays, 1598–1601* (London, 1949), I.ii.293, 296–99; reprinted in H. & S., XI, 364. Frank L. Huntley has recently argued strongly for Joseph Hall's authorship of the second part of

The Returne; see his *Bishop Joseph Hall, 1574–1656: A Biographical and Critical Study* (Cambridge, England, 1978), pp. 29–45.

7. Alexander Gill the younger, "Uppon Ben Jonsons Magnettick Ladye," Bodleian MS. Ashmole 38, p. 15, ll. 52–56; printed in H. & S., XI, 346–48.

8. Jonson may have had other children; see Mark Eccles, "Jonson's Marriage," *Review of English Studies,* 12 (1936), 257–72, and the cautionary discussion of Eccles' findings and conclusions in H. & S., XI, 574–77.

9. G. E. Bentley, "Ben Jonson," in *The Jacobean and Caroline Stage,* IV, 618, 625.

10. The citation is printed in H. & S., I, 220–22.

11. G. E. Bentley, *The Profession of Dramatist in Shakespeare's Time, 1590–1642* (Princeton, N.J., 1971), pp. 227–34.

12. Ibid., pp. 30–32.

13. Jonas A. Barish, "Jonson and the Loathed Stage," in *A Celebration of Ben Jonson,* ed. William Blissett et al. (Toronto, 1973), p. 38.

14. See Bentley, *Profession,* pp. 51–53.

15. Anonymous; first printed in *Wits Recreations* (London, 1640) as epigram 269, but circulated in manuscript much earlier.

16. W. David Kay, "The Shaping of Ben Jonson's Literary Career: A Reexamination of Facts and Problems," *Modern Philology,* 67 (1970), 236.

17. For an excellent discussion of Drummond's assessment of Jonson's personality, and of *Conversations* in general, see Ralph S. Walker, "Literary Criticism in Jonson's Conversations with Drummond," *English,* 8 (1951), 222–27.

18. Inigo Jones, "To his false friend mr: Ben Johnson," British Library MS. Harleian 6057, fol. 30, l. 42; printed in H. & S., XI, 385–86.

19. Robert Herrick, "His Prayer to Ben Johnson," *The Complete Poetry of Robert Herrick,* ed. J. Max Patrick (New York, 1963), p. 282.

20. Sir Edward Walker, Garter, August 17, 1637; quoted in H. & S., I, 115.

21. These are the labels of the two parts of the collection of satiric poems that apparently touched off the vogue for satire in the late 1590s, Joseph Hall's *Virgidemiarum* (1597–98); see Huntley, *Bishop Joseph Hall,* pp. 10–26. Cf. Jonson's acknowledgment of his own reputation for satirical bite: "And, howsoever I cannot escape, from some, the imputation of sharpnesse, but that they will say, I have taken a pride, or lust, to be bitter, and not my youngest infant but hath come into the world with all his teeth . . ." (*Vol.,* Dedication, ll. 47–50).

22. For a discussion of Jonson's critical principles, see the introduction to James D. Redwine, Jr., ed., *Ben Jonson's Literary Criticism* (Lincoln, Neb., 1970); this volume selects and categorizes various critical comments and passages from throughout Jonson's canon.

23. Douglas Bush, *English Literature in the Earlier Seventeenth Century, 1600–1660,* 2d ed., rev. (Oxford, 1962), p. 111.

Chapter Two

1. For detailed information on the social background of Jonson's comedies, see Knights, *Drama and Society.*

2. For some of the remarks by Jonson's contemporaries, see D. Heyward Brock's introduction to the Scolar facsimile of *The Workes of Benjamin Jonson, 1616* (London, 1976), p. [iii].

3. On this point, see Gabriele Bernhard Jackson, *Vision and Judgment in Ben Jonson's Drama* (New Haven, Conn., 1968), pp. 57–69.

4. See Edward B. Partridge, *The Broken Compass: A Study of the Major Comedies of Ben Jonson* (London, 1958); and Jonas A. Barish, *Ben Jonson and the Language of Prose Comedy* (Cambridge, Mass., 1960; reprinted New York, 1970).

5. H. & S., I, 288. Some scholars date the original version of the play later; see L. A. Beaurline, *Jonson and Elizabethan Comedy* (San Marino, Cal., 1978), p. 275. The best discussion of the play is J. A. Bryant, Jr., *The Compassionate Satirist: Ben Jonson and His Imperfect World* (Athens, Ga., 1972), pp. 160–80.

6. See John Jacob Enck, "*The Case Is Altered:* Initial Comedy of Humours," *Studies in Philology,* 50 (1953), 195–214; reworked and condensed in Enck's *Jonson and the Comic Truth* (Madison, Wis., 1957), pp. 21–33. The date of *The Case Is Altered* is usually ascribed to 1598, but Kay suggests 1597 as the more likely date in "The Shaping of Ben Jonson's Career," pp. 226–27.

7. See Joseph A. Bryant, Jr., "Jonson's Revision of *Every Man in His Humour,*" *Studies in Philology,* 59 (1962), 641–50; A. Richard Dutton, "The Significance of Jonson's Revision of 'Every Man in His Humour,' " *Modern Language Review,* 69 (1974), 241–49; and Ralph Alan Cohen, "The Importance of Setting in the Revision of *Every Man in His Humour,*" *English Literary Renaissance,* 8 (1978), 183–96.

8. See Chapter Two of Judd Arnold, *A Grace Peculiar: Ben Jonson's Cavalier Heroes* (University Park, Penn., 1972), especially pp. 16–17.

9. Edward B. Partridge, "Ben Jonson: The Makings of the Dramatist (1596–1602)," in *Elizabethan Theatre,* Stratford-upon-Avon Studies No. 9 (London, 1966), p. 228; see also Lawrence L. Levin, "Clement Justice in *Every Man in His Humor,*" *Studies in English Literature,* 12 (1972), 291–307.

10. For provocative discussions of the comical satires, see Alvin Kernan, *The Cankered Muse: Satire of the English Renaissance* (New Haven, Conn., 1959), pp. 156–64; C. G. Thayer, *Ben Jonson: Studies in the Plays* (Norman, Okla., 1963), pp. 25–49; Robert E. Knoll, *Ben Jonson's Plays: An Introduction* (Lincoln, Neb., 1964), pp. 45–65; R. B. Parker, "The Problem of Tone in Jonson's 'Comicall Satyrs,' " *Humanities Association Bulletin,* 28 (1977), 43–64; and Beaurline, *Jonson and Elizabethan Comedy,* pp. 110–55. On the importance of the comical satires to Jonson's literary career and on their

critical and popular reception by his contemporaries, see Kay, "The Shaping of Ben Jonson's Career," pp. 229–37.

11. See E. M. Thron, "Jonson's *Cynthia's Revels*: Multiplicity and Unity," *Studies in English Literature*, 11 (1971), 235–47.

12. See Ernest William Talbert, "The Purpose and Technique of Jonson's *Poetaster*," *Studies in Philology*, 42 (1945), 225–52; and Eugene M. Waith, "The Poet's Morals in Jonson's *Poetaster*," *Modern Language Quarterly*, 12 (1952), 13–19.

13. D. A. Scheve, "Jonson's *Volpone* and Traditional Fox Lore," *Review of English Studies*, N.S. 1 (1950), 242–44; amplified by Charles A. Hallett, "The Satanic Nature of Volpone," *Philological Quarterly*, 49 (1970), 41–55. See also R. B. Parker, "*Volpone* and *Reynard the Fox*," *Renaissance Drama*, N.S. 7 (1976), 3–42.

14. Although some of its readings are unconvincing, see S. L. Goldberg, "Folly into Crime: The Catastrophe of *Volpone*," *Modern Language Quarterly*, 20 (1959), 233–42.

15. See C. J. Gianakaris, "Identifying Ethical Values in *Volpone*," *Huntington Library Quarterly*, 32 (1963), 45–57. Cf. A. K. Nardo, "The Transmigration of Folly: Volpone's Innocent Grotesques," *English Studies*, 58 (1977), 105–109, which argues that Nano, Androgyno, and Castrone are the only characters in the play who neither gull others nor are themselves victimized.

16. For other thematic ties between the plots, see Jonas A. Barish, "The Double Plot in *Volpone*," *Modern Philology*, 51 (1953), 83–92; Judd Arnold, "The Double Plot in *Volpone*: A Note on Jonsonian Structure," *Seventeenth-Century News*, 23 no. 4 (1965), 47–48, 50–52; and Dorothy E. Litt, "Unity of Theme in *Volpone*," *Bulletin of the New York Public Library*, 73 (1969), 218–26.

17. See Charles A. Hallett, "Jonson's Celia: A Reinterpretation of *Volpone*," *Studies in Philology*, 68 (1961), 50–69; Ian Donaldson, "Volpone: Quick and Dead," *Essays in Criticism*, 21 (1971), 123–24; and the answer to Donaldson in G. A. E. Parfitt, "Volpone," *Essays in Criticism*, 21 (1971), 411–12.

18. See Arnold, *A Grace Peculiar*, p. 45. But for a contrary view, see John Creaser, "A Vindication of Sir Politic Would-be," *English Studies*, 57 (1976), 503–14.

19. But see Alexander Leggatt, "The Suicide of Volpone," *University of Toronto Quarterly*, 39 (1969), 19–32; and Stephen J. Greenblatt, "The False Ending in *Volpone*," *Journal of English and Germanic Philology*, 75 (1976), 90–104.

20. See Harriet Hawkins, "Folly, Incurable Disease, and *Volpone*," *Studies in English Literature*, 8 (1968), 335–48.

21. John Dryden, "An Essay of Dramatic Poesy," in *Essays of John Dryden*, ed. W. P. Ker, 2 vols. (Oxford, 1900; reprinted New York, 1961), I, 83. But see also Freda L. Townsend, *Apologie for Bartholomew Fayre: The*

Art of Jonson's Comedies (New York, 1947), pp. 91–97; and Ray L. Heffner, Jr., "Unifying Symbols in the Comedy of Ben Jonson," in *English Stage Comedy*, ed. W. K. Wimsatt, Jr. (New York, 1955), pp. 74–97.

22. Knoll, *Ben Jonson's Plays*, p. 115.

23. The best discussion of the gallants is in Arnold, *A Grace Peculiar*, pp. 47–54. But cf. Bryant, *The Compassionate Satirist*, pp. 92–111.

24. Dryden, "An Essay of Dramatic Poesy," I, 86.

25. See, for example, Edmund Wilson, "Morose Ben Jonson," in *The Triple Thinkers*, rev. ed. (New York, 1948), pp. 213–14.

26. First discussed extensively in Partridge, *The Broken Compass*, pp. 161–77.

27. For example, Knoll, *Ben Jonson's Plays*, p. 110.

28. Partridge, *The Broken Compass*, pp. 162–65; and Knoll, *Ben Jonson's Plays*, pp. 111–13.

29. Partridge, *The Broken Compass*, p. 165.

30. See Alvin B. Kernan, "Alchemy and Acting: The Major Plays of Ben Jonson," *Studies in the Literary Imagination*, 6 no. 1 (1973), 4–8.

31. On the recent tendency to ignore the play's good humor, see Richard Levin's excellent corrective, " 'No Laughing Matter': Some New Readings of *The Alchemist*," *Studies in the Literary Imagination*, 6 no. 1 (1973), 85–99. See also Donald Gertmenian, "Comic Experience in *Volpone* and *The Alchemist*," *Studies in English Literature*, 17 (1977), 247–58.

32. See Edgar Hill Duncan, "Jonson's *Alchemist* and the Literature of Alchemy," *Publications of the Modern Language Association*, 61 (1946), 699–710; the valuable Appendix I, "Jonson's Use of Alchemy and a Glossary of Alchemical Terms," in Alvin B. Kernan, ed., *Ben Jonson: The Alchemist*, The Yale Ben Jonson no. 7 (New Haven, Conn., and London, 1974), pp. 227–39; and Michael Flachman, "Ben Jonson and the Alchemy of Satire," *Studies in English Literature*, 17 (1977), 259–80.

33. See Johnstone Parr, "Non-Alchemical Pseudo-Sciences in *The Alchemist*," *Philological Quarterly*, 24 (1945), 85–89.

34. Jackson, *Vision and Judgment*, p. 68.

35. On this point see William Blissett, "The Venter Tripartite in *The Alchemist*," *Studies in English Literature*, 8 (1968), 333–34; and Judd Arnold, "Lovewit's Triumph and Jonsonian Morality: A Reading of 'The Alchemist,' " *Criticism*, 11 (1969), 151–66, some of which is incorporated into *A Grace Peculiar*, pp. 56–61.

36. Samuel Taylor Coleridge, "Table Talk," *The Complete Works*, ed. James Shedd, 7 vols. (London, 1871), VI, 426. The other two are Sophocles's *Oedipus Tyrannos* and Henry Fielding's *Tom Jones*.

37. On the play's patterns of separation and reunion, see Richard Levin, "The Structure of *Bartholomew Fair*," *Publications of the Modern Language Association*, 80 (1965), 172–79.

38. Beaurline, *Jonson and Elizabethan Comedy*, p. 252.

39. See Chapter Three, " 'Days of Privilege': *Bartholomew Fair*," in Ian

Donaldson, *The World Upside-Down: Comedy from Jonson to Fielding* (Oxford, 1970), pp. 46–77.

40. Brian Gibbons, *Jacobean City Comedy: A Study of Satiric Plays by Jonson, Marston, and Middleton* (Cambridge, Mass., 1968), p. 186.

41. Donaldson, *The World Upside-Down*, p. 71. See also W. David Kay, "*Bartholomew Fair:* Ben Jonson in Praise of Folly," *English Literary Renaissance*, 6 (1976), 299–316.

42. For detailed information concerning Jacobean monopolies and projectors and Jonson's accuracy in depicting them, see Knights, *Drama and Society*, especially pp. 71–88, 210–18.

43. For extended, generally sympathetic treatments of the play, see, e.g., Thayer, *Ben Jonson*, pp. 156–77; Larry S. Champion, *Ben Jonson's "Dotages": A Reconsideration of the Late Plays* (Lexington, Ky., 1967), pp. 22–44; and Gibbons, *Jacobean City Comedy*, pp. 192–99.

44. For an excellent discussion of this aspect of the play, see Devra Rowland Kifer, "*The Staple of News:* Jonson's Festive Comedy," *Studies in English Literature*, 12 (1972), 329–44. Also provocative are the analyses in Richard Levin, "The Staple of News, The Society of Jeerers, and Canters' College," *Philological Quarterly*, 44 (1965), 445–53; and Champion, *Ben Jonson's "Dotages*," pp. 45–75.

45. Knights, *Drama and Society*, p. 223.

46. This idea was first developed in Harriet Hawkins, "The Idea of a Theater in Jonson's *The New Inn*," *Renaissance Drama*, 9 (1966), 205–26.

47. In addition to the Hawkins study cited above, see, e.g., Partridge, *The Broken Compass*, pp. 189–205; Thayer, *Ben Jonson*, pp. 198–232; Champion, *Ben Jonson's "Dotages*," pp. 76–103; Douglas Duncan, "A Guide to *The New Inn*," *Essays in Criticism*, 20 (1970), 311–26; and Beaurline, *Jonson and Elizabethan Comedy*, pp. 256–75. But see also Richard Levin's protest, "The New *New Inn* and the Proliferation of Good Bad Drama," *Essays in Criticism*, 22 (1972), 41–47.

48. The most sympathetic discussion of the play is in Champion, *Ben Jonson's "Dotages*," pp. 104–30; and there are valuable analyses in Partridge, *The Broken Compass*, 205–12; and Thayer, *Ben Jonson*, pp. 232–46.

Chapter Three

1. Jonson may have written several tragedies early in his career. Francis Meres in his *Palladis Tamia* (entered in the Stationers' Register on September 7, 1598) includes Jonson among the best contemporary tragic playwrights, and Jonson collaborated with other authors on several tragedies. On this point, and for interesting speculation as to why Jonson may have suppressed his early tragedies, see Kay, "The Shaping of Ben Jonson's Career," pp. 225–26.

2. On this point, see Robert Ornstein, *The Moral Vision of Jacobean Tragedy* (Madison, Wis., 1965), pp. 85–86.

3. See Joseph A. Bryant, Jr., "The Significance of Ben Jonson's First Requirement for Tragedy: 'Truth of Argument,' " *Studies in Philology*, 49 (1952), 195–213; and A. Richard Dutton, "The Sources, Text, and Readers of *Sejanus:* Jonson's 'integrity in the Story,' " *Studies in Philology*, 75 (1978), 181–98.

4. For an interesting account of the topical applications of history and drama, see the first chapter of B. N. DeLuna, *Jonson's Romish Plot: A Study of Catiline and Its Historical Context* (Oxford, 1967), pp. 1–30.

5. Marvin L. Vawter, "The Seeds of Virtue: Political Imperatives in Jonson's *Sejanus,*" *Studies in the Literary Imagination*, 6 no. 1 (1973), 41–60. See also George A. E. Parfitt, "Virtue and Pessimism in Three Plays by Ben Jonson," *Studies in the Literary Imagination*, 6 no. 1 (1973), 23–40; Frederick Kiefer, "Pretense in Ben Jonson's *Sejanus,*" *Essays in Literature*, 4 (1977), 19–26; and Dutton, "The Sources, Text, and Readers of *Sejanus.*"

6. J. W. Lever, *The Tragedy of State* (London, 1971), p. 66.

7. On Jonson's interpretation of history in *Catiline*, see Joseph A. Bryant, Jr., "*Catiline* and the Nature of Jonson's Tragic Fable," *Publications of the Modern Language Association*, 69 (1954), 265–77.

8. Cf. Ornstein, *The Moral Vision of Jacobean Tragedy*, pp. 102–103.

9. DeLuna, *Jonson's Romish Plot*, argues that "*Catiline* . . . was both intended and in some circles understood as a classical parallelograph on the Gunpowder Plot of 1605 . . ." (p. 360).

Chapter Four

1. On the development of the masque and its conventions, see, e.g., Enid Welsford, *The Court Masque: A Study in the Relationship between Poetry & the Revels* (Cambridge, England, 1927; reprinted New York, 1962); Allardyce Nicoll, *Stuart Masques and the Renaissance Stage* (London, 1937); and Stephen Orgel, *The Illusion of Power: Political Theater in the English Renaissance* (Berkeley, Cal., 1975). The two fullest and most influential studies of Jonson's masques are Stephen Orgel, *The Jonsonian Masque* (Cambridge, Mass., 1965); and John C. Meagher, *Method and Meaning in Jonson's Masques* (Notre Dame, Ind., 1966). Other useful studies include Ernest W. Talbert, "The Interpretation of Jonson's Courtly Spectacles," *Publications of the Modern Language Association*, 61 (1946), 454–73; Dolora Cunningham, "The Jonsonian Masque as a Literary Form," *Journal of English Literary History*, 22 (1955), 108–24; W. Todd Furniss, "Ben Jonson's Masques," in *Three Studies in the Renaissance: Sidney, Jonson, Milton* (New Haven, Conn., 1958), pp. 89–179; Stephen Orgel, "To Make Boards to Speak: Inigo Jones's Stage and the Jonsonian Masque," *Renaissance Drama*, N.S. 1 (1968), 121–52, revised and expanded as "Introduction" in his edition, *Ben Jonson: The Complete Masques* (New Haven, Conn., 1969), pp. 1–44; and M. C. Bradbrook, "Social Change and the Evolution of Ben Jonson's Court Masques," *Studies in the Literary Imagination*, 6. no. 1 (1973), 101–38.

2. On Jonson's collaboration with Jones, and their quarrel, see D. J. Gordon, "Poet and Architect: The Intellectual Setting of the Quarrel between Ben Jonson and Inigo Jones," *Journal of the Warburg and Courtauld Institutes*, 8 (1945), 107–45; and Stephen Orgel and Roy Strong, *Inigo Jones: The Theater of the Stuart Court*, 2 vols. (Berkeley, Cal., 1973).

3. Sir Francis Bacon, "Of Praise," *The Essayes* (London, 1625; reprinted Menston, England, 1971), pp. 305–306.

4. Orgel, *The Illusion of Power*, p. 40.

5. Barish, *Ben Jonson and the Language of Prose Comedy*, p. 244.

6. An atypical but telling example of Jonson's daring in this regard is *The Gypsies Metamorphosed* (1621), where the poet may have intended to warn the king of the prodigality of his favorite, the Earl (later Duke) of Buckingham, who commissioned the masque. See the fascinating book by Dale B. J. Randall, *Jonson's Gypsies Unmasked: Background and Theme of* The Gypsies Metamorphos'd (Durham, N.C., 1975). An excellent study of the topical nature of Jonson's masques is Leah Sinanoglou Marcus, " 'Present Occasions' and the Shaping of Ben Jonson's Masques," *Journal of English Literary History*, 45 (1978), 201–25.

7. See, e.g., D. J. Gordon, "The Imagery of Ben Jonson's 'The Masque of Blacknesse' and 'The Masque of Beautie,' " *Journal of the Warburg and Courtauld Institutes*, 6 (1943), 122–41; Allan H. Gilbert, *The Symbolic Persons in the Masques of Ben Jonson* (Durham, N.C., 1948; reprinted New York, 1969); and Furniss, "Ben Jonson's Masques." Meagher's *Method and Meaning* is perhaps the best study of Jonson's assimilation of a wide variety of philosophical influences. Much of the symbolism in Jonson's masques is derived from popular mythographical handbooks, such as Cesare Ripa's *Iconologia*, Natilis Comes's *Mythologia*, and Vicenzo Cartari's *Imagini*.

8. Luckily, many of Jones's designs survive and are often reproduced. In their lavishly illustrated and beautifully printed *Inigo Jones*, Orgel and Strong reproduce many of Jones's sketches for masques. Orgel's distillation of that work, *The Illusion of Power*, includes photographs of three of Jones's designs for *The Masque of Queens:* the costume of one of the masquers, the headdress worn by Queen Anne, and a sketch of the House of Fame.

9. On this point, see Meagher, *Method and Meaning*, pp. 155–56.

10. See Orgel's introduction to *The Complete Masques*, pp. 9–25. But, as pointed out in Bruce Louis Jay, "The Role of Verse and the Dynamics of Form in Jonson's Masques," *Études Anglaises*, 29 (1976), 129–43, "Jonson's resistance to the encroaching glitter of Jones' spectacles was compromised by the royal taste and his own slim pocketbook" (p. 141).

11. For an excellent discussion of *Oberon*, see Jay, "The Role of Verse," pp. 136–38.

12. See Willa McClung Evans, *Ben Jonson and Elizabethan Music* (Lancaster, Penn., 1929; reprinted New York, 1965), pp. 78–121.

13. Orgel, *The Jonsonian Masque*, p. 162.

14. For an excellent discussion of the relationship between *Pleasure Reconciled to Virtue* and "A Maske," see ibid., pp. 151–53.

Chapter Five

1. Useful comparisons of Donne and Jonson include J. B. Leishman, *The Monarch of Wit* (London, 1951; reprinted New York, 1966), pp. 11–29; Wesley Trimpi, *Ben Jonson's Poems: A Study of the Plain Style* (Palo Alto, Cal., 1962), pp. 1–40; and Joseph H. Summers, *The Heirs of Donne and Jonson* (New York and London, 1970), pp. 13–40.

2. On Jonson's classicism, see, e.g., George A. E. Parfitt, "Compromise Classicism: Language and Rhythm in Ben Jonson's Poetry," *Studies in English Literature*, 11 (1971), 109–23; and Earl Miner, *The Cavalier Mode from Jonson to Cotton* (Princeton, N. J., 1971), pp. 84–99.

3. On this point, see Geoffrey Walton, "The Tone of Ben Jonson's Poetry," in *Metaphysical to Augustan* (London, 1955), pp. 23–44; Hugh Maclean, "Ben Jonson's Poems: Notes on the Ordered Society," in *Essays in English Literature from the Renaissance to the Victorian Age, Presented to A. S. P. Woodhouse*, ed. Millar MacLure and F. Watt (Toronto, 1964), pp. 43–68; L. C. Knights, "Ben Jonson: Public Attitudes and Social Poetry," in *A Celebration of Ben Jonson*, ed. William Blissett, Julian Patrick, and R. W. Van Fossen (Toronto, 1973), pp. 167–87; and Anthony Mortimer, "The Feigned Commonwealth in the Poetry of Ben Jonson," *Studies in English Literature*, 13 (1973), 69–79.

4. For discussions of Jonson's style, see Trimpi, *Ben Jonson's Poems*, pp. 96–237; G. A. E. Parfitt, "The Poetry of Ben Jonson," *Essays in Criticism*, 18 (1968), 18–31; William V. Spanos, "The Real Toad in the Jonsonian Garden: Resonance in the Nondramatic Poetry," *Journal of English and Germanic Philology*, 68 (1969), 1–23; Arthur F. Marotti, "All About Jonson's Poetry," *Journal of English Literary History*, 39 (1971), 208–37; and Richard C. Newton, " 'Ben. / Jonson': The Poet in the Poems," in *Two Renaissance Mythmakers: Christopher Marlowe and Ben Jonson*, ed. Alvin Kernan (Baltimore, Md., 1977), pp. 165–95.

5. T. K. Whipple, *Martial and the English Epigram from Sir Thomas Wyatt to Ben Jonson*, University of California Publications in Modern Philology, vol. 10 (Berkeley, Cal., 1925), 387ff.

6. On *Epigrams* as a coherent collection, see Rufus D. Putney, " 'This So Subtile Sport': Some Aspects of Jonson's Epigrams," *University of Colorado Studies*, Series in Language and Literature, 10 (1966), 37–56; David Wykes, "Ben Jonson's 'Chast Booke': The *Epigrammes*," *Renaissance and Modern Studies*, 13 (1969), 76–87; Edward Partridge, "Jonson's *Epigrammes*: The Named and the Nameless," *Studies in the Literary Imagination*, 6 no. 1 (1973), 153–98; Bruce R. Smith, "Ben Jonson's *Epigrammes*: Portrait-Gallery, Theater, Commonwealth," *Studies in English Literature*, 14 (1974),

91–109; R. V. Young, Jr., "Style and Structure in Jonson's Epigrams," *Criticism*, 17 (1975), 201–22; and Judith Kegan Gardiner, *Craftsmanship in Context* (The Hague, 1975), pp. 12–53.

7. See Young, "Style and Structure," pp. 214–15.

8. Robert Burton, *The Anatomy of Melancholy*, ed. Floyd Dell and Paul Jordan Smith (New York, 1955), p. 504.

9. See Young's discussion of this poem, "Style and Structure," pp. 207–208.

10. Partridge, "Jonson's *Epigrammes*," p. 198. See also Achsah Guibbory, "The Poet as Myth Maker: Ben Jonson's Poetry of Praise," *Clio*, 5 (1976), 315–29.

11. Homer, *The Odyssey*, Book I, l. 506, in *Chapman's Homer*, ed. Allardyce Nicoll, 2 vols. (New York, 1956), II, 12.

12. On this point, see Young, "Style and Structure," p. 212. For a discussion of the circle image which figures so prominently in the poem, see Thomas M. Greene, "Ben Jonson and the Centered Self," *Studies in English Literature*, 10 (1970), 325–48.

13. Spanos, "The Real Toad," pp. 6–7.

14. See Richmond Lattimore, *Themes in Greek and Latin Epitaphs* (Urbana, Ill., 1962), pp. 65–74.

15. The Christian context of the poem is discussed by the following: L. A. Beaurline, "The Selective Principle in Jonson's Shorter Poems," *Criticism*, 8 (1966), 64–74, revised and reprinted in *Ben Jonson and the Cavalier Poets*, ed. Hugh Maclean (New York, 1974), pp. 516–25; Francis Fike, "Ben Jonson's 'On My First Sonne,' " *Gordon Review*, 11 (1969), 205–20; W. David Kay, "The Christian Wisdom of Ben Jonson's 'On My First Sonne,' " *Studies in English Literature*, 11 (1971), 125–36; and J. Z. Kronenfeld, "The Father Found: Consolation Achieved through Love in Ben Jonson's 'On My First Sonne,' " *Studies in Philology*, 75 (1978), 64–83.

16. For discussions of "On the Famous Voyage," see J. G. Nichols, *The Poetry of Ben Jonson* (New York, 1969), pp. 105–11; and Peter E. Medine, "Object and Intent in Jonson's 'Famous Voyage,' " *Studies in English Literature*, 15 (1975), 97–110.

17. Summers, *The Heirs of Donne and Jonson*, p. 27.

18. See H. & S., XI, 366–67.

19. See Anne Ferry, *All in War with Time: Love Poetry of Shakespeare, Donne, Jonson, Marvell* (Cambridge, Mass., 1975), pp. 163–68.

20. On the relationship of neoplatonism and Petrarchanism, see Trimpi, *Ben Jonson's Poems*, pp. 280–81, n. 18.

21. H. & S., II, 389.

22. For example, see Nichols, *The Poetry of Ben Jonson*, pp. 23–29; and Summers, *The Heirs of Donne and Jonson*, p. 28.

23. See Beaurline, "The Selective Principle," revised reprint, pp. 523–24.

24. D. J. Palmer, "The Verse Epistle" in *Metaphysical Poetry*, ed. Malcolm Bradbury and David Palmer (London, 1970; reprinted Bloomington, Ind., 1971), p. 73.

25. Studies of the country house poem include G. R. Hibbard, "The Country House Poem of the Seventeenth Century," *Journal of the Warburg and Courtauld Institutes*, 19 (1956), 159–74; Charles Molesworth, "Property and Virtue: The Genre of the Country-House Poem in the Seventeenth Century," *Genre*, 1 (1968), 141–57; and William A. McClung, *The Country House in English Renaissance Poetry* (Berkeley, Cal., 1977).

26. J. C. A. Rathmell, "Jonson, Lord Lisle, and Penshurst," *English Literary Renaissance*, 1 (1971), 250–60. See also Gayle E. Wilson, "Jonson's Use of the Bible and the Great Chain of Being in 'To Penshurst,' " *Studies in English Literature*, 8 (1968), 77–89; Paul Cubeta, "A Jonsonian Ideal: 'To Penshurst,' " *Philological Quarterly*, 42 (1963), 14–24; Jeffrey Hart, "Ben Jonson's Good Society: On the Growth of a Place and a Poem," *Modern Age*, 7 (1963), 61–68; and Alistair Fowler, "The Locality of Jonson's *To Penshurst*," in *Conceitful Thought: The Interpretation of English Renaissance Poems* (Edinburgh, 1975), pp. 114–34.

27. See Lisle Cecil John, "Ben Jonson's 'To Sir William Sydney, on his Birthday,' " *Modern Language Review*, 52 (1957), 168–76.

28. See William Kerrigan, "Ben Jonson Full of Shame and Scorn," *Studies in the Literary Imagination*, 6 no. 1 (1973), 199–217.

29. Augustine, *De Civitate Dei*, I.xvi–xxvii. Cited by Kerrigan, pp. 202, 209.

30. *Biathanatos*, ed. J. William Hebel (New York, 1930), p. 121. Cited by Kerrigan, p. 210.

31. From a treatise on "The Practical Methode of Meditation," prefaced to Richard Gibbons's translation of *An Abridgment of Meditations . . . by the R. Father Vincentius Bruno . . .* (1614), quoted in Louis L. Martz, *The Poetry of Meditation* (New Haven, Conn., 1954), p. 14. See also Paul M. Cubeta, "Ben Jonson's Religious Lyrics," *Journal of English and Germanic Philology*, 62 (1963), 95–110.

32. On this point, see Cubeta, "Ben Jonson's Religious Lyrics," pp. 97–98.

33. Ibid., pp. 103–105.

34. H. & S., II, 392.

35. See A. B. Chambers, "Christmas: The Liturgy of the Church and English Verse of the Renaissance," *Literary Monographs*, vol. 6, ed. Eric Rothstein and Joseph Anthony Wittreich (Madison, Wis., 1975), especially pp. 140–42.

36. As Herford and Simpson explain, "The original is not by Petronius, but it was printed in Linocerius' edition, Paris, 1585. . . ." See H. & S., XI, 109; and Petronius, trans. Michael Heseltine, Loeb Classical Library (London, 1913), pp. 340, 358–61. That Jonson chose to translate this

supposed fragment, so different from the licentiousness of most of Petronius's authentic work, is telling. For an appreciation of Jonson as translator, see Nichols, *The Poetry of Ben Jonson*, pp. 135–37.

37. Baldassare Castiglione, *The Book of the Courtier,* trans. Sir Thomas Hoby, intro. Walter Raleigh (London, 1900; reprinted New York, 1967), p. 344. Subsequent quotations from *The Courtier* are from this edition and are cited by page number in the text.

38. Nicholas Caussin, *The Holy Court: Fourth Tome* (n.p., 1638), sig. A4v. Quoted in Meagher, *Method and Meaning in Jonson's Masques,* p. 126.

39. Hugh Richmond, *The School of Love: The Evolution of the Stuart Love Lyric* (Princeton, N.J., 1964), p. 207.

40. See Ferry, *All in War with Time,* pp. 168–71.

41. Ovid, *Amores* I.ix.3–4. Quoted from *Heroides and Amores,* trans. Grant Showerman, Loeb Classical Library (Cambridge, Mass., 1914), p. 35. In addition to those works of Horace, Ovid, and Castiglione discussed in the text, the *senex amans* debate includes, among other documents, *Anacreontea,* Odes 7 and 51; Plato, *The Symposium;* Cicero, *De Senectute;* Tibullus, I.viii; Seneca, *Epistles* XII and LXVIII; Ficino, *Commentary on Plato's* Symposium. Richard S. Peterson, "Virtue Reconciled to Pleasure: Jonson's 'A Celebration of Charis,' " *Studies in the Literary Imagination,* 6 no. 1 (1973), 219–68, suggests the importance of Ronsard's *Sonnets pour Helene* and of emblematic literature; see p. 221, nn. 3, 4, and 5. Trimpi, *Ben Jonson's Poems,* identifies the aging persona of "My Picture Left in *Scotland*" with Socrates as presented in *The Symposium* and interpreted by Ficino; see p. 228.

42. Patrick Cruttwell, "The Love Poetry of John Donne: Pedantique Weedes or Fresh Invention?" in *Metaphysical Poetry,* ed. Bradbury and Palmer, p. 16.

43. Peterson, "Virtue Reconciled to Pleasure," discusses the motif of secrecy, pp. 259–68. Ovid stresses the need for secrecy in *Ars Amatoria,* II.601–40; Castiglione, throughout *The Courtier,* but especially pp. 284–87. Peterson also suggests Montaigne's essay "Upon some verses of Virgill," Sidney's Songs 8 and 9 from *Astrophil and Stella,* and Chapman's *Ovids Banquet of Sense* as possible influences on Jonson's use of this motif.

44. Because *Underwood* 39 was printed with Donne's *Poems* in 1633, the authenticity of Jonson's authorship of it and of *Underwood* 38, 40, and 41 has sometimes been in doubt. Evelyn Simpson, "Jonson and Donne," *Review of English Studies,* 15 (1939), 274–82, argues convincingly for the ascription of *Underwood* 38, 40, and 41 to Jonson; and this attribution is now generally accepted. *Underwood* 39 probably is not by Jonson. In any event, it does not form part of the sequence under discussion.

45. See Paul Cubeta, " 'A Celebration of Charis': An Evaluation of Jonsonian Poetic Strategy," *Journal of English Literary History,* 25 (1958), 163–80; Trimpi, *Ben Jonson's Poems,* pp. 209–27; G. J. Weinberger, "Jonson's Mock-encomiastic 'Celebration of Charis,' " *Genre,* 4 (1971),

305–28; Peterson, "Virtue Reconciled to Pleasure"; and Sara Van Den Berg, "The Play of Wit and Love: Demetrius' *On Style* and Jonson's 'A Celebration of Charis,' " *Journal of English Literary History*, 41 (1974), 26–36. Peterson's essay and Trimpi's discussion are particularly important.

46. See Ian Donaldson, "Jonson's Ode to Sir Lucius Cary and Sir H. Morison," *Studies in the Literary Imagination*, 6 no. 1 (1973), 139–52; Mary I. Oates, "Jonson's 'Ode Pindarick' and the Doctrine of Imitation, *Papers on Language and Literature*, 11 (1975), 126–48; and Susanne Woods, "Ben Jonson's Cary-Morison Ode: Some Observations on Structure and Form," *Studies in English Literature*, 18 (1978), 57–74.

47. A useful history of this belief is Raymond Crawfurd, *The King's Evil* (Oxford, 1911). Cf. Robert Herrick's "TO THE KING, To Cure the Evill"; and see Claude J. Summers, "Herrick's Political Poetry: The Strategies of His Art," in *"Trust to Good Verses": Herrick Tercentenary Essays*, ed. Roger B. Rollin and J. Max Patrick (Pittsburgh, 1978), pp. 171–83.

Chapter Six

1. Many of these elegies were printed in *Jonsonus Virbius*, a collection compiled by Bishop Brian Duppa (London, 1638), reproduced in H. & S., XI, 428–81. The quotations in the text are from William Habington, p. 446, and Edmund Waller, p. 447. James Clayton begins his tribute by asking, "Who first reform'd our *Stage* with justest *Lawes,/* And was the first best *Judge* in his *owne Cause*" (p. 450).

2. Excellent studies of Jonson's influence on his contemporaries include Douglas Bush, *English Literature in the Earlier Seventeenth Century*, pp. 107–25; Joseph H. Summers, *The Heirs of Donne and Jonson*; and Earl Miner, *The Cavalier Mode from Jonson to Cotton*.

3. Robert Herrick, "An Ode for Him," *The Complete Poetry of Robert Herrick*, ed. Patrick, p. 380.

4. Dryden, "An Essay of Dramatic Poesy," *Essays*, ed. Ker, I, 82–83.

5. Jonas A. Barish, "Introduction," *Ben Jonson: A Collection of Critical Essays* (Englewood Cliffs, N.J., 1963), p. 4. Barish's concise historical survey of Jonson's reputation is very valuable.

6. *The Works of Ben Jonson*, ed. William Gifford, 9 vols. (London, 1816).

7. Coleridge, "Notes on Ben Jonson," *The Complete Works*, ed. Shedd, IV, 185–99; J. A. Symonds, *Ben Jonson*, English Worthies Series (London, 1886).

8. *The Works of Ben Jonson*, ed. William Gifford, with intro. and appendixes by Lieutenant-Colonel Francis Cunningham, 9 vols. (London, 1875).

9. Algernon Charles Swinburne, *A Study of Ben Jonson* (London, 1889); ed. Howard B. Norland (Lincoln, Neb., 1969), p. 3.

10. Ibid., pp. 6, 181.

11. T. S. Eliot, "Ben Jonson," *Selected Essays* (London, 1951), p. 147.

12. The "Introduction" to D. Heyward Brock and James M. Welsh, *Ben Jonson: A Quadricentennial Bibliography* (Metuchen, N.J., 1974), pp. 11–32, surveys the trends in twentieth-century criticism. See also William L. Godshalk, "Ben Jonson" in *The New Intellectuals: A Survey and Bibliography of Recent Studies in English Renaissance Drama*, ed. Terence P. Logan and Denzell S. Smith (Lincoln, Neb., 1977), pp. 3–116.

13. Eliot, "Ben Jonson," p. 148.

14. The quoted phrase is from Summers, *The Heirs of Donne and Jonson*, p. 18.

Selected Bibliography

[Only full-length studies are included here. Readers should also consult important essays cited in "Notes and References."]

PRIMARY SOURCES

1. Important Early Editions

The Workes of Benjamin Jonson. London: William Stansby, 1616; reprinted in facsimile, with an introduction by D. Heyward Brock, London: Scolar, 1976. Contains seven comedies, two tragedies, two collections of poems, and several masques and entertainments.

The Workes of Benjamin Jonson. 2 vols. London: R. Bishop et al., 1640–41. The first volume a reprint of the 1616 *Workes;* the second volume in two parts, the former prepared by Jonson, the latter assembled by Sir Kenelm Digby after Jonson's death.

2. Modern Critical Editions

Ben Jonson. Edited by C. H. Herford and Percy and Evelyn Simpson. 11 vols. Oxford: Clarendon Press, 1925–52. Contains a life, critical and textual introductions to each work, textual notes, commentaries, and corollary materials.

The Yale Ben Jonson. Edited by Alvin B. Kernan and Richard B. Young. In progress. New Haven, Conn.: Yale University Press, 1962–   . The individual volumes edited by noted scholars. Critical introductions, textual notes, and commentaries.

SECONDARY SOURCES

1. Biography and Bibliography

BROCK, D. HEYWARD, and WELSH, JAMES M. *Ben Jonson: A Quadricentennial Bibliography, 1947–1972.* The Scarecrow Author Bibliographies, No. 16. Metuchen, N.J.: Scarecrow, 1974. Supplements the Tannenbaum bibliographies (below). Lists articles, books, dissertations, editions, and some reviews. Many entries annotated. Subject index.

CHUTE, MARCHETTE. *Ben Jonson of Westminster.* New York: Dutton, 1953. Popular, well-written biography, but often questionable in its critical assessments.

TANNENBAUM, SAMUEL A. and DOROTHY R. *Ben Jonson: A Concise Bibliography.* Elizabethan Bibliographies 2. New York: privately printed, 1938. *Supplement*. New York: privately printed, 1947. Reprinted together in *Elizabethan Bibliographies*, vol. 4. Port Washington, N.Y.: Kennikat, 1967. Indispensable, but untrustworthy. Cryptic entries; no annotations.

2. Scholarly and Critical Books and Monographs

ARNOLD, JUDD. *A Grace Peculiar: Ben Jonson's Cavalier Heroes*. The Pennsylvania State University Studies No. 35. University Park: Pennsylvania State University, 1972. Emphasizes the importance of the witty gallants as keys to discerning the tone of many of the comedies. An important corrective.

BAMBOROUGH, J. B. *Ben Jonson*. British Writers and Their Work, No. 112. London and New York: Longmans, 1959; reprinted in the collected British Writers and Their Work, No. 11. Lincoln: University of Nebraska Press, 1966. Brief general introduction to Jonson and his work.
————. *Ben Jonson*. Hutchinson University Library. London: Hutchinson, 1970. An expanded version of the earlier pamphlet. Generally insightful discussions of the plays; slights the nondramatic poetry.

BARISH, JONAS A. *Ben Jonson and the Language of Prose Comedy*. Cambridge, Mass.: Harvard University Press, 1960; reprinted New York: Norton, 1970. Thorough and illuminating study of the complex variety in Jonson's prose comedies; contains incidental important remarks on the verse plays as well.

BEAURLINE, L. A. *Jonson and Elizabethan Comedy: Essays in Dramatic Rhetoric*. San Marino, Cal.: Huntington Library, 1978. Emphasizes the diversity of Jonson's rhetoric and the complexity of audience response demanded by his comedies. Important.

BRYANT, J. A., JR. *The Compassionate Satirist: Ben Jonson and His Imperfect World*. Athens: University of Georgia Press, 1973. Balanced discussion of the comedies; stresses Jonson's abiding faith in goodness.

CHAMPION, LARRY S. *Ben Jonson's "Dotages": A Reconsideration of the Late Plays*. Lexington: University of Kentucky Press, 1967. Sustained attempt to rehabilitate the last four comedies. Provocative insights.

DELUNA, B. N. *Jonson's Romish Plot: A Study of Catiline and Its Historical Context*. Oxford: Clarendon Press, 1967. Argues that *Catiline* was intended as a "parallelograph" on the Gunpowder Plot. Interesting, but not altogether convincing.

DESSEN, ALAN C. *Jonson's Moral Comedy*. Evanston, Ill.: Northwestern University Press, 1971. Discusses Jonson's debt to earlier dramatic modes and emphasizes the moral intention of the comedies.

DONALDSON, IAN. *The World Upside-Down: Comedy from Jonson to Fielding*. Oxford: Clarendon Press, 1970. Discusses *Epicoene* and *Bartholomew Fair* in the context of social disorder; traces Jonson's influence on later comic writing.

ENCK, JOHN J. *Jonson and the Comic Truth*. Madison: University of

Wisconsin Press, 1957. A chronologically arranged discussion of Jonson's achievements in comedy. Emphasizes Jonson's awareness of the ultimate imperfectibility of man and society. Provocative.

FERRY, ANNE. *All in War with Time: Love Poetry of Shakespeare, Donne, Jonson, Marvell*. Cambridge, Mass.: Harvard University Press, 1975. Includes an excellent consideration of Jonson's love poetry.

GARDINER, JUDITH KEGAN. *Craftsmanship in Context: The Development of Ben Jonson's Poetry*. The Hague: Mouton, 1975. Useful study of Jonson's poetic development, emphasizing the distinctive traits of each period of the poet's career.

GIBBONS, BRIAN. *Jacobean City Comedy: A Study of Satiric Plays by Jonson, Marston and Middleton*. Cambridge, Mass.: Harvard University Press, 1968. Discusses Jonson's city comedies from the comical satires through *The Devil Is an Ass*, emphasizing their relationships to Jacobean social, economic, and political life.

JACKSON, GABRIELE BERNHARD. *Vision and Judgment in Ben Jonson's Drama*. Yale Studies in English, Vol. 166. New Haven, Conn.: Yale University Press, 1968. Emphasizes Jonson's view of man's lofty potentiality and his poetic function as judge of human realities. Tends to ignore Jonson's good-humored compromises.

JOHNSTON, GEORGE BURKE. *Ben Jonson: Poet*. Columbia University Studies in English and Comparative Literature, No. 162. New York: Columbia University Press, 1945. An important attempt to revive interest in the nondramatic poetry; dated and impressionistic, but still valuable.

KNIGHTS, L. C. *Drama and Society in the Age of Jonson*. London: Chatto and Windus, 1937; reprinted New York: Norton, 1968. An important, pioneering study of the social and economic structures of Jacobean England as they are embodied in the plays of Jonson, Dekker, Heywood, Middleton, and Massinger. Offers invaluable insights into the drama it discusses.

KNOLL, ROBERT E. *Ben Jonson's Plays: An Introduction*. Lincoln: University of Nebraska Press, 1964. Chronologically arranged readings of the plays. Generally appreciative.

LEVER, J. W. *The Tragedy of State*. London: Methuen, 1971. Contains a provocative discussion of *Sejanus*.

McCLUNG, WILLIAM ALEXANDER. *The Country House in English Renaissance Poetry*. Berkeley: University of California Press, 1977. Important study of the intriguing subgenre initiated by "To Penshurst" and "To Sir Robert Wroth."

MEAGHER, JOHN C. *Method and Meaning in Jonson's Masques*. Notre Dame, Ind.: University of Notre Dame Press, 1966. Especially valuable for its exposition of the philosophical and thematic contexts of the masques.

MINER, EARL. *The Cavalier Mode from Jonson to Cotton*. Princeton, N.J.: Princeton University Press, 1961. Jonson is the central figure in this important critical account of cavalier poetry. Contains sensitive readings of individual poems.

NICHOLS, J. G. *The Poetry of Ben Jonson.* New York: Barnes and Noble, 1969. Interesting and informative study of the nondramatic poetry, emphasizing Jonson's variety and careful craftsmanship.

ORGEL, STEPHEN. *The Illusion of Power: Political Theater in the English Renaissance.* A Quantum Book. Berkeley: University of California Press, 1975. Jonson's masques discussed as the center of this study of theater at the Stuart court.

————. *The Jonsonian Masque.* Cambridge, Mass.: Harvard University Press, 1967. Thorough and perceptive study of Jonson's development as a writer of masques.

ORNSTEIN, ROBERT. *The Moral Vision of Jacobean Tragedy.* Madison: University of Wisconsin Press, 1960. Contains a provocative chapter on Jonson's two tragedies and provides a useful context in which to view them.

PARFITT, GEORGE. *Ben Jonson: Public Poet and Private Man.* London: Dent, 1976. Concentrates on the nondramatic poetry and attempts an integrated view of Jonson's life, social concerns, and artistry. Examines individual works in light of his total achievement.

PARTRIDGE, EDWARD B. *The Broken Compass: A Study of the Major Comedies of Ben Jonson.* London: Chatto and Windus; Cambridge, Mass.: Harvard University Press, 1958. A detailed study of imagery. Occasionally eccentric in its readings, but an important, provocative study.

SUMMERS, JOSEPH H. *The Heirs of Donne and Jonson.* New York and London: Oxford University Press, 1970. Argues that Jonson and Donne jointly influenced nearly all of the poets of the seventeenth century. Important both for its criticism of Jonson's poetry and for its documentation of his influence.

SWINBURNE, ALGERNON CHARLES. *A Study of Ben Jonson.* London: Chatto and Windus, 1889; annotated reprint, edited by Howard B. Norland, Lincoln: University of Nebraska Press, 1969. Highly impressionistic and dated, but offering many valuable insights.

THAYER, C. G. *Ben Jonson: Studies in the Plays.* Norman: University of Oklahoma Press, 1963. Chronologically arranged, appreciative analyses of the plays.

TRIMPI, WESLEY. *Ben Jonson's Poems: A Study of the Plain Style.* Palo Alto, Cal.: Stanford University Press, 1962. The best critical account of the nondramatic poetry and Jonson's characteristic style.

3. Collections of Essays

BARISH, JONAS, ed. *Ben Jonson: A Collection of Critical Essays.* Twentieth-Century Views. Englewood Cliffs, N.J.: Prentice-Hall, 1963. Reprints essays by T. S. Eliot, L. C. Knights, Harry Levin,

Edmund Wilson, C. H. Herford, Jonas Barish, Paul Goodman, Edward B. Partridge, Ray L. Heffner, Jr., Joseph Allen Bryant, Jr., and Dolora Cunningham. The introduction a useful historical survey of Jonson's reputation.

BLISSETT, WILLIAM; PATRICK, JULIAN; and VAN FOSSEN, R. W., eds. *A Celebration of Ben Jonson.* Toronto: University of Toronto Press, 1973. Contains previously unpublished essays by Clifford Leech, Jonas Barish, George Hibbard, D. F. McKenzie, Hugh Maclean, and L. C. Knights.

KERNAN, ALVIN, ed. *Two Renaissance Mythmakers: Christopher Marlowe and Ben Jonson.* Selected Papers from the English Institute, 1975–76, N.S. 1. Baltimore and London: Johns Hopkins University Press, 1977. Contains previously unpublished essays on Jonson by Gabriele Bernhard Jackson, Ian Donaldson, and Richard C. Newton.

THOMAS, MARY OLIVE, ed. "Ben Jonson: Quadricentennial Essays." A special issue of *Studies in the Literary Imagination,* 6 no. 1 (April 1973). Contains previously unpublished essays by Alvin B. Kernan, George A. E. Parfitt, Marvin L. Vawter, L. A. Beaurline, David McPherson, Richard Levin, M. C. Bradbrook, Ian Donaldson, Edward Partridge, William Kerrigan, and Richard S. Peterson.

Index

Adams, J. Q., 207n2
Admiral's Men, 27
Allen, Edward, 145–46
Amaltei, Girolamo, 180
Anacreon, 178, 218n41
Anne of Denmark, queen of James I, 30, 125, 126, 128, 214n8
Apollo Club, 17, 32, 192
Aristotle, 38, 39–40, 110, 140
Arnold, Judd, 209n8; 210nn16, 18; 211nn23, 35
Articles of Religion, 19, 176–77
Aubigny, Esmé Stuart, Seigneur of, 26, 164
Aubigny, Katherine, Lady, 164–65
Aubrey, John, 207n5
Augustine, St., 171, 217n29

Bacon, Sir Francis, 31, 33, 123, 204, 214n3
Barish, Jonas A., 30, 124, 203, 208n13, 209n4, 210n16, 214n5, 219n5
Beaurline, L. A., 92; 209nn5, 10, 211n38, 212n47, 216nn15, 23
Beaumont, Francis, 32, 147
Bedford, Lucy Harington, Countess of, 31, 150–51, 164, 165
Bentley, G. E., 29, 207n2, 208nn9, 11, 12, 14
Bernard of Clairvaux, St., 175
Blackfriars Theater, 58, 99, 101, 104, 107
Blissett, William, 211n35
Bodley, Sir Thomas, 31
Bradbrook, M. C., 207n2, 213n1
Brock, D. Heyward, 209n2, 220n12
Brome, Richard, 29
Bryant, J. A., Jr., 209nn5, 7; 211n23; 213nn3, 7
Buckingham, George Villiers, first Duke of, 24, 214n6
Burbage, James, 18
Burbage, Richard, 49, 112

Burton, Robert, 114, 216n8
Bush, Douglas, 40, 208n23, 219n2

Caesar, Julius, 117, 118–19, 146, 168
Calvin, John, 20, 172
Cambridge University, 25, 61, 70
Camden, William, 23, 25, 136, 147–48, 207n4
Carew, Thomas, 32, 202
Cartari, Vicenzo, 214n7
Cary, Sir Henry, 146
Cary, Sir Lucius. See Falkland
Castiglione, Baldassare, 161, 179–80, 182, 218nn37, 41, 43
Catullus, 40, 161, 162
Caussin, Nicholas, 218n38
Chambers, A. B., 217n35
Champion, Larry S., 212nn43, 44, 47, 48
Chapman, George, 29, 32, 40, 61, 110, 112, 218n43
Charles I, 19, 20, 21, 24, 36, 121, 128, 132, 195, 196–97
Charles II, 196
Chaucer, Geoffrey, 127, 130
Chettle, Henry, 27
Children of the Chapel Royal (also Children of Queen Elizabeth's Chapel and Children of Her Majesty's Revels), 27, 58, 71
Chute, Marchette, 207n5
Cicero, 36–37, 111, 116–19, 134, 135, 169, 218n41
city comedy, 42, 45, 47, 49–51, 57, 58, 61, 80–81, 91, 99, 101
Clayton, James 219n1
Cohen, Ralph Alan, 209n7
Coleridge, Samuel Taylor, 90, 203, 211n35, 219n7
comedy of humors, 45, 47, 48, 49, 53, 58, 64, 73, 76, 107
comedy of manners, 42, 49, 53, 62–63, 64, 70, 71, 80

Comes, Natilis, 214n7
comical satire, 17, 31, 47, 48, *57–61*, 71
Condell, Henry, 35, 49, 112, 198
Corbet, Vincent, 194
Corbett, Richard, 202
Cornwallis, Sir William the elder, 125
Cotton, Sir Robert, 31
country house poem, *166–70*, 217n25
Covell, Lady, 194
Crawfurd, Raymond, 219n47
Creaser, John, 210n18
Cruttwell, Patrick, 183, 218n42
Cubeta, Paul M., 217nn26, 31–33;
218n45
Cunningham, Dolora, 213n1
Cunningham, Colonel Francis, 203,
219n8
Curtain Theater, 49

Davis, John, of Hereford, 139
Dekker, Thomas, 27, 28–29, 59–60, 158
DeLuna, B. N., 213nn4, 9
Digby, Sir Kenelm, 174
Digby, Venetia Stanley, Lady, 194
Dion Cassius, 113, 116
Domitian, Roman emperor, 144
Donaldson, Ian, 210n17, 211–12n39,
212n41, 219n46
Donne, John, 32, 34, 40, *133–34*, 141,
163, 172, 174, 178, 183, 188, 191, 194,
202, 204, 215n1, 217n30, 218nn42,
44
Dorset, Sir Edward Sackville, Earl of,
194
Dryden, John, 71, 72, *202–203*, 210n21,
211n24, 219n4
Drummond, William, of Hawthornden,
25, 27, 28, *34–35*, 134, 137, 144, 158–
59, 167, 176, 197, 208n17; *see also*
Jonson, Ben: *Conversations with
William Drummond of Hawthornden*
Duncan, Douglas, 212n47
Duncan, Edgar Hill, 211n32
Duppa, Brian, 36, 219n1
Dutton, A. Richard, 209n7, 213nn3, 5

Eccles, Mark, 208n8
Edmonds, Clement, 146
Edward VI, 19
Eliot, T. S., 204, 219n11, 220n13

Elizabeth I, 17, 18, 19, 20, 21, 22, 23, 24,
27, 59, 151
Enck, John Jacob, 209n6
epigram, 17, 37, 134, *138–39*
epitaph, 134, *151–55*
Erasmus, Desiderius, 61, 81
Essex, Robert Devereux, second Earl of,
19
Evans, Willa McClung, 214n12

Falkland, Sir Lucius Cary, Viscount,
192–94
Felice, Constanzo, 116
Ferrabosco, Alphonso, 121
Ferry, Anne, 216n19, 218n40
Ficino, Marsilio, 180, 218n41
Fike, Francis, 216n15
Flachman, Michael, 211n32
Fletcher, John, 29
Fowler, Alistair, 217n26
Fuller, Thomas, 207n5
Furniss, W. Todd, 213n1, 214n7

Gardiner, Judith Kegan, 216n6
Gertmenian, Donald, 211n31
Gianakaris, C. J., 210n15
Gibbons, Brian, 93; 212nn40, 43
Gifford, William, 203, 219nn6, 8
Gilbert, Allan H., 214n7
Gilchrist, Octavius, 203
Giles, Thomas, 121, 128
Gill, Alexander the younger, 26, 208n7
Globe Theater, 58, 61, 80
Godshalk, William L., 220n12
Goldberg, S. L., 210n14
Goodyere, Sir Henry, 147
Gordon, D. J., 214nn2, 7
Gower, John, 130
Greenblatt, Stephen J., 210n19
Greene, Thomas M., 216n12
Gregory XII, Pope, 20
Gresham College, 35
Guibbory, Achsah, 216n10
Gunpowder Plot, 20, 119, 146, 213n9

Habington, William, 202, 219n1
Haddington, John Ramsey, Lord, 125
Hall, Joseph, 207–208n6, 208n21
Hallett, Charles A., 210nn13, 17

Harbage, Alfred, 207n2
Hart, Jeffrey, 217n26
Hawkins, Harriet, 210n20, 212n46
Hayward, Edward, 192
Heffner, Ray L., 210–11n21
Heinsius, Daniel, 39–40
Heminges, John, 35, 49, 112, 198
Henry VII, 18
Henry VIII, 19, 22
Henry, Prince of Wales, son of James I,
    129, 168
Herbert, George, 177
Herford, C. H., Percy and Evelyn
    Simpson, eds., *Ben Jonson*, 161, 176,
    204, 207n5, 208n8, 209n5, 216nn18,
    21; 217nn34, 36; 219n1
Herrick, Robert, 32, 35, 202, 208n19,
    219nn47, 3
Herrick, Robert, 32, 35, 202, 208n19,
    219nn47, 3
Heywood, Thomas, 29
Hibbard, G. R., 217n25
Holland, Philemon, 25
Homer, 40, 127, 148–49, 202, 216n11
Hope Theater, 91
Horace, 37, 40, 42, 60, 98, 126, 134, 141,
    159, 163, 169, 182, 218n41
Howard, Charles, Lord High Admiral,
    19
Howell, James, 32
Hunsdon, George, Lord Chamberlain,
    19
Huntley, Frank L., 207–208n6, 208n21

Jackson, Gabriele Bernhard, 209n3,
    211n34
James I, 17, 19, 20, 21, 23, 24, 26, 28,
    30, 32, 35, 121, 122, 125, 126, 127,
    132, 133, 144–45, 168, 196, 197
Jay, Bruce Louis, 214nn10, 11
Jephson, Sir William, 144
John, Lisle Cecil, 217n27
Jones, Inigo, 35, 36, 48, 121, 122, 126,
    129, 192, 195, 198, 208n18, 214nn2,
    8, 10
Jonson, Anne Lewis (wife), 26, 28, 152–
    53
Jonson, Ben, artistic stance, 17, 28–33,
    36–41, 42–47, 109–12, 121–25, 133–

38, 200–201, 204–205; as love poet,
    134, 138, *158–63*, 174, *177–91*, 197,
    201; as poet of friendship, 35, 147–49,
    191–94; as political poet, 111, 115, 119,
    122–25, *144–45*, *196–97*; as religious
    poet, 28, 152–55, *171–74*, *175–77*, 192,
    194–95; as social poet, 30–31, 32–33,
    37–38, 40, *42–43*, 59, 109, 110, 111,
    115–16, 120, *121–25*, 133, *134–35*,
    138, 139, 140, 142, *145–47*, 155–57,
    163, 166–70, 175, 196, 200; birth, 24;
    classicism, 17, 25, 33, *37–41*, *42–46*,
    50–55, 57, 61, *110–12*, 116, 125, *134–*
    35, 138, 148–49, 150, 153, 155–57,
    162, 163, 167, 168, 169, 170, 182, 192,
    193, 199, 200, 203; collaborative
    writing, 27, *28–29*, 61, 112–13; *Con-*
    versations with William Drummond of
    Hawthornden, 25, 26, 27, 28, 33, *34–*
    35, 39, 134, 137, 144, 167, 176, 198,
    207n5, 208n17; death, 36; education,
    25; influence, 32, 35, 64, *202*, 219n2;
    marriage and children, 26, 28, 151,
    152–55, 208n8; political stance, 17, 21,
    24, 26, *33*, 111, 115–16, 119, 123, 144–
    45, 169–70, 197; religious stance, *27–*
    28, 152, 171–74, 175–77

WORKS–COLLECTIONS:
Works of Benjamin Jonson, The (1616),
    29, *31–32*, 43, 49, 61, 138, 157–58;
    enlarged ed. (1640–41), 158, 174
WORKS–MASQUES AND ENTERTAIN-
MENTS:
Chloridia, 129
Entertainment at Althorp, The, 121,
    125
Entertainment at Highgate, The, 125
Golden Age Restored, The, 128, 130
Gypsies Metamorphosed, The, 129,
    130–31, 214n6
Hue and Cry after Cupid, The (also
    The Haddington Masque), 125
Hymenaei, 122, 125
King's Entertainment in passing to his
    Coronation, The, 125
Love Restored, 129
Lovers Made Men, 129
Love's Triumph through Callipolis,
    38, 121, 123, 129, 159

Masque of Beauty, The, 125
Masque of Blackness, The, 32, 122, 125
Masque of Queens, The, 124, *125–28,* 129
Mercury Vindicated, 129
Neptune's Triumph, 129, 130, 131
Oberon, 129, 131
Pan's Anniversary, 122
Pleasure Reconciled to Virtue, 130, *131–32*
Time Vindicated, 128
WORKS—PLAYS:
Alchemist, The, 30, 31, 37–38, 42, 43, 46, 47, 55, *80–90,* 91, 99, 101, 108, 169
Bartholomew Fair, 32, 42, 46, 47, *90–99,* 102
Case Is Altered, The, 27, 47, *48–49*
Catiline, 31, 110–12, *116–19,* 120
Cynthia's Revels, 31, 32, 47, 57, *58–59,* 60, 91
Devil Is an Ass, The, 46, 90–91, *99–101,* 103
Eastward Ho!, 28–29, 61
Epicoene, 31, 42, 44, 46, 47, *70–80,* 91
Every Man in His Humour, 27, 30, 31, 39, 42, 44, 45, 46, 47, 48, *49–57,* 58, 61, 71, 80, 85, 91, 96
Every Man out of His Humour, 27, 30, 31, 42, 47, 57, *58,* 59, 60, 91
Hot Anger Soon Cold, 27
Isle of Dogs, The, 27
Magnetic Lady, The, 26, 101, *107–108,* 109
New Inn, The, 36, 101, *103–107,* 109, 196
Page of Plymouth, The, 27
Poetaster, 31, 47, 57, 58, *59–61,* 120
Robert the Second, King of Scots (also *The Scot's Tragedy*), 27
Sad Shepherd, The, 36, 107
Sejanus, 29, 31, 40, 110, 111, *112–16,* 117, 119–20, 164
Staple of News, The, 36, *101–103,* 109
Tale of a Tub, A, 47, 48, 107
Volpone, 30, 31, 32, 37, 39, 42, 43, 46, 47, 55, *61–70,* 71, 74, 80, 87, 89–90, 91, 101, 162, 208n21

WORKS—POETRY:
COLLECTIONS:
Epigrams (1616), 32, *138–57,* 158, 174, 197
Forest, The (1616), 32, *157–74,* 178, 183
Underwood, The (1640–41), 158, 161, *174–98*
Ungathered Verse, 198–200
INDIVIDUAL POEMS:
"And must I sing? what subject shall I chuse?" (*F.* 10), 158, *160*
"Another [in the person of Woman-kind]. In defence of their Incon-stancie. A Song." (*U.* 6), 178
"Celebration of Charis in ten Lyrick Peeces, A" (*U.* 2), 184, *187–91*
"Come my Celia, let us prove" (*F.* 5), 162; *see also* 66–67
"Drinke to me, onely, with thine eyes" (*F.* 9), 136, *162–63*
"Elegie, An" (*U.* 22), 138, *181,* 182–83
"Elegie, An" (*U.* 38), *184–85,* 187
"Elegie, An" (*U.* 40), 184, *185–86,* 187
"Elegie, An" (*U.* 41), 184, *186–87*
"Elegie On the Lady Jane Pawlet, An" (*U.* 83), 136, *194–95*
"Epigram on the Princes birth, An" (*U.* 65), 196
"Epigram. To a Friend, and Sonne" (*U.* 69), 191
"Epigram. To K. *Charles* for a *100.* pounds he sent me in my sicknesse, An" (*U.* 64), 197
"Epigram. To our great and good K. *Charles* On his Anniversary Day, An" (*U.* 64), 197
"Epigram. To the honour'd [Eliza-beth] Countesse of [Rutland], An" (*U.* 50), 194
"Epigram, To the House-hold, An" (*U.* 68), 196
"Epistle answering to one that asked to be Sealed of the Tribe of *Ben,* An" (*U.* 47), 191–92
"Epistle to a friend, An" (*U.* 37), 191
"*Epistle* To Elizabeth Countesse of Rutland" (*F.* 12), *163–64,* 165
"*Epistle.* To Katherine, Lady Aubigny"

(F. 13), 164–65

"Epistle to Master *Arthur Squib*, An"
(*U.* 45), 191

"Epistle to Mr. *Arthur Squib*" (*U.* 54),
196

"Epistle to Master *John Selden*, An"
(*U.* 14), 123, 145, *192*, 205

"Epistle. To my Lady *Covell*" (*U.* 56),
194

"Epistle to Sir *Edward Savile*, now
Earle of *Dorset*, An" (*U.* 13), 194

"Epitaph on Elizabeth, L. H." (*E.*
124), 151, 152

"Epitaph on Master *Vincent Corbet*,
An" (*U.* 12), 194

"Epitaph on S[alomon] P[avy]" (*E.*
120), 138, 151, *155*

"Epode" (*F.* 11), 159, *160–61*

"Eupheme" (*U.* 84), 194

"Execration upon *Vulcan*, An" (*U.* 43),
196

"Expostulacion with Inigo Jones, An"
(*U. V.* 34), 198

"Fragment of Petronius Arbiter, A"
(*U.* 88), *278–80*, 181, 191

"*Ghyrlond* of the blessed Virgin *Marie*,
The" (U. V. 41), 198

"Horace. Ode the first. The fourth
Booke. To Venus" (*U.* 86), 159

"Houre-glasse, The" (*U.* 8), 180

"Humble Petition of poore Ben. To . . .
King *Charles*, The" (*U.* 76), 196

"In the person of Woman-kind. A Song
Apologetique" (*U.* 5), 178

"Inviting a Friend to Supper" (*E.* 101),
139, *155–57*, 168

"My Picture left in *Scotland*" (*U.* 9),
138, 158, *181–82*, 183, 187

"Ode, or Song, by all the Muses. In
celebration of her Majesties birthday, An" (*U.* 67), 196–97

"Ode. To himselfe, An" (*U.* 23), 196

"Ode. To Sir William Sidney" (*F.* 14),
170–71

"Of Death" (*E.* 34), 152, 155

"Of Life, and Death" (*E.* 80), 144, 152

"Oh doe not wanton with those eyes"
(*U.* 4), 136, *183–84*

"On Court-worme" (*E.* 15), 143

"On English Mounsieur" (*E.* 88), 143

"On Giles and Jone" (*E.* 42), 143

"On Lieutenant Shift" (*E.* 12), 143

"On Lucy Countesse of Bedford" (*E.*
76), *150–51*, 165

"On Margaret Ratcliffe" (*E.* 40), 151

"On My First Daughter" (*E.* 22), 138,
151, *152–53*

"On My First Sonne" (*E.* 45), 151,
153–55, 195, 200

"On Sir Cod the Perfumed" (*E.* 19),
144

"On Sir John Roe" (*E.* 27), 151

"On Sir John Roe" (*E.* 32), 151

"On Sir Voluptuous Beast" (*E.* 25), 144

"On Some-thing, That Walkes Some-
where" (*E.* 11), 143–44

"On Spies" (*E.* 59), 157

"On the Famous Voyage" (*E.* 133),
139, 157

"On the Same Beast [i.e., Sir Volup-
tuous]" (*E.* 26), 144

"On the Union" (*E.* 5), 144–45

"*Poems* of Devotion" (*U.* 1), 137, *175–
77*

"Song, A" (*U.* 4), 136, *183–84*

"Song. That Women Are But Mens
Shaddowes" (*F.* 7), 161

"*Song*. To Celia" (*F.* 5), 162; *see also*
66–67

"*Song*. To Celia" (*F.* 9), 136, *162–63*

"Sonnet, To the noble Lady, the Lady
Mary Wroth, A" (*U.* 28), 169, 194

"That Women Are But Mens Shaddowes" (*F.* 7), 161

"To a Friend [i.e., Inigo Jones] an
Epigram Of him" (U. V. 36), 198

"To Alchymists" (*E.* 6), 142

"To All, to Whom I Write" (*E.* 9), 144

"To Clement Edmonds" (*E.* 110), 146

"To Edward Allen" (*E.* 89), 145–46

"To Esme, Lord 'Aubigny" (*E.* 127),
164

"To Fine Lady Would-bee" (*E.* 62),
144

"To Francis Beaumont" (*E.* 55), 147

"To Heaven" (*F.* 15), 171–74

"To His Lady, Then Mrs. Cary" (*E.*
126), 150

"To Inigo Marquess Would be A
Corollary" (U. V. 35), 198

"To John Donne" (*E.* 96), 141

"To K. *Charles* and Q. *Mary.* For the losse of their first-borne, An Epigram Consolatorie" (*U.* 63), 196

"To King James" (*E.* 4), 144

"To Mary Lady Wroth" (*E.* 103), 169

"To Mary Lady Wroth" (*E.* 105), 150, 169

"To Master *John Burges*" (*U.* 57), 196

"To my Booke" (*E.* 2), 139

"To My Booke-seller" (*E.* 3), 141

"To My Lord Ignorant" (*E.* 10), 144

"To My Meere English Censurer" (*E.* 18), *139*, 140

"To My Muse" (*E.* 65), 145

"To Penshurst" (*F.* 2), 22, 79, 137, *166–68*, 169

"To Pertinax Cob" (*E.* 69), 142–43

"To Robert Earle of Salisburie" (*E.* 43), 146

"To Sir Cod" (*E.* 50), 144

"To Sir Henrie Cary" (*E.* 66), 140, 146

"To Sir Henrie Savile" (*E.* 95), 146

"To Sir Henry Goodyere" (*E.* 85), 147

"To Sir Henry Nevil" (*E.* 109), 144

"To Sir Ralph Shelton" (*E.* 199), 172

"To Sir Robert Wroth" (*F.* 3), 123, *168–69*, 170

"To Sir Thomas Overbury" (*E.* 113), 147

"To Sir Thomas Roe" (*E.* 98), 149, 171

"To Sir William Jephson" (*E.* 116), 144

"To Susan Countesse of Montgomery" (*E.* 104), 146–37, 150–51

"To the Ghost of Martial" (*E.* 36), 144

"To the immortall memorie, and friendship of that noble paire, Sir *Lucius Cary,* and Sir *H. Morison*" (*U.* 70), *192–94*, 195

"To the King. On his Birth-day. An Epigram Anniversarie" (*U.* 72), 196–97

"To the Learned Critick" (*E.* 17), *140–41*, 205

"To the memory of . . . *Mr. William Shakespeare*" (U. V. 26), 31, 35, 38, *198–200*

"To the most noble . . . Robert, Earle of Somerset" (U. V. 18), 198

"To the Reader" (*E.* 1), 140

"To the Right Honourable, the Lord high Treasurer of *England.* An Epistle Mendicant" (*U.* 71), 196

"To the Same [i.e., Celia]" (*F.* 6), 161–62

"To the Same [i.e., Sir John Roe]" (*E.* 33), 151

"To the Same Sir Cod" (*E.* 20), 144

"To the World" (*F.* 4), *171*, 172–73

"To William Camden" (*E.* 14), 25, *147–48*, 192

"To William Earle of Pembroke" (*E.* 102), 146

"To William Lord Mounteagle" (*E.* 60), 146

"To William Roe" (*E.* 128), *148–49*, 192

"Why I Write Not of Love" (*F.* 1), 158, *159–60*

WORKS–PROSE:
Timber, or Discoveries, 25, 33, 54, *37–41*, 44, 133, 136, 137, 140, 145, 157, 198–99, *200–201*, 204, 205

Jonson, Benjamin the younger (son), 26, 151, *153–55*

Jonson, Mary (daughter), 26, 151, *152–53*

Jonsonus Virbius, 202, 219n1

Juvenal, 37, 113, 169

Kay, W. David, 32, 208n16, 209n6, 209–10n10, 212nn41, 1; 216n15

Kempe, Will, 49

Kernan, Alvin, 209n10, 211nn30, 32

Kerrigan, William, 217nn28–30

Kiefer, Frederick, 213n5

Kifer, Devra Rowland, 212n44

King's Men, 61, 80, 99, 101, 104, 107, 112, 116; *see also* Lord Chamberlain's Men

Knights, L. C., 207n1, 209n1, 212nn42, 45; 215n3

Knoll, Robert E., 209n10, 211nn22, 27, 28

Kronefeld, J. Z., 216n15

Kyd, Thomas, 28, 199, 200

Lady Elizabeth's Men, 91

Lattimore, Richard, 216n14

Laud, William, Archbishop of Canterbury, 21

Leggatt, Alexander, 210n19
Leishman, J. B., 215n1
Lever, J. W., 116, 213n6
Levin, Lawrence L., 209n9
Levin, Richard, 211n31, 37; 212nn44, 47
Libanius, 71
Lisle, Sir Robert Sidney, Lord, 22, 31, 166–68, 169, 170
Litt, Dorothy E., 210n16
Livy, 156
Lord Chamberlain's Men, 27, 28, 49, 58, 61; *see also* King's Men
Lovelace, Richard, 202
Lucan, 127
Lydgate, John, 130
Lyly, John, 199, 200

McClung, William A., 217n25
Machiavelli, Niccolo, 110, 112, 114, 118
Maclean, Hugh, 215n3
Marcus, Leah Sinanoglou, 214n6
Marlowe, Christopher, 40, 47, 67, 88, 110, 111, 157, 199
Marotti, Arthur F., 215n4
Marston, John, 28–29, 34, 35, 59–60, 61
Martial, 40, 134, 139, 144, 155, 156, 167, 168
Martz, Louis L., 217n31
Mary Tudor, Queen of England, 19, 20
Massinger, Philip, 29
Meagher, John C., 213n1, 214nn7, 9; 218n38
Medine, Peter E., 216n16
Meres, Francis, 212n1
Mermaid Club, 32, 156, 192
Milton, John, 132, 202, 204, 215n14
Miner, Earl, 215n2, 219n2
Molesworth, Charles, 217n25
Montaigne, Michel de, 218n43
Monteagle, William Parker, Baron, 146
Montgomery, Susan, Countess of, 146, 150–51
Morison, Sir Henry, 192–94
Morley, George, 36
Mortimer, Anthony, 215n3
Munday, Anthony, 49
Murray, John Tucker, 207n2

Nardo, A. K., 210n15
Nashe, Thomas, 27

neoplatonism, 30, 101, 105, 160–61, *178–81*, 183, 190–91, 216n20
Nevil, Sir Henry, 144
Newton, Richard C., 215n4
Nichols, J. G., 216nn16, 22; 217–18n36
Nicoll, Allardyce, 213n1

Oates, Mary I., 219n46
ode, 134, 138, 158, *170–71*
Orgel, Stephen, 123, 213n1, 214nn 2, 4, 8, 10, 13; 215n14
Ornstein, Robert, 212n2, 213n8
Overbury, Sir Thomas, 147
Ovid, 60, 67, 85, 161, 173, 182, 218nn41, 43
Oxford University, 25, 31, 35, 61, 70

Palatine, Frederick V, Elector, 21
Palmer, D. J., 163, 217n24
Parfitt, G. A. E., 210n17, 213n5, 215nn2, 4
Parker, R. B., 209n10, 210n13
Parr, Johnstone, 211n33
Partridge, Edward B., 146, 209nn4, 9; 211nn26, 28, 29; 212nn47, 48; 215n6, 216n10
Paul, St., 172
Pavy, Salomon, 138, 151, *155*
Pawlet. *See* Winchester
Pembroke, William Herbert, Earl of, 31, 36, 138–39, 146
Peterson, Richard S., 218nn41, 43; 219n45
Petronius Arbiter, 38, 178, 217–18n36
Pius V, Pope, 20
Plato, 218n41
Plautus, 40, 49, 50, 71, 81
Plutarch, 116, 118
Poley, Robert, 157
Porter, Henry, 27
Puritanism and Puritans, 20, 21, 22, 33, 82, 86–87, 88, 90, 93, 95, 96, 97, 98, 99, 170, 197
Putney, Rufus D., 215n6

Ralegh, Sir Walter, 31
Randall, Dale B. J., 214n6
Randolph, Thomas, 202
Ratcliffe, Margaret, 151
Rathmell, J. C. A., 166, 217n26

Index

Redwine, James D., Jr., 208n22
Returne from Parnassus, The, Part II, 26
Richmond, Hugh, 180, 218n39
Ripa, Cesare, 214n7
Roe, Sir John, 151
Roe, William, 148–49
Ronsard, Pierre, 218n41
Rowley, William, 29
Rutland, Elizabeth Sidney, Countess of, 163–64, 194

Salisbury, Sir Robert Cecil, Earl of, 29, 146, 167
Sallust, 116, 118
Scheve, D. A., 210n13
Selden, John, 31, 32, 36, 192
Seneca, 113, 134, 163, 218n41
Shakespeare, William, 29, 31, 34, 35, 38, 40, 49, 50, 59, 92–93, 110, 112, 178, 183, *198–200*, 202–204
Shelton, Sir Ralph, 172
Shirley, James, 29, 202
Sidney, Sir Philip, 18, 34, 39, 40, 163, 168, 218n43
Sidney, Sir Robert. *See* Lisle
Sidney, Sir William, 170–71
Simpson, Evelyn, 218n44
Smith, Bruce R., 215n6
Socrates, 218n41
Somerset, Robert Carr, Earl of, 198
"Sons of Ben," 32, 161, 192, 202
Spanos, William V., 215n4, 216n13
Spencer, Gabriel, 27
Spenser, Edmund, 130, 183
Squib, Arthur, 196
Strong, Roy, 214nn2, 8
Suckling, Sir John, 202
Suetonius, 113
Summers, Claude J., 219n47
Summers, Joseph H., 215n1, 216nn17, 22; 219n2, 220n14
Swinburne, Algernon Charles, 203–204, 219nn9–10

Symonds, J. A., 203, 219n7

Tacitus, 113, 156
Talbert, Ernest William, 210n12, 213n1
Taylor, John, the Water Poet, 33
Thayer, C. G., 209n10, 212nn43, 47, 48
Theatre, The, 18
Thron, E. M., 210n11
Tibullus, 60, 218n41
Townsend, Freda L., 210–11n21
Townshend, Sir Robert, 26
Trimpi, Wesley, 215nn1, 4; 216n20; 218nn41, 45

Van Den Berg, Sara, 219n45
Vawter, Marvin L., 115, 213n5
Vergil, 40, 60, 127, 148–49, 156, 169, 202–203
verse epistle, 37, 134, 138, 158, *163–65*

Waith, Eugene M., 210n12
Walker, Ralph S., 208n17
Waller, Edmund, 202, 219n1
Walton, Geoffrey, 215n3
War of the Theaters, 59–60, 61
Weever, John, 139
Weinberger, G. J., 218–19n45
Welsford, Enid, 213n1
Welsh, James M., 220n12
Westminster School, 25, 147
Whipple, T. K., 139, 215n5
Whitefriars Theater, 71
Wilson, Edmund, 211n25
Wilson, Gayle E., 217n26
Winchester, Lady Jane Pawlet, Marchioness of, 194–95
Woods, Susanne, 219n46
Wroth, Mary, Lady, 31, 150, 169, 194
Wroth, Sir Robert, 168–69
Wykes, David, 215n6

Young, R. V., Jr., 216nn6, 7, 9, 12